Quod scriptura, non iubet vetat

The Latin translates, "What is not commanded in scripture, is forbidden:'

On the Cover: Baptists rejoice to hold in common with other evangelicals the main principles of the orthodox Christian faith. However, there are points of difference and these differences are significant. In fact, because these differences arise out of God's revealed will, they are of vital importance. Hence, the barriers of separation between Baptists and others can hardly be considered a trifling matter. To suppose that Baptists are kept apart solely by their views on Baptism or the Lord's Supper is a regrettable misunderstanding. Baptists hold views which distinguish them from Catholics, Congregationalists, Episcopalians, Lutherans, Methodists, Pentecostals, and Presbyterians, and the differences are so great as not only to justify, but to demand, the separate denominational existence of Baptists. Some people think Baptists ought not teach and emphasize their differences but as E.J. Forrester stated in 1893, "Any denomination that has views which justify its separate existence, is bound to promulgate those views. If those views are of sufficient importance to justify a separate existence, they are important enough to create a duty for their promulgation ... the very same reasons which justify the separate existence of any denomination make it the duty of that denomination to teach the distinctive doctrines upon which its separate existence rests." If Baptists have a right to a separate denominational life, it is their duty to propagate their distinctive principles, without which their separate life cannot be justified or maintained.

Many among today's professing Baptists have an agenda to revise the Baptist distinctives and redefine what it means to be a Baptist. Others don't understand why it even matters. The books being reproduced in the *Baptist Distinctives Series* are republished in order that Baptists from the past may state, explain and defend the primary Baptist distinctives as they understood them. It is hoped that this Series will provide a more thorough historical perspective on what it means to be distinctively Baptist.

The Lord Jesus Christ asked, *"And why call ye me, Lord, Lord, and do not the things which I say?"* (Luke 6:46). The immediate context surrounding this question explains what it means to be a true disciple of Christ. Addressing the same issue, Christ's question is meant to show that a confession of discipleship to the Lord Jesus Christ is inconsistent and untrue if it is not accompanied with a corresponding submission to His authoritative commands. Christ's question teaches us that a true recognition of His authority as Lord inevitably includes a submission to the authority of His Word. Hence, with this question Christ has made it forever impossible to separate His authority as King from the authority of His Word. These two principles—the authority of Christ as King and the authority of His Word—are the two most fundamental Baptist distinctives. The first gives rise to the second and out of these two all the other Baptist distinctives emanate. As F.M. lams wrote in 1894, "Loyalty to Christ as King, manifesting itself in a constant and unswerving obedience to His will as revealed in His written Word, is the real source of all the Baptist distinctives:' In the search for the *primary* Baptist distinctive many have settled on the Lordship of Christ as the most basic distinctive. Strangely, in doing this, some have attempted to separate Christ's Lordship from the authority of Scripture, as if you could embrace Christ's authority without submitting to what He commanded. However, while Christ's Lordship and Kingly authority can be isolated and considered essentially for discussion's sake, we see from Christ's own words in Luke 6:46 that His Lordship is really inseparable from His Word and, with regard to real Christian discipleship, there can be no practical submission to the one without a practical submission to the other.

In the symbol above the Kingly Crown and the Open Bible represent the inseparable truths of Christ's Kingly and Biblical authority. The Crown and Bible graphics are supplemented by three Bible verses (Ecclesiastes 8:4, Matthew 28:18-20, and Luke 6:46) that reiterate and reinforce the inextricable connection between the authority of Christ as King and the authority of His Word. The truths symbolized by these components are further emphasized by the Latin quotation - *quod scriptura, non iubet vetat*— i.e., "What is not commanded in scripture, is forbidden:' This Latin quote has been considered historically as a summary statement of the regulative principle of Scripture. Together these various symbolic components converge to exhibit the two most foundational Baptist Distinctives out of which all the other Baptist Distinctives arise. Consequently, we have chosen this composite symbol as a logo to represent the primary truths set forth in the *Baptist Distinctives Series*.

THE
APOSTOLIC CHURCH

WILLIAM EDWARDS PAXTON
1825-1883

THE
APOSTOLIC CHURCH;

BEING

AN INQUIRY INTO THE

CONSTITUTION AND POLITY

OF THAT

VISIBLE ORGANIZATION

SET UP BY

JESUS CHRIST AND HIS APOSTLES.

BY

W. E. PAXTON

FIRST THOUSAND.

With a Biographical Sketch of the Author
By John Franklin Jones

MEMPHIS:
Southern Baptist Publication Society
W. D. Mayfield, Business Manager.
1876.

he Baptist Standard Bearer, Inc.
NUMBER ONE IRON OAKS DRIVE • PARIS, ARKANSAS 72855

Thou hast given a *standard* to them that fear thee;
that it may be displayed because of the truth.
-- Psalm 60:4

Reprinted 2006

by

THE BAPTIST STANDARD BEARER, INC.
No. 1 Iron Oaks Drive
Paris, Arkansas 72855
(479) 963-3831

THE WALDENSIAN EMBLEM
lux lucet in tenebris
"The Light Shineth in the Darkness"

ISBN# 1579786421

PREFACE.

IN the work here presented to the public, I have endeavored to meet a recognized want in our denominational literature—the discussion, in a single volume, of the underlying principles of that church polity which we derive from the New Testament. Our people have scarcely enough appreciated the strength which our simple, popular government gives us, to make those principles prominent in our discussions. We have too much relied upon our Scriptural Baptism as our main pillar of strength, when in truth it is but one of many. A converted church membership, the want of power in the church to alter its forms, the local and independent character of the Apostolic Churches, the essential equality of the Christian brotherhood, the subordination of the clerical order to the church, the rights of conscience and private judgment—these and other principles, discussed in this volume are readily admitted; but we scarcely realize how peculiarly these are our own, and how certainly we derive them from the Scriptures. These are no minor questions, but they involve the authority of the Scriptures themselves; and present the only safeguard against the Spirit of innovation that would sweep away the whole fabric of the church, with all its precious and consoling doctrines.

Most of the questions discussed are living ones, though a few of them, necessarily embraced in the subject of our inquiry may not be so regarded. The law of religious liberty has made wonderful progress during the present century; yet it is but imperfectly understood out of our own country. It is true that almost everywhere dissenters enjoy the privilege of worshiping God according to the dictates of their own conscience; but in most countries this is regarded as an act of generous toleration, rather than the enjoyment of a natural right; and even in our own country we encounter a power that denies the right of private judgment.

The subject of Baptism is regarded as one of the settled questions, and I have only aimed to gather up and classify the results.

In a few instances I have dared to follow the inexorable deductions of logic to advanced conclusions, from which many of my brethren may shrink, who deprecate a denominationalism rigidly distinctive in practice, if not in theory. But I have not sought to give these matters an undue prominence or thrust them into connections where they do not properly belong; and altogether they occupy less than a dozen pages of the volume.

In the original plan of the work I included the Doctrines of the Apostolic Church. But I found that the proper discussion of these would extend the book beyond the limits I had assigned myself; and a mere compend would hardly serve any useful purpose. I preferred therefore to defer these to some future volume, if God should graciously spare my life.

In regard to the execution of the task I have assigned myself, I invite fair, candid and respectful criticism; and for the benefit of those who may essay the role of critics I am constrained to confess that I cannot plead in extenuation either the indiscretion of youth, or haste in the preparation of the work. It is the work of mature age, and the fruit of years of study. My studies in this direction began previous to the year 1859, when I published a little work on the Rights of Laymen; but in 1864 I began to collect the material for a more extended work on the Apostolic Church. Most of these questions I have had occasion to discuss in the regular or occasional discharge of my duty as a minister; and I have devoted my leisure moments—those precious fragments of time which it has been my habit to improve— in arranging and unifying the material thus accumulated.

There is one respect in which I ask indulgence; I am at too great a distance to personally supervise the publication, and am compelled to depend upon the care and intelligence of compositors and proof readers for the accuracy of the typography.

Thus I send forth this child of my brain to battle with the world and to accomplish its destiny, invoking the blessings of the Great Head of the Church, and praying that he may sanctify my labors to the good of his cause.

SHREVEPORT, LA., Aug. 13, 1876.

TABLE OF CONTENTS.

PAGE.

Introduction—Authority of the "Fathers"—The Apostolic Church Polity may be learned from the Scriptures. 9

PART I.—THE CHARACTER OF THE CHURCH.

I. Its government spiritual, not temporal 13
II. An executive not a legislative body 24
III. The object and uses of church government 32
    Section 1—Nature of Government in general 32
    Section 2—Rights of conscience 33
IV. The object and uses of Church Government, continued 41
    Section 1—The Preservation of Doctrine 41
        Guilt of Corrupting the Word 47
        This may be committed:
        1. By transmitting incorrect copies of the original 47
        2. By wrong translation 47
        3. By handling the Word of God deceitfully 47
        4. By decrees of Councils and Bulls of Popes 48
    Section 2—How the Doctrine of Christ is to be Preserved 49
        1. By upholding the truth 49
        2. By assailing error 51
    Section 3—Right of Private Judgment 52
V. Objects and uses of church government, continued. 60
    The Preservation of order 60
    Section 1—Preventive Discipline 60
        1. By giving right direction to Energies of the Church 61

	PAGE.
2. By watching over each other in Brotherly Love	62
3. By faithfully maintaining the truth	63
4. By maintaining a lively state of Religion	64
Section 2—Punitive Discipline	64
Corrective and excisive	64
1. Personal offences	65
2. Moral offences	67
Section 3—The participation of the whole church in discipline, and the finality of its action	70
VI. Further characteristics of the church	77
Section 1—Ekklesia	77
Section 2—Selected material	79
Section 3—Qualifications for membership	81
1. Conversion	81
2. Baptism	87
VII. Characteristics continued:	
Section 1—The basis of association	89
Section 2—Its local character	90
Section 3—Church independence	93

PART II—ORGANIZATION.

I. Its organization may be ascertained	96
II. Its component parts	100
Section 1—The ministry	100
1 Divine call	101
2. Ordination	105
Section 2—Apostles	106
III. Primacy of Peter	111
Section 1—The supremacy of Peter	111
Section 2—The right of Peter to transfer his authority	124
Section 3—Peter at Rome	126
IV. Pastors or Bishops	131
Section 1—Their qualifications	131
Section 2—Their rights	141

	PAGE.
Section 3—Their duties.	149
Section 4—Episcopal jurisdiction.	154
V. Elders or Presbyters	159
Ruling Elders	162
VI. Deacons:	
Section 1—The office.	169
Section 2—Qualifications.	171
Section 3—Duties.	173
VII. The Laity	176
Section 1—Their rights	176
VIII. Relation of woman to the church	185
Section 1—Her rights and duties	186
Section 2—Her subordination	190
IX. The sovereignty of the church	193
Rights of minorities	193
X. Laws of the church	198
Section 1—Moral law.	198
Section 2—Positive law	202
Sacramental efficacy	203
XI. Baptism, Action of	209
Section 1—Testimony of the Lexicons	210
Section 2—Testimony of critics and commentators.	216
Section 3—Testimony of the classics	220
Section 4—Testimony of versions and usage	222
Section 5—Monumental testimony	225
1. Baptisteries	225
2. Practice of Greek church	226
Section 6—Scripture usage	227
XII. Subject of Baptism	237
Section 1 - Infant baptism not an institution of Christ	237
Section 2—Not in the Old Testament	243
1 Not a substitute for circumcision	243
2. Identical relation of children consi'd.	243
Section 3—Historical view	247
1. Proselyte baptism	247
2. Catechumens	249
3. Apostolic fathers	249
4. Later fathers	250

	PAGE.
Section 4—Evils of Infant baptism	255
XIII. The design of baptism	258
1. Not sacramental	263
2. An outward sign	264
3 Baptismal remission	264
4. Its emblematic character	264
XIV. The administrator	265
Alien immersion	267
XV. The Lord's Supper	271
Section 1—Nature and design	271
Section 2—Its limitation	276
Section 3—Feet washing	281

PART III.—INSTITUTION AND PERPETUITY.

I. Identity of church under both dispensations	288
II. Setting up the church	297
Section 1—Mission of John the Baptist	297
Section 2—Collection of material	301
III. Perpetuity of the church	304
IV. Source of knowledge	309
V. Church succession	317
VI. Treatment of Heretics and Schismatics	323
VII. Basis of Christian union	328
1. The basis	329
2. Obstacles to Christian union	333
3. In what Christian union consists	335

INTRODUCTION.

I PROPOSE, in the spirit of Christ, to institute an inquiry into the organization, external form, rights and powers of the Apostolic Church, so far as the same may be deduced from the Holy Scriptures. If I shall have occasion to refer to those writings immediately succeeding the Apostolic age, usually denominated the Apostolic Fathers, it will be with that caution with which it is necessary to examine all merely human writings. Many who have undertaken to investigate this subject lay too much stress upon the authority of those fathers who wrote during the first three hundred years of the Christian Era, forgetting that corruptions began to creep into the church polity even during the days of the Apostles ; for Paul declares that the mystery of iniquity had already begun to work, and that these corruptions went on until they subverted the original constitution.

In the application of their writings we should not loose sight of the fact that the lust of power is the ruling passion of man, from which not even good men are always exempt, and that the natural tendency of those who are invested with temporary authority, is to endeavor to establish, perpetuate and extend that power, and to enlarge the prerogatives of office. The few who govern are apt to be more vigilant than the many who are governed. Men are disposed to suffer some encroachments upon their rights rather than to disturb the peace and order of society by an effort to redress their wrongs Hence gradual inroads may be made upon their rights without resistance. All history proves that there is a tendency in all governments, administered by man, to centralize and consolidate power in the hands of the few ; and what was at first permitted in an emergency, is afterwards construed into a precedent and finally claimed *jure divino*. No part of history more clearly illustrates this than the first centuries of the Christian Era Now, in examining the writings of this period, as I may occasionally do in the course of these pages, this fact must be kept constantly in view. They must be treated as all other witnesses, and their admissions against themselves allowed more weight than their declarations in favor of themselves.

These writers were the bishops and presbyters, the rulers in their respective churches, and may be supposed to be careful not to admit anything against their own order, while at the same time they were not so exempt from ordinary human frailties as not to desire to extend their prerogatives as far as circumstances would permit. Thus any concessions made by them as to the rights of the laity are to be taken as sufficient proof of their tradition from the Apostles, unless contradicted by Apostolic authority. While on the other hand if we find them laying claim to powers neither expressed nor implied in the inspired writings, we may justly suspect that the powers are usurped. Judged by this rule, they may serve to throw light upon the Sacred Record.

It is plain that in an inquiry of this kind the principle authority must be the Holy Scriptures. Where these speak, it is the duty of man to be silent and obey. When they are silent, man may safely leave off doing.

While I am not disposed to disparage the real difficulties of the investigation I have undertaken, I by no means adopt the opinion of Dr. Bangs:

"Perhaps there are few subjects of a religious nature involved in greater obscurity, and which have occasioned sharper disputes than the question: *What was the primitive mode of church government?* Its obscurity, indeed, affords a very obvious reason why ecclesiastical writers have been so much divided concerning it; for those truths which are expressly revealed as articles of faith, or may be easily deduced from given principles, do not readily admit of controversy, and therefore respecting all such, Christians are more generally agreed.

* * * * * This imperfect manner in which the order of the church is sketched out in the Holy Scriptures affords no small proof that no specific mode is essential to constitute an evangelical church."—Original Church of Christ, page 6.

If this argument is worth anything, it proves that all revelation is a crude mass of obscurities, for there is not a single doctrine of the New Testament that is not disputed by some class of persons, calling themselves Christians; and some of its plainest teachings are most hotly contested. Dr. Bangs himself does not more widely differ from his Presbyterian brethren on the form of church government than he does on the essential doctrines of grace.

I cannot think that God, who revealed the most minute particulars respecting the form, dimensions, material and construction of the temple at Jerusalem, which was the antetype of the Christian Church, would leave his spiritual building at the caprice of every bungling journeyman, who might choose to set up his own model and exercise his skill in erecting this Holy Tabernacle of the Lord. If God has left no designs upon the tresel-board, whereby the workmen may pursue their labors, who shall arrogate to himself the exclusive right to become master builder ? If God has given no directions upon the subject, it becomes the common property of all, and each may set up his own model. And so, Jo. Smith, the Mormon, had as clear a right to set up a new church as Luther or Calvin, Henry VIII. or John Wesley

I believe a candid examination of the Holy Writings will satisfy any unprejudiced mind that this question is susceptible of as clear and definite an answer as any question concerning the doctrines taught, and the duties enjoined in the Sacred Scriptures. I am not surprised that men, who start with their own ecclesiastical organizations, and look in the New Testament to find a counterpart, should discover any amount of obscurities. But he who divests his mind of his preconceived notions of what the church *should be*, and comes to the Scriptures to learn what it *is*, I dare say will be able to learn the leading characteristics of the church, the qualifications of its members, its officers, and their qualifications and powers, and the manner of administering discipline. This is all that need be known, for this knowledge *practically* applied, will constitute all that Christ intended his church to be—an executive, not a legislative body. To adopt the language of an earnest advocate of original church order : "That these principles can be found together, embodied in specific articles in any one chapter of the New Testament, I do not claim; nor can the Apostles' creed, or the acknowledged articles of evangelical faith, but like these they run through the whole body of the teachings of Christ and his Apostles; and I do maintian that the principles of church constitution, order and discipline, are as clearly and specifically taught as are the doctrines which Christian churches are to hold and teach." (J. R. Graves.)

THE APOSTOLIC CHURCH.

PART I.
The Character of the Church.

CHAPTER I.

ITS GOVERNMENT SPIRITUAL—NOT TEMPORAL.

Before proceeding to inquire as to the end of church government, it may clear the subject of some obscurity to anticipate the discussion of its nature, so far as to consider some points of vital importance to a proper understanding of the subject.

The government of the church is spiritual—not temporal; that is, it is established for the attainment of spiritual ends by spiritual means. It is no rival of human governments for temporal domination, and it is in no way an auxiliary of the State, except in so far as by moral appliances it makes better men and consequently better citizens. The proper office of civil government is to ensure to every citizen protection in the enjoyment of life, liberty, and the pursuit of happiness; and as an incident to this pursuit of happiness the right to worship God according to the dictates of his own conscience. The Church does not displace the State in these things.

Our Saviour taught his disciples to render unto Cæsar the things which are Cæsar's, and unto God the things which are God's; the obvious meaning of which is, that the church was not meant to disturb the relation of a citizen to his government. Paul taught the subordination of the Christian to the State, when he said: "Let every soul be subject unto the higher powers." He admonishes Titus to put the Cretans in mind "to be subject to principalities and powers, to obey magistrates." In all matters of civil concernment, the State is supreme, and no man may claim exemption from its requirements, within the scope of its proper jurisdiction. No one's ecclesiastical relations dissolve that just allegiance which he owes to the government under which he lives; nor can the church rightfully afford sanctuary to the violators of the civil law. But there is a limit to the supremacy of the State. If it transcend the province for which it was ordained of God, and undertakes to regulate religious concernments, the subject is not bound to obey. It is not for the State to define God's laws and enforce obedience to them. Neither may it govern the church, as such. It is not the creature of the State, and in all matters that pertain strictly to itself, it is independent of the State.

But there is no conflict of jurisdiction. It may be difficult sometimes to define the boundary lines of each, because they lay along side, and our duties to God and to society overlap and blend until it is often impossible to tell how far either may go. But it is a safe rule, sanctioned by the example of Christ, for the church to keep aloof from all civil matters, and for the State to abstain from every attempt to enforce the laws of God beyond that moral code, upon which the existence of society depends.

So long as the church and State both confine themselves to their legitimate sphere of action there can be no conflict between them. The proper ends of human government are attained without any violation of the law of God; and the ends of God's spiritual government in his church do not interfere with any legitimate functions of the State. Neither may invade the dominion of the other. Each is independent within its own sphere.

The church has "a higher mission, a sublimer struggle, a more lasting victory. 'My Kingdom is not of this world.' He never intended it to be linked to the State; or sustained by human enactment. Radiant with light, and panoplied with the armor of heaven, Christianity wins with her smiles and conquers with her charms; but she does not ask for, nor seek human aid or alliance. Her weapons are not carnal but spiritual and mighty." (S. H. Ford.)

" The Church," says the excellent Richard Watson, "is a society, founded upon faith, and united by mutual love, for the personal edification of its members in holiness, and for the religious benefit of the world. The nature of its government is thus determined. It is concerned only with spiritual objects. It cannot employ force to compel men into its pale, for the only door of the Church is faith to which there can be no compulsion: 'he that believeth and is baptized' becomes a member. It cannot inflict pains and penalties upon the disobedient and refractory like civil governments, for the only punitive discipline authorized in the New Testament is comprised in 'admonition,' 'reproof,' 'sharp rebuke,' and finally excision from the society." (Institutes vol. 2 p. 573.)

When Jesus was brought before Pilate he declared: "My Kingdom is not of this world; if my Kingdom were of this world, then would my servants fight that I should not be delivered to the Jews: but now is my Kingdom not from thence."

And when Peter would have defended the person of his Master, and, drawing his sword, smote off the ear of Malchus, a servant of the high priest, Jesus rebuked him and commanded him to put up his sword; for they that take the sword shall perish by the sword. Force was not to be used in the propagation of the gospel; or to be employed by the church to suppress the wickedness of men.

The great error of the Jews consisted in supposing that the Messiah was to be a temporal prince, who would restore the glory of their ancient kingdom; but when he came, seeking no alliance with the civil power, and asking no aid from the arm of the State to enforce his divine precepts notwithstanding the moral sublimity of his teachings, his wonderful miracles, the dignity of his person, and the purity of his life, they rejected his mission and crucified him as a blasphemer. Their poets had sung of the magnificence of his kingdom, and visions of its glories flitted before the prophetic eye; but they failed to see, in the glowing discriptions of their sacred penmen, the perfection of moral beauty, the excellence of that higher morality which he taught, and whose practical effects he embodied in the organization of the church. When they witnessed his miracles no doubt their hopes were raised and they expected to see him assume temporal authority; and so impatient did they become at the development of what they supposed would attend his movements, that the "Pharisees demanded when the kingdom of God should come, and he answered them and said: 'The kingdom of heaven cometh not with observation.' The kingdom which God will set up in the world will not become conspicuous and remarkable by any outward splendor or worldly pomp, but by its inward power and efficacy on the hearts and minds of men. 'Neither shall they say: Lo! here or lo! there! for behold!

the kingdom of heaven is within you.'" It is a government of the heart, the will, the affections. These are its subjects and these no human authority can control. The civil power may force an external compliance. Nothing but the power of God can rule the heart, control the will, and administer the affections according to the law of perfect love. Lying lips may be forced to repeat a stereotyped formula; but God alone can command the faith. Inquisitorial judges may chain the body, but tyranny never yet invented a cord to bind the enlightened mind. Hence we see the folly of attempting to establish religion by human enactments, and forcing conformity under pains and penalties. Christianity possesses a vitalizing power that renovates the heart and reforms the life; but in this work it needs not the adjuncts of civil authority. It may win its way to the heart by its native beauty, but every effort to force it there closes the heart against it. Like a sensitive guest, it enters not—save when invited, and when the desires of the heart stand ready to welcome it. The blessed Saviour did not address himself to the potentates of earth and invoke their aid in setting up his kingdom. He needed not their assistance. He and his apostles seem to have acted upon the injunction of the Psalmist, "Put not your trust in princes." They relied alone upon the word, which, under the influence of the Holy Spirit, became "quick and powerful, sharper than a two-edged sword, piercing even to the dividing assunder of the soul and spirit, and joints and marrow, and is a discerner of the thoughts and intents of the heart." Christianity did not need the endorsement of the State to commend it to the hearts prepared by the Spirit, and none others will receive it, while every touch of the State is pollution, and its embrace death.

The declaration of the founder of the Christian

religion, "My Kingdom is not of this world," seems even yet to be imperfectly comprehended by His professed followers. The relation of the Church to the State is one of those problems which has more than any other agitated the world, and is not yet fully settled. For more than fifteen centuries the great mass of Christian people have thought the enforcement of religion was a part of the functions of the State. But there have always been a large number who possessed the original spirit of Christianity, and have plead for the rights of conscience, believing the alliance of Church and State to be unnatural and unholy; and when they have been molested in the exercise of their religious opinions they have sternly demanded in the language of the ancient Donatists: *Quid est imperitori cum ecclesia?* "What has the emperor to do with the church?" But the present century has done much to divorce Church and State and to recognize more fully the rights of conscience.

The government of the United States was founded upon the principle that Congress should not establish any form of religion or prohibit the free exercise thereof. It was intended that the State should attend strictly to civil matters, leaving each individual free to follow the dictates of his own conscience. The Church has been left to take care of itself, and has found enough to do in its own legitimate sphere without meddling in affairs of State. Under this form of government the vital principles of Christianity have flourished as they flourish no where else in the world.

But even here there are those who would change this order and establish at least a qualified alliance of Church and State. Recently this idea has produced an organized movement. A national association was formed in 1875 and is to meet again in June of this present year (1876). Circulars are being scattered broadcast over the land soliciting every prominent minister and layman to co-operate in the movement. This association proposes to amend the Constitution of the United States so as to recognize God and to declare the Christian religion, the religion of the nation; to authorize Congress to enact laws enforcing the Christian Sabbath, and to require the Holy Scriptures to be read in the Public Schools.

Those who are solicited to join in this movement would do well to consider several points.

1. God is in no need of such an endorsement. The only recognition of Him which will be received is that which exists in the hearts of the people; and manifests itself in obedience to His laws. God-fearing rulers will do more to honor God than all the paper declarations in the world. It would be an act of rediculous folly for the people of the United States to assemble in convention and solemnly resolve that God is God.

2. It is a mistake to suppose that the Christian religion cannot take care of itself without the aid of the State. It is no mere human philosophy that requires human authority to enforce it. It is stamped with the authority of God. There is a divine sanction manifest in its teachings that no human enactment can enhance, or render more authoritative. God himself speaks in his word and what folly in man to suppose that kings and rulers, the mere creatures of God, can by any act of theirs add dignity to His commands.

But in addition to the inherent divinity of the Gospel which alone might win its way in the world by its superior moral philosophy as have done some systems of human science in spite of formidable opposition, God has himself provided sufficient means for its propagation without the aid of government. He has charged the heralds of the Cross with this work. He said "Go ye into all the world and preach the Gospel to every creature," with the promise: "Lo! I am with you alway even unto the end." The Gospel has the adjunct of the Holy Spirit to open and prepare the hearts of men and enforce the teachings of the Gospel; and no human authority can do this office half so well. He does not need the aid of the State to enable Him to do His work.

3. The attempt to enforce the recognition of Christianity might produce a great many hypocrites, but no sincere believers. He who adopts the Christian religion merely to enjoy the rights of citizenship is the merest hypocrite. And the union of Church and State produces this. How many men there are in Germany who scoff at the Christian religion yet who profess it and attach themselves to the established church merely to be able to hold office and exercise the rights of citizenship! What is that man's religion worth who merely professes for the sake of some worldly advantage? It will neither benefit him spiritually, nor will he reflect any honor upon religion. Yet this is what it is proposed to institute in our government. Infidels and scoffers who would hold office must swear to obey the Constitution and thus in form adopt the Christian religion as their faith while in their hearts they hated and despised it.

4. To adopt the Christian religion as a part of the Constitution which every office-holder must swear to support, would exclude from a participation in the government many citizens who pay large taxes for its support, and thus would violate that principle which lies at the foundation of government, viz: that taxation and representation go together. It was upon this very principle that the colonies revolted from the mother country. America was taxed, but allowed no representation in the

Parliament. A large part of our population consists of Jews who are a thriving, industrious people. In point of intelligence, morals and property, they will compare favorably with any other class. As a people they are peaceable and orderly. They have given to the nation some of its finest statesmen and orators. And yet the councils of the nation are to be deprived of these, or they must violate their consciences by recognizing a religion which they abhor. If a wealthy and intelligent Chinaman should desire to become a citizen he must either renounce his religion or play the role of hypocrite by pretending to do what he would not voluntarily do.

5. To adopt such a provision would make it necessary for Congress to enact a law defining in what the Christian religion consists. This would be to adopt, as the established religion, some one of the various sects as the highest type of Christianity, and thus exclude the rest. Just think of a Congress like that now in session, or any other that has assembled in fifty years, or that is likely to assemble soon, sitting as an umpire to choose the form of Christianity to receive the patronage of the government! Strangers to godliness, mere men of the world, they would choose a religion like themselves. The church that would offer the freest indulgence to their lusts and required the least self-denial would be that which would please them most. This would offer to ambitious ecclesiastics the temptation to modify the sterner and more exacting duties of the church so as to adapt it to the tastes of the rulers and secure their suffrage. Thus corrupted at the start, it would become more and more corrupt in time. This is the history of all State Churches.

6. It would be a step backward centuries in the path of human progress, and to assume a yoke under which the nations of the old world have groaned

for ages, but which has become so intolerable that they are everywhere preparing to shake it off. Even Spain, the home of the Inquisition and the birth place of Ignatius Loyola, despite of Papal threats, has proclaimed religious freedom.

7. The observance of the Sabbath can better be enforced by cultivating a higher tone of public sentiment than by the enactment of Sunday Laws. There is no country in the world where the Sabbath is so orderly and so universally observed as in the United States, where there is so little interference on the part of the government to enforce religious duties. The disregard of this day is due in a great measure to the large influx of populations from those States of Europe having established churches, where the desecration of the Sabbath is universal.

But the observance of Sunday cannot be enforced by law without violating the principle of religious liberty. Why should I violate the conscience of my Jewish fellow-citizens by compelling them to do that which their religion teaches them to regard as sacrilegious, any more than they—if they were in the ascendency—should violate mine by requiring me to observe the Jewish Sabbath instead of the Christian?

But the enforcement of one holiday by the government would soon give rise to another and we would soon have, as in some parts of Europe, a constant round of days to be held sacred.

8. Another subject connected with this movement is the use of the Bible as a text book in the public schools. The excuse for it is that if the Bible is not read in our public schools the young will grow up without reverence for the word of God and its sacred teachings. But an ample and most effective remedy for this is found in the Sunday Schools of the various denominations, where Bible-teaching is a specialty; and at the same time without any of

the difficulties which occur in the public schools. Here the attendance is voluntary and each may select the school of his own denomination; and the zeal of Christian workmen, to say nothing of the rivalry of opposing sects, secures a more thorough and universal system of Bible teaching than could possibly be attained in the public schools often conducted by godless teachers. And thus no violence would be done to the conscience of any.

But there are insuperable difficulties in the way of forcing the Bible into the public schools. The question of versions meets us at the very threshold. The common English version, while excellent in many respects, is full of admitted deficiencies. So that during the past twenty-five years two independent movements have been set on foot to revise the common version, and we will soon have two rival revised versions. Now if we adopt either of these we offend the friends of the other. If we fall back upon the version of King James we must take it with all its faults. This perhaps Protestants and Baptists could do; but the Catholic regards it as full of damnable heresies, and the Jew is offended by the New Testament in any version. But why should we violate the conscience of these citizens by forcing them to have their children taught what is contrary to their religious belief? If the Protestants would not suffer the Catholic version to be used in the public schools, why should they force theirs upon Catholics?

CHAPTER II.

THE CHURCH AN EXECUTIVE—NOT A LEGISLATIVE BODY.

In the last chapter I demonstrated that the government of the church is spiritual—that its subjects are spiritual, and the ends to be attained of a spiritual character. This being the case all its laws must be of divine origin, for only such can be adapted to spiritual uses.

I now propose to show that the church is an executive, not a legislative body; that its province is to enforce the laws which God has given for its government, not to make new ones. And as this is the starting point of error I may be excused for giving considerable space to the consideration of the subject.

Such is the extent to which men have been drawn as a logical sequence of the rejection of this conservative principle, that they have exalted the church, in some of its co-ordinate branches, into the vicegerent of God on earth. The bull of Pio Nono, making the Immaculate Conception of the Virgin Mary an article of Faith, essential to salvation; and the decree of the recent council of Rome declaring the dogma of Papal Infallibility, are legitimate deductions from the false assumption that the church possesses legislative power.

But this fundamental error is not confined to the Church of Rome. It is the foundation upon which most of the errors of Protestantism are based, under pretext of "modeling the church according to the circumstances of time and place so long as they do not transcend a known law of Christ." [Dr. Bangs.] Assuming that the form of Church Government "may vary with the other varying circumstances of human society; with the extent of a country; the manners of the inhabitants (!!) the nature of its civil government, and many other peculiarities which might be named," [Bishop Tomline]. men have changed the original institution of Christ and set aside His laws for the commandments and ordinances of men.

The only barrier to this innovation is absolute restriction upon the power of legislation. Concede to man the right to make laws for his own moral government, and the legislation will partake of his own character, and the door be opened for every change that the caprice of man can suggest. But to concede this, is to admit that man is better able to judge what his moral wants require than God himself.

I am not now discussing the question whether God has given His church any government at all, and what is the form of that government. That will be reserved for subsequent chapters. But I am only seeking to find where the legislative power is lodged. In every government there is a power that makes laws, and the inquiry I am now instituting is, whether God has chosen to reserve to himself the right of making laws for the government of His church, or has conceded a part of that right to man. Will any deny that the original right belongs to God? Then if he has granted to the church the right to make laws for its government is it at all unreasonable, that one who is affected thereby should demand to see the patent under the sign manual of the Great King? Until such authority is produced, I must continue to believe that no such power exists.

The government of God is an absolute one. He is an absolute sovereign, and no one can claim to share his government with Him, unless He chooses to delegate that power. If that authority has been conferred, the burden of proving the express permission of God rests upon those who claim the right to exercise it. Where is it written in the King's Book, that man may remodel the church, which Christ has established to suit his own notions of propriety?

I have elsewhere remarked that the church is the visible manifestation of God's moral government. Nowhere else do we find His laws embodied and arrangements made for their administration. The whole business of the church is to promulgate those laws; to make known to God's rebellious subjects the terms of reconciliation; to collect the reconciled into organized bodies for their mutual support, encouragement, instruction and correction. The admission and excision of members is merely incidental and consists in the exercise of a fallible judgment as to the persons who ought to compose the visible body of Christ. All strictly judicial powers God has reserved to himself because He alone can discern the thoughts and intents of the heart. What is called the punitive discipline of the church consists only in withdrawing the fellowship of the brotherhood from a person who is supposed to be disorderly, and withholding from him the privileges of membership; but this must be done in strict accordance with the regulations of Christ. Has God prescribed who shall compose His church? Then, man cannot admit others, or exclude any who possess the prescribed qualifications. Has God declared for what offences one shall be excluded? Can man establish other requirements than those which God has established and debar those who disregard them? Or can he restrict the law of God so as to retain in fellowship those who are punishable by the law of Christ? Can man change any law of Christ, or any law of the Gospel? Can he alter the terms of reconciliation to God or the manner of making these known? If he possesses any such power God has given it. Then we ask with renewed emphasis, where is it?

But say those who advocate the power of legislation in the church, we may not change the fundamentals, but we may legislate upon matters indifferent! Then who is to be the judge of what is indifferent? The assumption subjects the whole law of God to the supervision of man, who is by nature inclined to evade God's requirements. Once admit this power in man, and you furnish him a lever to upset the whole law of God; for he will not be long in concluding that whatever does not suit his taste or convenience is indifferent.

The safe rule of conduct in matters of religion is to do literally what God has commanded, or expressly permitted, and let alone entirely what He has considered too indifferent to make the subject of a command; for if a thing is of too little importance for God to prescribe it, then it can be no matter if it be left undone entirely; and if a thing is of sufficient importance to be commanded then it is important enough to be done. Better be content with doing what is commanded, lest we sin attempting to help God make laws. He knows what we need, and we cannot commend ourselves to His favor by attempting works of supererogation.

If God has given the church any legislative power surely it can be shown. The express grant can be pointed out; and as I remarked in the outset, the burden of proof rests upon those who assert its existence.

Here I might leave the subject, confident that no such permission has been given, either expressly or by fair inference from the powers conferred; and that whoever waits for the production of the authority of God to abrogate, alter or amend His law, will always leave the institution of Christ intact. But I propose to examine the subject further, and to show affirmatively that God has prohibited us from adding to or taking from what He has been graciously pleased to reveal as His will.

The national establishment of the Jews is frequently referred to as a prototype of the Christian Church—a question I will hereafter consider. But there is at least one respect in which the parallel holds good. They are both strictly theocratic. When God led the children of Israel out of the land of Egypt by the hand of Moses, and set them up as a nation, he gave them not only the fundamental laws of their government, but even minutely prescribed the smallest affairs. He not only enunciated the great code of moral law, but He enacted the penal statutes and the minutest forms of worship. Nay, He even went so far as to prescribe the manner of purification and to regulate the food of the people, and the very clothing of the priests, in the neglect of which no man could be held guiltless.

It is a remarkable feature in the Jewish economy that they possessed no legislative body, with power to make and alter their laws like other nations. God was their sole law-giver, and there could be no such defects as pertain to mere human codes and which require to be changed to conform to the experience of men.

At first the execution of the laws was entrusted to judges; an institution they dared not abolish until they obtained the express permission of the Almighty. Indeed, God gave them a King as a punishment for that very spirit of discontent which led them to seek a change.

If under the Jewish dispensation, which related to temporal and external things, and was merely preparatory to that which should follow, the power of legislation was withheld, may we not reasonably infer that under the new dispensation where eternal interests are involved, God has much more reserved to himself the making of even the smallest regulations. And if the Lord smote Uzzah because he dared to put forth sacrilegious hands to the ark of wood, which had been made in all things according to the pattern shown in the Mount, how will He hold men guiltless who presume to lay profane hands upon the ark of the better covenant? The motive of Uzzah seems to have been a good one; for it is said that the ark shook; and he was evidently prompted by the desire to prevent its falling. So, no doubt, many who touch the sacred structure of God's church, vainly imagine that they do God a service by propping up His house by some contrivance of their own. But let them beware lest they meet the fate of Uzzah.

To the Jews this plain law was given: "Now, therefore, hearken, O Israel, unto the statutes and unto the judgments which I teach you, to do them; that ye may live and go in, and possess the land which the Lord God of your fathers giveth you. Ye shall not add unto the word which I command you, neither shall ye diminish aught from it, that ye may keep the commandments of the Lord your God which I command you." (Deut. iv: 1-2). And although they did change these laws in many respects the Saviour rebukes them for making void the law by their traditions.

If God demanded such a strict compliance with His laws under the old dispensation, does He require less under the new? Indeed an examination of the New Testament will satisfy any impartial inquirer that Christ is the only law-giver of His church. He himself declares (Matt. xxviii: 18) "All power is given unto me in heaven and *in earth;*" and He gives this as a reason why He commands them to "Go disciple all nations." If *all* power *in earth* is given to Jesus Christ, then the church possesses none but such as He sees proper to confer upon her. But as if foreseeing that men would pervert authority, he added, "teaching them to observe all things whatsoever I have commanded you." The command is to *observe* the regulations *He* has given—no others; for the direction to do a particular thing is a prohibition to do another instead, according to the well known principle of legal interpretation *expressio unius, exclusio alterius.*

Again (Col. i : 16). "For by Him were all things created that are in heaven and that are in earth, visible and invisible, whether thrones or DOMINIONS or PRINCIPALITIES or POWERS." Here is a positive declaration that all power emanates from the Lord Jesus Christ. If he has conferred upon any body of men the power to legislate for His church, surely the clause can be found in this musty old charter of Christian liberty.

The Lord is expressly declared to be the law-giver (Isaiah xxxiii: 22) "The Lord is our law-giver and king." Then any other law-giver is a usurper of the divine prerogative. The apostle James declares (James iv: 12) "There is one law-giver." This necessarily implies that there is but one. Any other interpretation would destroy its force in the passage, for the declaration occurs in the climax of a rebuke to those to whom it is addressed for presuming to prescribe a law for the government of their brethren.

To assume that there is any other law-giver than Christ, even in the smallest particulars, is to impeach His wisdom and foresight. It implies that He lacked either the will or the ability to provide sufficient laws for the government of His people. God forgive the presumption of those who would exalt man above his Maker.

It seems, therefore, that the church has no power

to enact new laws or to abrogate old ones; and that nothing ought to be established in the church but what is commanded in the Word of God, or is deducible from the apostolic example. And if as Richard Hooker, the learned apologist of innovation declares, "the application of this principle affects all churches," it cannot change the truth of the principle, but only proves that all have been unfaithful to their trust. It is but a poor apology for wrong doing, to show that others are equally guilty.

But I will discuss more fully the perpetuity of the laws established by Christ in another part of this work.

CHAPTER III.

THE OBJECT AND USES OF CHURCH GOVERNMENT.— SECTION I.—GENERAL REMARKS.

Government is a necessary concomitant of man in his social relations. Religion is based upon the social principle and grows out of our relations to each other and to God. And as man cannot abstract himself from those relations, it follows that government is an essential condition of his being.

All human governments grow out of a community of interests, and the mutual dependence and reciprocal obligations of the individuals that compose each respectively. Church government results from the very institution of Christianity, and he who accepts the latter has no option but to receive the former. It is the visible manifestation of God's moral government, so far as He has entrusted the execution of His laws to human hands.

I make no scruple in adopting the following judicious remarks of Richard Watson:

The Christian church," says he, "being then a visible and permanent society, bound to observe certain rites and obey certain rules, the existence of government is necessarily supposed. All religious *rites* suppose *order*, all order *direction* and *control;* and these a *directive* and *controlling power*. Again all laws are nugatory without enforcement in the present mixed and imperfect state of society; and all enforcement supposes an *executive*. If baptism be the door of admission into the church, some must judge of the fitness of candidates, and administrators of this rite must be appointed; if the Lord's supper must be partaken of, the times and the modes are to be determined, the qualifications of communicants judged of and the administration placed in proper hands; if worship must be social and public, here again must be an appointment of times, order and administration; if the word of God is to be read and preached, then readers and preachers are necessary; if the continuance of any one in the fellowship of Christians be conditioned upon good conduct so that the purity and credit of the church may be guarded, then the power of enforcing discipline must be lodged somewhere. Thus government flows necessarily from the very nature of the institution of the Christian church; and since this institution has the authority of Christ and His apostles, it is not to be supposed that its government was left unprovided for; and if they have in fact made such a provision, it is no more a matter of mere option with Christians whether they will be subject to government or not, than it is optional with them 'to confess Christ by becoming its members" [Inst. vol. 2; p. 572.

The nature of Church government has already been discussed in part and will be resumed hereafter; and also the inquiry as to the persons to whom it is intrusted. The subject of the present inquiry is the ends of church government without respect to the means to be employed to attain those ends.

And I remark in general that as the object of human government is to improve the material condition of its subjects, so the object of God's moral government as embodied in the church is to promote the spiritual good of His followers.

In succeeding chapters I will take up these subjects in detail, and I invoke the guidance of the Great Head of the Church to lead me into all truth, and to imbue my heart with love to all His children, even to those whom I may consider erring.

But there is a limit to the extent of church power which I now proceed to consider.

SECTION II.—THE RIGHTS OF CONSCIENCE.

Upon one occasion the disciples came to Jesus, saying: "Master, we saw one casting out devils in thy name, and he followeth not us; and we forbade him, because he followeth not us." But Jesus said, "Forbid him not." The evident teaching of the Saviour is that we may not prohibit the free exercise of religion, even though it may be a false religion, assuming to act in the name of Jesus.

The history of the Christian religion is but a history of the triumphs and defeats of principles involving the rights of conscience. And although these rights in the present century have received a more general recognition than in times past, yet they are still but imperfectly understood and inadequately enforced.

This question does not, as many suppose, involve the discussion of the question which has puzzled some casuists, whether a man has the natural right to do wrong; but it does involve the question whether one man may rightfully assume to be the keeper of another's conscience.

The mistakes of the past have grown out of two fundamental errors: the supposed responsibility of one man for the faith of another, and the necessity for universal conformity to some established form of doctrine at whatever cost.

The lesson referred to in the beginning of this section was meant to rebuke the assumption of authority on the part of His disciples to restrict the freedom of other men's consciences. These were His true disciples and those they would have forbidden were not; for they followed Him not. It was not theirs to forbid. That is the prerogative of God, who alone is the Master of the conscience. He alone possesses this authority, because He alone can exercise it with unerring wisdom.

No man has the right to forbid another the free exercise of his religious faith, or prescribe for him what he shall believe, or how he shall worship.

No man's own conscience can be relied on as an unerring guide to his own duty, much less can anothers. But imperfect a guide as is conscience, God has given one to each individual, and he is responsible alone to Him who gave it for its abuse. If God had given the moral sense to only a few then we might conclude that He intended them to be the directors of others, but as He has given the moral sense to all men it is clearly deducible therefrom that He meant each to make use of it in determining his own line of duty.

There are two reasons why one man cannot take cognizance of the conscience of another. One man is just as liable to err as another, and he who undertakes to regulate the duty of another may himself be in the wrong. Besides, he is wholly unable to control the mind of another, or to inflict adequate punishment for disobedience. Hence the conflicts of conscience must of necessity be adjourned to the arbitrament of a higher tribunal than man can erect, and one whose decisions cannot err.

What one may not do in this respect, an aggregate of individuals calling themselves the church, may not do. Those who associate religiously may and indeed ought to make a declaration of their faith, and so long as one continues a member of that society, he is bound to conform to its creed. And the church may rightfully exercise discipline over its members, and insist upon their conformity to the authorized standards under pain of excision from its privileges. It is absurd to suppose that a man has the right to enjoy all the benefits and privileges of an association and yet set its laws at defiance. This would be to subordinate the rights of the many to the will of the few. But the church has no jurisdiction over any but its own members. It has no right to judge them that are without. It may punish its erring members by withdrawing its fellowship, because it is commanded to withdraw from every brother that walketh disorderly. It may cast the heretic out of its pale, but it may pursue him no further. There, its authority over him ceases.

Alas! what tyranny has been perpetrated in the

name of the church! What vain efforts to bind the consciences of men and to coerce them to a compliance with established forms, as if conviction of duty were a thing of volition, and as if the forced, outward compliance were not hypocrisy that imperils the souls of men as much as the worst forms of heresy.

Nor can the State prescribe the faith of individuals. Christ taught His disciples to render unto Cæsar the things that be Cæsar's. Thus while He recognized Cæsar as the civil sovereign He bestowed upon him no authority to rule in the church, but charged His disciples to render unto God the things that are God's. To concede to the State the authority to regulate matters of religion would be to place the interests of Christianity at the disposal of ungodly men, who have no love for God or His government, and who are disposed to punish severely an act of non-conformity in some trifling external and leave the grossest sins unpunished.

Human governments are established to provide for the temporal, not the spiritual interests of the people. The founder of Christianity himself declared, "My kingdom is not of this world." The unholy connection of Church and State is destructive to that spiritual character which belongs to the Kingdom of Christ. To presume to forbid the free exercise of religion is to assume the prerogative of God, and to undertake to regulate that which is beyond the reach of human enactment.

The teaching of the Saviour referred to at the beginning of this section, prohibits persecution for religion's sake. One may not prohibit another the free exercise of his religious convictions nor punish him for the use of his rights of conscience. This case is very much in point, for the persons in question confessedly did not follow Chirst. But, notwithstanding, He commanded: "Forbid them not."

The Apostolic Church. 37

To lodge such a power in any organization, composed of fallible men, would have been to jeopardize the interests of true religion, because false religion, gaining the ascendency, might suppress the true.

Religion must be voluntary. God will not accept a constrained service. It must be a freewill offering. He uses persuasions but He will not accept the service of the lips while the heart is far from Him. He hates every form of sin; but most especially the sin of hypocrisy—an outward, but not an inward compliance with the law.

The spirit of persecution is cruel and wholly at war with the peaceful and gentle teachings of Christ. The bloody annals of Rome teem with examples of the most shocking cruelties. The reeking vallies of Piedmont; the butcheries perpetrated in the Crusades against the Albigenses in France, and the horrible massacre of St. Bartholomew, all attest that the spirit of persecution is not the spirit of Christ.

But persecution always has and always will fail to produce the desired uniformity of faith. In spite of prisons and gibbets and glowing fagots, conscience ever has and ever will assert its rights. That which was denounced as heresy and sought to be exterminated, has always proved like the fabled hydra; as fast as one head was stricken down, another rose in its stead. The martyrdom of John Huss and Jerome of Prague, filled Bohemia with followers, who like Ziska, were ready to bequeath their skins to cover a drum to rally the scattered forces of those who determinedly resisted the oppression of their tyrants. Bigotry in its mad rage dug up and burned the bones of Wickliffe, and scattered the ashes upon the Avon. "But the Avon bore them to the Severn, the Severn to the sea, the sea to the ocean and the ocean to all lands." The Church of England persecuted John Wesley, but now his followers outnumber the partizans who pursued him. The established clergy imprisoned the Baptists in Virginia, and now more than one tenth of the population of the State are Baptists. The weapons of persecution have ever rebounded to the injury of those who have invoked them, thus verifying the words of Jesus, "they that take the sword shall perish by the sword."

But Christ did not mean to teach that a man's religious belief is of no consequence and that we are to make no effort to reclaim men to the truth. This would involve the suppression of truth itself. While we may not forbid one in the free exercise of his convictions of duty; we may and ought to labor to convince him of his errors and persuade him to abandon them.

In order that men may do right, it is necessary that they should believe right. The connection between doing and believing is so close that the salvation of men is made dependent upon their faith. And as all men are more or less guided by their conscientious convictions of duty, how important that we labor to enlighten their consciences by the presentation of the truth.

Jesus could not have revealed a system of faith and then taught men to disregard it. This would have been to disparage His own teachings and to set at nought His own precepts. Indeed, it would have been to little purpose that He announced the truths of the Gospel if men were not taught to obey them. The mere fact that He dignified the Gospel by preaching it himself is an evidence that He meant that its requirements should be obeyed. Religion is too serious a subject for its very author to trifle about it.

Neither could the Saviour have meant that it is a matter of indifference whether men follow Him or not. I have known this example to be quoted to prove that the differences between Christians are of no consequence, and that one form of worshipping God is about as good as another; that it is all a matter of taste. But this idea is a snare of the devil, and is only one step removed from infidelity, for he who is not attached to some form of religion, in reality cares but little for any. With him religion is a mere accident, and under different circumstances he would as readily become a Pagan or Mahommedan, a Jew or Christian.

Christ made following Him the test of discipleship: "Whosoever doth not bear his cross and come after me, he cannot be my disciple." Obedience to Him is the standard of allegiance: "Ye are my friends if ye do whatsoever I have commanded you." The Saviour did not therefore mean to inculcate the idea that the person who was the occasion of this lesson, was as acceptable to Him as one of His followers.

If we are absolutely to let men alone in their errors, truth would make no headway, and as error has more ready access to the minds and hearts of men, truth itself would soon retire into the bosom of God, and the world be given over to hardness of heart and reprobacy of mind to believe a lie and be damned. But truth is aggressive. It fights its way to victory over prostrate error. It knows no compromise and gives no quarter.

We are to labor to bring men to the truth, but the weapons of our warfare are not carnal but spiritual. We are to appeal to the conscience and to reason by sound arguments and facts. The rack and the torture may terrify and intimidate but they cannot convince. They may cause the heretic to feign and dissemble, but they can never truly convert him to the truth.

The commission to His followers was: "Go disciple all nations, teaching them to observe all things whatsoever I have commanded you." This command could never be complied with if Christians are to be passive and wink at the existence of false doctrine. But persuasion, not coercion, is the Christian's prescribed mode of procedure. We may not depreciate the value of firm religious faith. This is absolutely necessary to piety. He who is without it is not far from being an infidel. He who attaches no importance to the faith he holds will be careless of his conduct. Hence Paul admonishes the Romans: "Let every one be fully persuaded in his own mind." What is piety but an earnest conviction of truth. But a "double-minded man" (one who has no fixed and settled views of religion) says James, "is unstable in all his ways." That religion makes but little impression upon the heart that has had no definite effect upon the mind. It is only when truth becomes vivid to the mind that it becomes warm to the heart. The most zealous Christians are those who are most established in the faith.

Thus, we have seen that one man has no right to coerce the conscience of another, or forbid the free exercise of his religious views. But at the same time a correct religious faith is of the highest importance and Christ demands nothing less than the most implicit obedience. While He forbade His disciples to interfere with the freedom of the heretic, He did not mean to depreciate the truth and place errorists on the same footing with His true followers.

CHAPTER IV.

THE OBJECTS AND USES OF CHURCH GOVERNMENT CONTINUED.

Section 1. The Preservation of Doctrine.

The general object of church government is to promote the spiritual good of its proper subjects, and to convert the world to its faith. So far all are agreed; but when we descend to particulars and inquire in what manner it should be applied to the promotion of that general end, and whether it may extend beyond this legitimate object, these are questions about which Christians are more or less unhappily divided.

I proceed now to consider in detail some of the particular uses of church government, and first among these, the preservation of the doctrines and laws of Christ's kingdom. In this general statement there is no disagreement, but in the application of this use great abuses have been perpetrated. Indeed it has been pushed so far as to destroy the right of private judgment, and to require a blind submission to the pretended infallible decrees of the church, not only in the interpretation of the word, but in the enunciation of new *dogmata;* as if the assembly of a number of fallible men could render the aggregate infallible. Nay, men have even gone further than this, and in addition to the right to add to the articles of religion, they have required their acceptance with the same unquestioning obedience as the revealed teachings of the Bible.

Such a power God never entrusted to fallible men. He has revealed in his word all that is necessary to be believed or done in order to salvation; and man may not diminish his requirements or make the terms more difficult. To assert otherwise is to charge him with leaving his work incomplete and permitting man to finish it for him. To assume that he has thus omitted anything of importance is to impeach his benevolence and wisdom. If on the other hand it be assumed that the church may add things unimportant, then it may be replied that if they are so unimportant that God has not commanded them, they cannot be of sufficient importance to require any action of the church to enforce them.

Christ revealed a distinct form of doctrine and practice, embracing all that is needful to be believed and to be done, and he entrusted to his church the preservation and propagation of his doctrines and ordinances. Said he: "Go disciple all nations, baptizing them in the name of the Father, and of the Son, and of the Holy Spirit, TEACHING THEM TO OBSERVE ALL THINGS WHATSOEVER I HAVE COMMANDED YOU." In his word are recorded his teachings. As a system of religious faith it is complete. All that God requires is here found with reasonable certainty. To do less than he has required is sinful neglect, to do more is presumptuous folly.

Paul said, (2. Thes. ii. 15,) "Therefore, brethren, stand fast, and hold the traditions ye have been taught." It was his boast that he had "not shunned to declare the whole council of God." Jude exhorts the church to "contend earnestly for the faith once delivered unto the saints." The precious treasure of divine truth was "committed to earthen vessels that the excellence of the power might be of God and not of man." This precious truth with all its sanctifying power upon the heart was to be handed down by the church as an heirloom of priceless value from generation to generation. The church was to bear witness to the truth of the gospel, to exemplify the divine power of the word in its practical effects upon its members; to transmit the written word pure and unaltered from age to age; to expound its teachings through its chosen officers; and to exert all its influence to induce men to embrace the truth in the love of it. But while its interpretations of the divine law are always entitled to respect they have no binding force upon the conscience further than they are in conformity to the truth. And that all men may be able to judge of the correctness of her interpretations, the written word of divine truth, carefully and faithfully preserved must be open and accessible to all. That word is the only touchstone of truth. Here every opinion must be tried.

The duty to preserve and extend the truth is further evident from the fact that the doctrines of the Gospel are the chief instrumentalities to be employed in the conversion of the world. The gospel is the power of God unto salvation to every one that believeth. It is the sword of the Spirit. This word enforced by the Holy Spirit is the power of God. It is not within the scope of my present remarks to speak of how this is accomplished, but to enforce the truth that through the propagation of the gospel this end is attained by the church. The gospel embraces all the doctrines, precepts and injunctions of the New Testament, and while all its truths are not equally important and vital, they are parts of a harmonious whole, each important in its place and it is the mission of the church to uphold them all, each in its own order. It does not become the obedient, faithful Christian, to inquire how little of the gospel may be made the power of God unto the salvation of the soul. We should leave the adjustment of so delicate a question to God himself, and strive to know all the gospel teaches, to do all it requires, and to communicate nothing less to our fellow men.

There is no doubt more or less error in every human effort to impart religious instruction, but error never yet converted and ministered to the spiritual growth of a single soul. Only gospel truth has that power. If we could always realize this and were concerned for the salvation of souls and the promotion of truth rather than our favor with the people, how anxious we would be to crowd our discourses with as much gospel truth as possible. The flowers of rhetoric and the graces of composition would give us less concern; and the great question would be what does the gospel teach in regard to this doctrine or duty, and how can I best communicate it to my fellow men.

There are some who think that only the great fundamental truths about which the mass of Christians are agreed should be enforced. But this would be to leave much of the gospel untaught Every part of that truth has its office to perform and whoever out of deference to his fellow men suppresses any part of the gospel even the most unimportant, (if it be right to call anything unimportant which God has established,) he that far fails in his duty. How dare any man trifle with the souls of men by withholding any part of the truth. How shall he know that the very truth he withholds is the truth ordained of God for the salvation of some soul that hears. While God has honored certain great truths more than others, if the lesser truths had not their office to perform in the work of salvation, they would not encumber his word. It is therefore the duty of the church to preserve and transmit all the truth.

While the gospel is the great instrumentality by which sinners are called to repentance it is also the principal means employed by the Holy Spirit in sanctifying the hearts of Christians. There is a native power in truth which by its own inherent excellence tends to enlighten and elevate the world. And if there were no other agency than this sanctifying power, the reading of the word and the preaching of the gospel would benefit mankind. The sacred precepts of its divine morality partake so much of the nature of God from whom they emanate that the gospel must leave its impress upon the characters of those with whom it comes in contact. However excellent the code of morals taught in ancient philosophy they all related to external intercourse of man with his fellow men. But the morality of the gospel reaches a higher plane. It springs from the principle of holiness implanted in the heart by the Spirit of God, and respects our relations to God. Its precepts are not the dry and lifeless deductions of human reason, but they are full of the life and power of the Spirit. They are life-giving. The soul (Spirit) of God is in them, and they awaken spiritual life wherever they are received into the heart. Pure and holy they render those who yield to them not only blameless in outward life, but pure in the inner man. And this is true not only of the moral precepts of the gospel but the doctrines and ordinances all tend to the same end. "It is written that man shall not live on bread alone, but on every word that proceeds out of the mouth of God." His truth is the food by which our spirtual natures are sustained. The purer that word the more spiritual nourishment is afforded. In proportion as the dross of human invention mingles with it in that proportion does it become unwholesome, and as the truth is suppressed just in that ratio is the soul dwarfed and impoverished.

The obligation of the church to preserve the revelation of God, pure and intact may be seen in the fearful denunciation at the close of Revelations: "If any man shall add unto these things, God shall add unto him the plagues written in this book.

And if any man shall take away from the words of the book of this prophecy, God shall take away his part out of the book of life, and out of the Holy City, and from the things written in this book."

While it is true that this language has a special application to the Book of Revelations, the reason of the thing makes it equally applicable to every part of God's word. For whatever reason would make it a crime to tamper with any part of God's word, would apply with equal force to every other. It cannot be supposed that God meant to protect a single book of his sacred volume from sacrilegious hands, while all the balance was to be desecrated with impunity. I take it therefore that these warnings and denunciations apply to the whole word of God and the passage was placed thus at the end of the last God-given writing not only to show that he had closed the revelation of his will and that the spirit of inspiration had been withdrawn, but that this awful sentence like a beacon light might shed its warning rays backward over the whole volume of His word. It supposes the reader to have begun with the dim outline of the earth's early history as contained in the Book of Genesis—that he has traced the remarkable history of the Jews—that he has been thrilled with the devotional poetry of the book, and has followed the shadowy visions of prophecy; that he has sat at the feet of the God-man and heard his teachings as detailed in the gospels; that he has noted the wonderful didactic sentences of the Epistles; and that with the last lingering apostle he has stood and gazed through the Gates ajar into the invisble world, and now as he closes the Sacred Volume, oppressed with its great thought, these fearful words thunder in his ears the curse of God against the impious mortal who would dare to attempt to add to or take from the Book.

It will be observed that the great crime against which God hurled such a fearful curse may be committed either by suppressing any part of the word, or by adding anything to it. It will be sufficient to consider these together, and thus save much unnecessary subdivision and repetition.

1. This crime may be committed by the transmission of imperfect copies of the Sacred Writings. To the first churches was entrusted the custody of the autograph books of the New Testament as written by the apostles. To keep these and to cause exact copies to be made was the peculiar duty of the church. And when in the lapse of time the original autographs had perished or were lost, it was necessary to preserve accurate copies and cause others to be made of them; to see that no additions, omissions, or variations occurred. And if errors crept into the text from accident or design to faithfully restore as far as possible the original words.

2. As the Gentile nations, who were not acquainted with the original languages in which the Scriptures were written received the gospel, it became necessary for their Spiritual improvement to make translations into their vernacular. To have this faithfully done was the duty of the churches; not to do it was a crime. To lock up the word of truth from the masses of the people in unknown languages, is a high spiritual offense. The church was to be the light of the world. It was to spread, not to hide the truth of God. Hence the church should seek out and cause to be made the best possible translations into all languages from the most accurate copies of the original.

3. This offense may also be committed by ministers of the gospel handling the word of God deceitfully. They are set in the church of God for the interpretation of the Word. But if they permit

their prejudices, their ignorance, or worldly interests to color their elucidation of divine truth, and pervert the teachings of the Scriptures, they are guilty of adding to or taking from God's word. Hence it behooves the church to admit none to teach but such as are apt, sound in the faith, and who are honest and faithful, and if any pervert the way of truth to be careful not to bid them Godspeed. False teachers should receive no countenance from the church. "Beware of false prophets," said the Saviour. Paul said to the Gentiles: "If any man preach any other doctrine unto you than that ye have recieved, let him be accursed." John says: "Whosoever transgresseth, and abideth not in the doctrine of Christ, hath not God. He that abideth in the doctrine of Christ, he hath both the Father and Son. If there come any unto you, and bring not this doctrine receive him not into your house, neither bid him Godspeed, for he that biddeth him Godspeed is partaker of his evil deeds." How unlike the charity of to-day that places the teachers of falsehood on a par with the teachers of the truth, and invites the propagaters of error to teach in the pulpits of the church. Certain it is that he who found admittance into the apostolic church was required to be a man sound in the faith.

4. The crime of suppressing or adding to God's truth may be committed by the decrees of councils and the bulls of Popes. Wherever an ecclesiastical assembly or papal order presumes to enact any new law for the government of God's church, or to add new *dogmata* to the articles of religion, or seeks to abolish or to lesson the obligation of any law which Christ has established, they incur the curse of God. The council held at Jerusalem, sometimes called erroneously, the first ecumenical council of Jerusalem, furnishes no authority for

the assumptions of subsequent councils. The decree passed at Jerusalem was but declarative of the Holy Spirit. "It seemed good unto the Holy Spirit and unto us," is the acknowledgment of the body as recorded in Acts xv: 28. They claimed no authority to decree anything, but the Holy Spirit spoke through them as it spoke through the writers of the New Testament. Any enactment of an assembly not exactly in accord with God's revealed word is worthless and nugatory. And the law of Christ endorsed by the church receives no additional authority.

It is the duty of the church to preserve the truth of God in its purity, because it is the light of the world. But if any part of it is withheld to that extent is the world in darkness. If any word is added it can only have the effect to mar the beauty and excellence of that which was before absolutely perfect and pure. Its alteration misguides souls in the most important concern of life. The gospel is ordained to be the power of God unto salvation to every one that believeth. But in so far as any part of that law is suppressed, in so far as the terms are altered by an attempted amendment, in so far is its power weakened: because God's work cannot be improved upon.

SECTION 2. *How the doctrine of Christ is to be preserved.*—There are two ways in which this is to be done, by bearing testimony to the truth and by exposing error.

1. By upholding the truth. The Saviour when about to depart from the world gathered his chosen disciples about him, and appointed them to the high mission of bearing witness for himself. It is plain that the public instructors—the ministry—are the principal agents in the dissemination of the doctrines of Christ. These are the heralds of God,

the ambassadors of Christ, who go forth bearing the precious truths of the gospel.

But they are not exclusively entrusted with this work. The whole church is an organized *propaganda* of the truth. It is the aggregate of many faithful witnesses, all of whom should concur in the same testimony. It is the City set upon a hill which cannot be hid, harmonious in all its parts, the adorned, the loved of God. It is the church that commissions and sends forth the ministers of the word, and upholds the truth in her recognized standards; for what are creeds but the voice of the church declaring what is taught by Christ.

Indeed each individual Christian is designed to be a living witness for Christ. an epistle known and read of all men. He is a candle set to give light in all the house.

All thus co-operating, we must bear no uncertain or partial testimony. A tree is known by its fruit, and our fruit must be of unmistakable quality. We must neither obscure nor pervert the testimony we bear. We may not compromise or suppress any part of the truth. Though all men should be offended, we may not shrink from a faithful maintainance of what Jesus taught. This often requires much firmness and decision of character.

We can better bear to be reproached as narrow-minded and bigoted than to withhold fellowship from those we love, but who lack the necessary qualifications to share in our privileges. But we must be equally deaf to the tender voice of affection and the sharp rebuke of hatred, if they seek to win us from faithful allegiance to Christ. The constant sentiment of every Christian should be: "Though all shall be offended because of thee, I will never be offended."

No doctrine taught in his word; no duty inculcated therein should be suppressed or its proper enunciation be avoided lest men should be offended. To do so is to be unfaithful to the Master. We are required to be ready at all times to give a reason of the hope within us, to "contend earnestly for the faith once delivered to the saints," "to be instant in season and out of season, to exhort, rebuke, reprove with all long suffering and doctrine."

2. But it is much easier to uphold and defend the truth than to assail error. Many errorists are willing to enter into terms with the cause of truth by which each may sustain his own grounds undisturbed. But when we cross the boundary line and attack error in its own entrenchments we awaken all its forces. "Let us alone!" cry the adherents of error. "Let them alone!" re-echo those whose hearts have never been sufficiently impressed with the truth to feel its importance. But the voice of God is: "Cry aloud: spare not: lift up thy voice as a trumpet and show my people their transgressions and the house of Jacob their sins!"

It may be said that this course will lead to religious controversy and bad feelings be engendered. If so the responsibility is not upon the advocates of truth. Paul who did more than any other in building up the Apostolic Churches, was constantly involved in controversy. It was his boast near the close of life that he had not shunned to declare the whole counsel of God, and he sharply reproved every form of error. This brought him into constant collisions. Of him it is said: "He went into the synagogues and spake boldly for the space of three months, disputing and persuading the things concerning the kingdom of God." He afterwards "disputed daily in the school of one Tyrannus, and this he continued by the space of two years." Paul was in no way responsible for the uproar at Ephesus, though he had "persuaded and turned away much people; saying that they be no gods, which are made with hands." Christ recognized the irrepressible antagonism between truth and error when he said: "Think not that I am come to send peace on the earth: I came not to send peace but a sword. For I am come to set a man at variance with his father, and the daughter with her mother, and the daughter in-law with her mother-in-law. And a man's foes shall be they of his own household." The church was born amid the clash of arms, and bitter controversy has marked every step of its progress and will do so as long as sin and hatred to God and His truth exist in the world.

Armed with the sword of the Spirit which is the word of God, the church goes forth upon its mission. It alone has power to kill and make alive. The church needs no carnal weapons to enforce the truth. There is a power in the doctrine of Christ which gains a triumphant victory over every heart prepared by the Spirit of God. It uses no coercion but that of persuasion, and thus from age to age its mission is accomplished.

SECTION 3. *The Rights of Private Judgment.*—While it is the duty of the church to expound and preserve the truth, its expositions are entitled to respect only when in accordance with God's word. Its decisions are not so ultimate as to preclude the exercise of private judgment.

Religion is a personal matter. Its duties and obligations are all personal. Faith, the foundation of the whole, is personal. It would be strange indeed if God required of me correct faith, and held me responsible for my religious belief, and yet required me to submit my judgment to others and to receive without question whatever might be prescribed by men as fallible as myself. God would never require me to receive the opinion of another, and yet hold me responsible for its correctness. Responsibility and choice necessarily go together. The voice of the church is but the sum of private judgments; and the responsibility of the whole is but the aggregate of individual responsibility. There can be no corporate moral responsibility because a corporation has no soul, and cannot therefore commit any crime. As such it is incapable of thought, choice or any action, which implies a moral quality. Whatever capability the assembled church may have for determining the truth, it is but the individual judgment of those who compose it.

If it be said that the voice of the church is the voice of the Holy Spirit speaking through the aggregate of individuals, it may be answered that it is not certain that all the individuals are in communication with the Holy Spirit. The voice of the majority cannot be relied on absolutely as the voice of truth. Christ said: "If ANY MAN will do his will he shall know of the doctrines." Says James: "If ANY OF YOU lack wisdom let him ask of God who giveth abundantly and upbraideth not; and it shall be given him." From this it appears that the promised spiritual guidance is accessible to every man who will do the will of the Father and ask his direction. But how can it be known that the majority have thus sought and obtained the guidance of the Holy Spirit? In such deliberations all cannot be directed by the Holy Spirit or else all would reach the same conclusion. But how can one be sure without the exercise of private judgment whether the apparently good man in the majority is any more in communication with God than the man of like character in the minority. Is it a matter to be determined like a game of chance by the highest throw of the dice? Then a number of wicked men in the church must often be supposed to be more guided by the Spirit than a few righteous ones. But the very fact that spiritual direction is promised to each individual who seeks it properly, is an evidence in favor of the right of private government, for God could not invite him to follow and then prohibit him from doing so. And there is no promise to the assembled church in this respect that is not made to every individual disciple.

But some one may say: Does not Peter condemn the right of private interpretation? "Knowing this first that no prophecy of Scripture is of any private interpretation." (2 Peter 1: 20.) Taken thus separated from its connections the passage does seem to oppose the exercise of the right of private interpretation, at least so far as the prophetic writings are concerned.

The only question presented is whether this passage teaches that we are bound to receive that construction which is given to the Scriptures by ecclesiastical councils and forbids the right of private judgment. This theory presents many objections, some of the most obvious of which I present.

1. It necessarily supposes that all or at least a majority of the members of councils are inspired, so as to be able to give an infallible exposition of the true faith as revealed in the word of God, and that God by His Holy Spirit specially qualifies a particular class for the work of infallible interpretation.

If the gift of inspiration conferred upon the primitive disciples be continued in the church, it affects all who are the subjects of it alike. Paul was as much inspired as Peter. Indeed the inspiration fell upon all the disciples on the day of Pentecost. Each was fully inspired, and the utterances of all agreed in every respect because they proceeded from the same Spirit. If such a gift remained in the church, after the full work of setting up the Kingdom was completed, it remained with individuals separately. A number of uninspired men congregated together could not be essentially different in the aggregate from the individuals that composed the assembly. Now, if the individuals were uninspired the assembly must be also. If individual Christians are inspired it follows that each man's interpretation would be infallibly correct, for the Spirit could not contradict Himself, and we must expect to find all Christians exactly agreeing. But the contrary is the case. Hence we conclude that no such inspiration resides in individuals.

But if it be said that this gift of the Holy Spirit descends in a particular line, and is transmitted by the imposition of hands in ordination then it follows that all who are in the succession are equally invested with this power by virtue of their office. But bishops have agreed no more than private Christians. As each is supposed to be invested with this wonderful gift, we are unable to determine without an appeal to the Scriptures for ourselves whether Athanasius and his followers, or the bishops who followed Arius were in possession of the truth.

But the Scriptures nowhere intimate that this divine gift continued in the church after the days of the apostles. So far as we are informed, when the apocalyptic John closed his divine reveries on the isle of Patmos the Spirit of inspiration took its flight from earth forever. No longer the divine *afflatus* fills the prophetic soul with heavenly visions, imparting a second sight that discerns divine truth with unmistakable certainty. If God has promised the light and guidance of his Holy Spirit it is to each individual Christian who earnestly seeks it. Whatever his degree, he who dwells most in the light of God's countenance enjoys most of this spiritual guidance. It is the best Christian without respect to his office, who is most nearly inspired; and not a particular class by reason of their orders. At least I hope it is no irreverance to insist that those who lay claim to this extraordinary gift, should give some proofs of it, as the apostles did, in the miracles they wrought. They did not consider it any impiety to be required to furnish such proof.

On the other hand if it be said that this inspiration resides in councils or in popes there is a sufficient answer to this in the facts of history. Different councils and different popes have decreed different and antagonistic things, and it is certain both cannot be right; both cannot reflect the will of that God who is without variableness or even a shadow of turning.

2. It is hardly probable that Peter would condemn what the writer of Acts strongly approves. The Bereans are commended because they searched the Scriptures to see if the things preached by Paul and Silas were true. Here we find the people sitting in judgment upon the teachings of an inspired apostle and the act commended as a noble one. The blessed Saviour tells the unbelieving Jews to search the Scriptures in order to learn the truth concerning himself. The First Epistle to the Thessalonians was addressed by Paul, Sylvanus and Timothy to the whole church; and that there might be no mistake on that score, Paul charges them by the Lord that this Epistle be read to all the holy brethren. What benefit to read the Epistle to the church if they were not to become informed thereby, if they were to form no conclusions from it. In the last chapter of the Epistle thus addressed to the Thessalonians they are exhorted not to despise prophesying, but to prove all things and hold fast that which is good. How could they try the doctrines pre-

sented to them by the pretended prophets without the exercise of a discriminating judgment?

The apostolic writings abound in warning to the brotherhood against false teachers and damnable heresies. How else could they detect these than by comparing their teachings with the divine record? If it is said that these injunctions are to be obeyed by a comparison between such teachings and the established articles of the church, it may be replied that these articles themselves, this injunction requires to be subject to examination. Besides this argument assumes, either that God is purposely obscure in the teachings of the Bible, or that man can express himself more intelligibly than God; and that we can more effectually guard against heresy by comparing it with the teachings of the church than with the original writings from which they are deduced. All articles of faith must be expressed in human language and to understand them requires the use of reason and judgment to discriminate between what they teach and what they condemn. There is always more or less obscurity about human language and the same powers of understanding are required to comprehend the canons of the church as those of the apostles. If both are equally inspired, and the former and latter correspond, what reasonable objection can apply to interpreting one that does not equally apply to the other? For there is the same liability for the interpreter to make a mistake in one case as in the other. But if the conformity does not exist, it furnishes a reason why the canon of the church should not be received, because we should obey God rather than men.

But if the decrees of councils and the bulls of popes are as truly inspired as the Scriptures, they can no more be subjected to private interpretation than the Holy Writings. They themselves require to be interpreted for us, and so the interpretation must be interpreted *ad infinitum*, and no one could ever know what to believe.

3. The context does not warrant the supposed construction of the passage in question. The best way to understand an author's meaning is first to inquire what is the subject of his discourse. Now it is evident that Peter was endeavoring to confirm those to whom his Epistle is addressed in the faith of the gospel. In order to do this he reminds them that the apostles were eye witnesses of the majesty of Christ. They had witnessed his transfiguration, his resurrection, his ascension. They had heard the voice of God declare: "This is my beloved Son in whom I am well pleased." "Moreover they had a more sure word of pophecy." They were divinely inspired to impart the truths they had taught, and by way of enforcing the truth of his declaration, he uses the language under consideration. He is discussing the authority of the Scriptures themselves, and not how we may arrive at their meaning. The expression "private interpretation" (*idias epilusios*) does not refer to the explanation of a prophecy when given, but to the original inception of the prophecy itself, as if he had said: No prophecy of the Scripture is the work of the prophet himself, but is the work of the Holy Spirit through him as the instrument of revelation. That this is the force of *idias*, rendered *private*, is evident from the following verse, which is given as a *reason* for the previous assertion: "For prophecy came not in the old time BY THE WILL OF MAN, but holy men of old spake as they were moved by the Holy Ghost." I omit the article before "prophecy" in the quotation because it is not in the original, and its use obscures the meaning. The fact that men did not anciently utter prophecies *proprio motu* is certainly a conclusive argument against their doing so in

the days of the apostles. With this view the whole context is consistent; but if you make the passage refer to the explanation of a prophecy when given, you place the apostle in the attitude of introducing a statement that had no necessary connection with the subject he was discussing, and then giving in proof of its truth, a reason which does not apply.

CHAPTER V.

THE OBJECTS AND USES OF CHURCH GOVERNMENT CONTINUED.—THE PRESERVATION OF ORDER.

The existence of law implies the obligation of obedience on the part of the subjects and the infliction of penalties upon the disobedient. The enforcement of law and the maintainance of order in the churches is called discipline; because its principal object is to train and instruct the subjects of it; and by the salutary influence of example to check the tendency to lapse into the former mode of life. The church is a school where men are taught the law of God and trained in the habit of obeying it.

The power of discipline is necessary to the very existence of the church. Those who despise government would throw off all restraints, turn Christian liberty into licentiousness and entirely destroy "the unity of the spirit in the bonds of peace." If every member of the church were allowed to think what he pleased and to do what he pleased without at all affecting his relations to the church, it is plain that all order would be destroyed, and religion itself be overthrown.

The discipline of the church may be divided into two kinds, *preventive* and *punitive*.

SECTION I.—PREVENTIVE DISCIPLINE.

This consists in the use of such means as tend to prevent the occurrence of cases of discipline of the severer kind, by giving such direction to the mind and conduct of the brotherhood as will avoid error. Members do not fall into disorder at a single bound. It is by gradual departures from duty that in time they diverge a long way from the path of truth and rectitude. If taken in time men are much more easily diverted from a course of sin than reclaimed when once confirmed in their ways. It is much easier to keep an object balanced when once poised than to restore the equilibrium when lost. The old adage: "An ounce of prevention is worth a pound of cure," applies as well to the affairs of the church as to those of domestic economy. The neglect of this truth has occasioned much trouble in the church and has lost to the cause of true religion the activities of many a man with capacities for usefulness if properly directed by the timely applicacation of those means which are within the reach of the church, and which would have given a different direction to the course of his life.

1. This preventive discipline is best employed in giving a proper direction to the energies of each individual; or, in the language of the Scripture, "by watching over one another to provoke unto love and good works." To prevent a man going in the wrong direction, he should be drawn in the right direction, developing love by calling his affections into exercise; and preventing him from doing evil by keeping him constantly employed in doing good.

There are a thousand channels in which Christian activities may flow. The occasions for doing good are scattered profusely around; and God has wisely so arranged that whilst the objects of our benevolence are benefitted, we are ourselves the recipients of the greatest good. As soon as a young member is brought into the church he should be put to work. He should be encouraged to talk with his companions on the subject of religion, to visit the sick, to solicit others to attend u on the regular services of religion; to attend the Sabbath School, either as a teacher or member of the Bible class. A number of young members might be induced to form a private prayer meeting, where they would be schooled for public exercises; then as they become accustomed to pray in the presence of others they may be drawn out in the public meetings of the church. Thus their talents for usefulness may be developed, the heart kept warm in the cause of religion, and the brain and heart kept too busily engaged with the Lord's work to find time to do the works of the devil. Let every one do something if it be no more than to give away a tract, introduce a religious topic in conversation, drop a word in passing for the truth; induce some one to read a good book, or subscribe for a religious paper, say a word in favor of the pastor that will increase his influence, attend the services regularly and encourage others to do so.

2. This kind of discipline is also maintained by watching over each other in brotherly love. Is one thrown into peculiar temptations? he should be supported, and encouraged to resist. Many a one has been lost to the church by being abandoned to struggle alone with some overpowering evil. Is he going in the way of sinners? Help him to break off evil associations and direct his footsteps in the right course. We are social beings, and will seek some kind of intercourse with our fellow men. A large portion of every community of Christians consists in single persons disconnected with the families where they live—mere waifs upon the surface of society. If left alone, distasteful as the society of the wicked and abandoned may be at first, they are gradually drawn into it for the want of better companionship, until at last they spend all their leisure moments lounging about the saloons and other places of wicked resort. It is the duty of those who are the heads of families and have the *entree* of society, to look out for such young men, and open to them such social advantages as will be at once attractive and elevating. Do

you find a brother's feet totter? strengthen him. Do his purposes waver? encourage him. At first, he may be easily recalled, but if neglected, habits are formed; shame, despair, the loss of interest in duty, and the growth of sinful appetite all combine to draw him still further away.

A large part of our duty to each other as Christians is faithfully to watch over each other and guard against the incipient deviations from rectitude. This affectionate subjection of one to another was a marked feature in the simple manners of apostolic times. But this tender watch-care bears no resemblance to the suspicious espionage established by Jesuits to secure power and control men by a knowledge of their weaknesses. But it is like the unselfish solicitude of the mother as she carefully watches the tottering steps of her infant, ever ready to catch him when he stumbles, to guide him when he wanders, and to help him to his feet when he falls.

3. The faithful maintainance of the truth will prevent many disorders, and guard against the ingress of error. Familiarity with the genuine coin enables the tradesman readily to detect the spurious. So constant contact with truth enables us to discover error, however well disguised under the appearance of truth. The apathy of the church breeds heresy. It was while the good man of the house slept that the enemy sowed tares. When truth conceals itself then error comes forth to deceive the people.

It often happens that well meaning Christians appear as the apologists of some form of sin, and thus encourage irregularities, and lay the foundations for wider breaches of Christian obligation. If Christians were only united in the condemnation of many evils that exist in society, there would be fewer young persons who would fall away from the church. Encouraged in the first step by worldly minded professors, they break away from wholesome restraints, and are soon swallowed up in the vortex of sinful pleasure and are necessarily cut off to save the credit of the church. At first they repel the admonitions of wiser Christians by quoting the authority of those thoughtless ones whose loose views have encouraged them to go astray.

4. By maintaining a lively state of religion in the church the zeal of all is kept alive. If a man has a spark of religion in his heart it will kindle up when others around are awake. There is an irresistible power in the warmth of Christian love, that tends to rouse into life and activity all who come within the sphere of its influence. A living, active piety in the church is the surest safe guard against every species of disorder.

SECTION II.—PUNITIVE DISCIPLINE.

When the means of Preventive Discipline have been neglected or have failed to restrain the evilly inclined, it becomes necessary to inflict punishment upon the offenders. This is called *Punitive Discipline*, and is of two kinds, *corrective and excisive*. The former is applied to minor offences, committed under such circumstances as give hope of the reformation of the offender. It consists in admonition, reproof, censure, and such mild penalties as the nature of the case may warrant. One object of punishment is to make the offender better, to restore him to duty. But this is by no means the only or even principal object of punishment, which is the protection of the good and obedient, in which is involved the very existence of society itself. When the offence is often repeated and the offender incorrigible, or when it is so grossly immoral as to indicate an entire destitution of religious principles, then excision is applied as the last remedy to preserve the purity of the body, just as a diseased limb is amputated when we despair of its cure.

But this is as far as the church may go. It may not pursue him into the world, and invoke the sword of the magistrate to press him further. "Let him be unto you as a heathen man and a publican," said the Saviour. While the Jews refused to associate with the heathen and publicans, they did not seek otherwise to molest them. The disciples understood by this allusion to the Jewish practices that they were to withdraw all association with such persons. "Withdraw yourselves from every brother that walketh disorderly," says Paul. But the same apostle settles this point beyond cavil in 1 Cor. v: 12–13. After directing the expulsion of an unworthy member, he adds: "For what have I to do to JUDGE them that are WITHOUT. Do ye not judge them that are WITHIN? But them that are WITHOUT GOD JUDGETH." Here is an express disclaimer of any jurisdiction over the offender after he has been cast out of the church. He is turned over not to the secular power, but to the judgment of God.

The punitive discipline of the church relates to two classes of offences: *personal* and *moral*. Some offences partake of the nature of both and therefore may be termed *mixed* offences. But for all practical purposes it is sufficient to class them as I have done below.

I. PERSONAL OFFENCES.

These relate to private grievances which break the fellowship of brethren, but do not affect the moral character of the offender. The conflicting interests of men, the officious intermeddling of third persons, the carelessness, mistakes and forgetfulness of men, often bring brethren into unpleasant relations to each other. An unadjusted variance continues to put them further apart until the harmony of the church is broken. To meet such cases the Saviour provided a rule which may be found in the eighteenth chapter of Matthew: "Morever if thy brother shall trespass against thee, go and tell him his fault between him and thee alone. If he shall hear thee thou has gained thy brother. But if he will not hear thee then take with thee one or two more, that in the mouth of two or three witnesses every word may be established. If he shall neglect to hear them, tell it unto the church. But if he neglect to hear the church, let him be unto thee as an heathen man and a publican."

Here are four distinct steps to be taken:

1. The private interview. Perhaps the offended brother is laboring under some mistake. The brother may be unconscious of any offense. It may be that unforseen circumstances have intervened to prevent him from discharging his obligation. An interview conducted in a Christian spirit, may explain the mistake, or give satisfaction. A calm and dispassionate discussion of the matters of difference, and a comparison of the facts and figures, may convince one or the other party of his wrong and induce him to do justice and thus he has gained his brother.

2. The interview before one or more brethren. Disinterested parties may discover what is right between the brethren at variance and point it out to them. Neither might be willing to yield to the other, but might consent to abide by the decision of an umpire. Perhaps both might make concessions to a third party that they would not to each other. Some compromise might be suggested equally satisfactory to both and thus the matter be adjusted.

3. Before the church. Here the united wisdom and influence of the whole church is brought to

bear to reconcile the difference and to judge between the parties.

It is plain that these steps must be taken in the order in which they are given, and any attempt to reverse them is injurious to good order.

4. If the party who is thus judged to be in fault still refuses to make amends it is evident that his heart is fully set in him to do evil, and this leads to his expulsion from the church; for his neglect to hear the body is a contempt of his brethren, and therefore their fellowship is withdrawn.

II. MORAL OFFENCES.

These are offences against the *order*, the *faith* and the *purity* of the church. To disturb the peace of the church, to despise, neglect or pervert its ordinances, to refuse to submit to the lawful authority of the church, or to encourage others to resist it, these are offences against good order. Some may object to this classification of offences against church order, but to violate that order which God has established in his church is to disobey Him, and disobedience to God is sin.

Offences against the faith, called heresy, consist in the rejection of any part of the doctrines revealed in God's Word; and the substitution of any thing else as religious belief.

Any kind of immorality is an offence against the purity of the church.

1. Minor offences are to be treated according to the rule in Galatians vi: 1: "Brethren, if a man be overtaken in a fault, ye which are spiritual restore such a one in the spirit of meekness, considering thyself, lest thou also be tempted." The word "fault" (*paraptoma*) does not apply to a gross, deliberate, continued act of immorality, but to those lesser offences that result from surprise rather than deliberation, and which do not import a cor-

rupt state of the heart, and this is implied in the word "overtaken." Such are to be treated with lenity. An endeavor in the spirit of meekness must be made to reclaim them. Admonish kindly such a one. Point out his error in the spirit of Him of whom it was said: "A bruised reed He will not break, and smoking flax He will not quench." Reason with him, and if he prove not incorrigible restore him to your fellowship.

But if after proper steps taken, one continues in any disorderly practice, contrary to the law of Christ; if he persists in propagating error to the subverting of the truth; if he is obstinate in strife, as a last resort he may be excluded. And in doing so the church does him no injustice. "For how shall two walk together except they be agreed?" The duty of the church to maintain the faith once delivered unto the saints, will not allow her to retain error in her bosom.

By the last remark it is not meant that the church should exclude every member who does not fully comprehend and receive the whole truth. The fewest number, perhaps none since the days of inspiration, do this entirely. Paul said: "Him that is weak in the faith receive ye, but not to doubtful disputations," and certainly one may be retained under the same circumstances in which he was received. The apostle does not contemplate the case of an active heretic propagating error, while sheltered in the bosom of the church, but one who has not yet sufficiently comprehended the truth as to receive it fully; one who is open to conviction, but silent where he doubts, not striving to win others to his views, but seeking by a careful study of the word to conform his views as far as he can to the recognized standards. Of such a one there is hope that he will in time "learn the way of the Lord more perfectly." But if he trouble the church with "disputations and doubts" he is neither to be received nor retained.

2. Gross offences are such as consist in scandalous immoralities and are incompatible with the renewed nature of the Christian. The rule in such cases is prompt and absolute excision. It is found in the directions of Paul, 1 Cor. 5th chapter, in a case which occurred in that church, and he there enumerates the class of offences that are to be governed by this rule—"a fornicator, or covetous, or an idolater, or a drunkard, or a railer, or an extortioner." Perhaps a single act of incontinency under strong temptation, or being drunk on a single occasion, under peculiar circumstances, followed by immediate contrition and confession, would not constitue one a fornicator or drunkard in the meaning of the apostle. Such cases should probably be governed by the rule in Gal. vi: 1. But the habitually licentious and drunken are to be dealt with severely. The other offences are of such a character as to denote deliberate pravity of heart. Covetousness or inordinate love of gain can only exist in the heart of one devoid of religion. The idolater deliberately renounces God without even the plea of temptation to palliate his sin. The railer and extortioner lack that good will (charity) without which all else pertaining to religion is "as sounding brass and a tinkling cymbal."

It is not meant that this catalogue embraces all the gross moral offences of which the church takes cognizance. They are only selected to represent a class. In Rom. i: 29, 30, 31 and elsewhere, we find other crimes classed with these which are no doubt to be dealt with according to this rule.

Immediate and prompt excision is the only remedy in such cases, the nature of which clearly shows the want of grace. Such were improperly received into the church, and the sooner she retraces her steps the better for the credit of religion. It is only thus that she can purge herself from the scandal and stamp with marked disapprobation such conduct.

In the simpler, direct and faithful discipline of the apostolic churches, the offender was required to bring forth fruits meet for repentance before the fellowship of the church was confirmed towards him. Offenders of this class may not evade the just consequence of their immorality by confession and promise of reformation. They must be cut off, and if by their subsequent life they give evidence of thorough repentance and amendment, then they may be restored. The rule "if thy brother trespass against thee rebuke him, and if he repent forgive him, and if he trespass against thee seven times in a day, and seven times in a day turn to thee saying, I repent, thou shalt forgive him," does not apply to cases of this kind, but to personal offences, which do not bring scandal upon the church. These are not offences which the church can forgive; but she may receive the offender back into her membership when assured that God has forgiven him.

SECTION III. THE PARTICIPATION OF THE WHOLE CHURCH IN DISCIPLINE, AND THE FINALITY OF ITS ACTION.

It is a question of some practical importance to determine by whom the discipline was administered, whether by the pastor or preacher; by a select number appointed to rule over the church; or by the assembled whole. I think it is evident that this power was exercised by the whole church duly assembled.

1. The Saviour in directing the proceeding in the case of personal offences after the previous steps have been taken to no purpose, says: "Tell it to the

church." To lay the complaint before the pastor, or the session of a chosen body of ruling elders, would not be to tell it to the church, but only to a part of the church. Dr. George Campbell translates the passage: "acquaint the congregation with it," and remarks that "it would be contrary to all the rules of criticism to suppose that Christ would say congregation, for so the word literally imports, when He meant a few heads or directors."—(*Com. in loco.*

Olshausen says: "The *ekklesia* like *rahal* is the assemblage of all the believers in one place, to which assembly the separate individual belongs as a member."

That this power was exercised by the whole church is also evident by the example in 1 Cor. v: 4–5: "When ye are gathered together * * * to deliver such an one to Satan," and Paul aftewards interceding for this excluded person, says: (2 Cor. ii: 6) "Sufficient unto such a man is this punishment which was inflicted by many. So that contrary wise ye ought to forgive him, and comfort him, lest perhaps such a one should be swallowed up of over much sorrow. Wherefore, I beseech you that ye would confirm your love toward him."

Daniel Whitby remarks on this case: "Some learned persons who exclude the laity from having any share in the excommunication or absolution of public offenders tell us this punishment was inflicted only by the clergy or presbytery of Corinth in the presence of the laity. But it seems clear in both of these epistles that the apostle writes to the Church of Corinth in general, for when he commanded that the incestuous person should be excluded from the society and be delivered up to Satan, he speaks to all that were assembled together; (1 Cor. v: 5.) to all that ought to have mourned for that fact, ver. 2; to all that were obliged to abstain from eating with him, ver. 11; and asserts the power they had of judging those that were within the church, ver. 11, and here speaking of the execution of this sentence he saith it was *epitimia* "punishment" inflicted, not *pro*, before only, but *hupo toon pleionoon*, "by the community." Hence he exhorts them all to forgive and comfort him, ver. 8, adding, ver. 10: "To whomsoever ye forgive anything I forgive also," but there is not in all this thing the least mention of any of the clergy separately from the church either executing or relaxing the censure."—(*Annot. in loco.*)

It in no way militates against the view I have taken, viz: that the church in the aggregate, the local assembly composed of its officers and members, exercised discipline; that Paul in writing to the Corinthians in relation to this case, says, "I have judged already concerning him who hath done this deed, and to whom ye forgive anything I forgive also," for he is careful to declare the capacity in which he speaks: "In the name of the Lord Jesus Christ"—"with the power of the Lord Jesus Christ"—for if I forgave anything, to whom I forgave it for your sakes, I forgave it in the person of Jesus Christ." By these expressions he expressly renounces any authority in his ministerial character —but because he was inspired to declare the will of Christ. Paul had formed his own opinion of the case: "For I verily as absent in the body, but present in spirit, have judged already;" but he rests his judgment not upon his apostolic authority but upon the will of Christ, which he makes known. And he expressly recognizes the jurisdiction of the church, ver. 12: "Do ye not judge them that are within?" He does not himself expel and afterwards restore the offender; but in the name of the Lord directs them to do it, thereby recognizing that the church was competent to execute the sentence against him and to restore him again to his forfeited privileges.

2. We may readily see the propriety of lodging this power in the whole church, if we consider:

1. The whole is affected by the act that requires the application of discipline. Whatever scandal is attached to the conduct of an offender it affects all alike; and therefore each has an equal interest in removing this stain, whatever it may be.

2 The many are less liable to be governed by wrong motives. If this duty devolved upon the pastor alone he would have no check upon his prejudices for or against the offender. He might expel a worthy member because he was his enemy, or retain an unworthy one because he was his friend. His decree would be but the judgment of a single man perhaps, no more capable of judging of a matter of fact than nine-tenths of the church. If he should be corrupt there is no other to restrain him. But if all the members take cognizance of the matter there are many minds and experiences concurring to produce a correct judgment.

3. If this power were exercised by a less number than the whole, a person very obnoxious to the whole might be retained, and thus the harmony of the body be broken; or one deemed worthy by the church expelled, and the church be deprived of the comforts of his society. In either event the effect upon the prosperity of the church would be deleterious.

4. The moral influence of discipline administered by the whole church is greater than if inflicted by a fewer number. If condemned by a single person he may claim that it was done through wrong motives; whereas, if all are concerned in it he is more ready to feel its justice, because it is the united voice of many. In the former case he could prop

himself by the hope of sympathy among his brethren, but here he has no such refuge. He feels "rebuked by all."

5. There is another consideration that renders it improper that this power should be exercised by the pastor, even if he were in a situation to exercise it with the same justice and prudence as others. His influence for good over the church and those who come within the scope of his ministry, depends not upon their fears but their affections. That he may pursuade all, he should not be embarrassed with the discipline of the church. He should be accessible as the common friend and counselor of all. If he should err in his decision in the estimation of the church, his influence over them is diminished if not destroyed. Hence he should keep aloof from discipline as much as possible.

6. The action of the church is final so far as it is itself concerned. There is no higher tribunal to revise, and compel it to set aside its decisions. If another power could annul its action it might be compelled to retain in fellowship a person entirely distasteful; and thus the unity and harmony of the church be broken. The victory of the successful appellant would tend to make him insolent towards the members of the church, and they would feel that the many were subjected to the one unworthy one. The zeal of the church would be cooled and its activity paralyzed.

But I may be asked if there is no remedy when a church may, through prejudice or ignorance, wrongfully and oppressively deal with a brother. Must he be debarred unworthily of the privileges of Christian association? If the church is composed of the kind of persons required by the gospel, such a case can but seldom occur, and if they should thus err they would readily retrace their steps if shown to be wrong.

But if such a thing should occur, the action of one church does not absolutely bind another. It is true there is and properly should be a con.ity between the several churches, situated in the same neighborhood, by which the acts of each other should be respected, so long as the law of Christ has not been violated. But as each is responsible to God for its own acts another church may examine into the case, and if found to be manifestly wrong, may receive the injured brother into its own fellowship; but it cannot compel the erring church to take him back. I say if the decision be manifestly wrong, for in a doubtful case it is better that a single individual should suffer awhile than that the peace of churches be broken. Churches should act with great prudence in their proceedings in such cases. If they have reason to believe that wrong has been done, they should first endeavor in a fraternal spirit to induce the erring church to retrace its steps. But if this should prove ineffectual they may invite a council of judicious brethren, in which the erring church should be invited to cooperate, and upon the advice of the council receive the injured brother.

A word in conclusion on the binding force of the action of the church. The language of the Saviour "Whatsoever ye shall bind on earth shall be bound in heaven, and whatsoever ye loose on earth shall be loosed in heaven," has been strangely perverted and made the engine of oppression. It is assumed that the decision of a church right or wrong, is ratified in heaven, and therefore absolutely binding upon all. There is an evident misunderstanding of the Saviour's meaning, as if heaven would approve and ratify that which is wrong. A Diotrephes rises and by his influence causes the good men of the church to be cast out. Will any one dare to say that God will endorse the act? Then the Saviour can mean no more than this: Whatsoever is rightly done on earth shall be approved in heaven. The church can only bind and unloose in strict accordance with the law of Christ. Otherwise the church might defeat the very ends for which it was constituted, and heaven be pledged to sanction it.

If the act must be taken as absolutely binding, then it is the local church that thus binds, and it cannot be revised by any appellate court—not even heaven itself—for right or wrong it is ratified in heaven and has thus become right and final. But more of this when I come to consider the rights of minorities.

CHAPTER VI.

FURTHER CHARACTERISTICS OF THE CHURCH.

SECTION 1. *Ekklesia.*—It may serve to throw some light upon the subject of our inquiry to examine the term employed by the sacred writers to designate the institution of Christ, which we denominate *church*. I do not propose to inquire what is embraced in the English word church, but the Greek word used by the Evangelists to represent the mind of the Holy Spirit.

Words are the representatives of ideas and the inspired writers made use of terms familiar to those for whom they wrote. They desired to be understood, and therefore chose words in which to express themselves, that conveyed definite ideas. The heathen oracles were purposely clothed in ambiguous words; but the Holy Spirit, charged with the revelations of God, could have no motives for obscurity, and therefore clothed the oracles of God in words easy to be understood. The writers did not coin new words for the purpose, nor use old words in a sense hitherto wholly unknown, but applied those in common use without any material change in their radical signification.

The word employed by Christ and his apostles translated into English by the word church, is *ekklesia*, a word familiar to the Greeks, in whose language the gospels were first written. It is derived from two other words, which literally mean to *call out*, and primarily signifies an assembly of the people called together for the purpose of deliberating on public affairs. It was originally applied to the popular assemblies of the Greeks at Athens, convoked by heralds to transact public business relating to the common interests. It determined the *status* of citizens and exercised both judicial and legislative powers. It admitted foreigners to the rights of citizenship and frequently expelled obnoxious citizens from the commonwealth. The basal idea of the word is "an assembly of the people called together to deliberate on public affairs." This was its secular usage when applied to the Christian Institution. Is it likely that the inspired writers arbitrarily applied the word to a new idea radically different from that attached to it in its original use? Is it not more reasonable to suppose that the resemblance between the primitive assemblies of the Christians and the *ekklesiai* of the Greeks suggested the application of the term to them? A material change in the basal idea of the word would have provoked remark and called forth some explanation to satisfy those who used the Greek language, and this comprised all the countries in and near the Mediterranean Sea, when the gospel was first preached. But we find no such remark or explanation, and hence we must infer that the word is employed in its ordinary signification.

To have called an assembly which never assembled, and from its nature could not assemble, or in which the *people* did not participate, an *ekklesia*, would have been to mock the common sense of every one who spoke the Greek language; and no sensible reason can be given why the writers of the New Testament should have done so. The power of the Greeks had but a short time before passed into the hands of Romans; and they naturally cherished the memory of everything that pertained to their once glorious republics. And it is not reasonable to suppose that the apostles would, without obvious necessity have insulted their national prejudices by a mere caricature of their most cherished institutions. Hence the *ekklesia* of the Christians must have borne a strong resemblance to the *ekklesia* of the Greeks. The *people* largely composed the church and were an important part of the *ekklesia*, the whole was accustomed to *assemble*, and the *assembly*, composed of the *people* and their officers as a body, transacted the business that pertained to its interests. Its government was therefore congregational.

Some have supposed that the government of the church was copied from the synagogue service of the Jews and was therefore *presbyterial*. If this were true the Greek language furnised another word which had long been applied to this kind of assembly, *synagogue*, and would most naturally have continued in use to express the Christian assemblies organized on the same plan. But never once is a Christian church called a *synagogue*. But a different word is employed and the thing represented must be different in some material point. Both words signified originally an assembly, but by usage one was employed to designate an assembly governed by Elders, the other an assembly governed by the whole body of people assembled. The latter was the word chosen to designate the Christian organization, and those who deny that the popular element prevails in the Christian assembly must show affirmatively that the word underwent a material change in its signification.

We may therefore deduce from the word this definition of a Christian church, viz.: an assembly of the disciples of Christ, called out of the world by the heralds of the cross, qualified according to the law of Christ, voluntarily associated and meeting in one place, and independent of every other similar organization.

SECTION 2. *Selected Material.*—The church was

not composed of persons indiscriminately coming together. It did not comprise the whole mass of people in any one community—but as the original term implies, persons selected—chosen, *called out*—separated from the world—persons called of God through the instrumentality of the gospel. Christ declared to his first disciples: "Ye have not chosen me, but I have chosen you." In the apostolic letters to the churches they are often addressed as "elect," "chosen." Paul admonishes the Colossians to "put on as the elect of God bowels of mercies." Peter addressing a general letter to the churches speaks of their members as "elect according to the foreknowledge of God, through sanctification of the Spirit unto obedience and sprinkling of the blood of Christ." He also speaks of "the church at Babylon, elected together with you." Of the Thessalonians Paul speaks: "Knowing, brethren, the election of God." "Ye are a chosen generation." (1 Pet. ii: 9). Paul speaks of the Thessalonians: "God has chosen you," and he admonishes them to "walk worthy of God who hath called you unto his kingdom and glory."

These expressions and many others that might be quoted are addressed, not to individuals, but to the churches, and were expressive of their general character. It was a body of selected material. These terms could not have been applied to the aggregate, unless they were equally applicable to each individual.

God through His Spirit renders the gospel effectual. Jesus commissioned his disciples to "go into all the world and preach the gospel to every creature." In obedience to that command the ministers of the gospel go forth as the heralds of God calling upon men to separate themselves from the world. God's Spirit disposes them to obey and they become the disciples of Jesus Christ. Then they are "called," "chosen unto salvation through the sanctification of the Spirit and the belief of the truth." And of the persons thus selected by the Spirit is the church composed.

SECTION. 3. *Qualifications for Membership.*—They must be holy. If one unholy person may be admitted, then another and another may, until the whole body is composed of unholy persons; a Christian church in which there are no Christians, which is an absurdity.

There are various terms expressive of the character of the members of the Apostolic Church.

The term elect taken in connection with the manner in which the election takes place, indicates the character of the persons chosen. It could hardly be supposed that God made a selection of bad persons to compose his church. But the very act of choosing necessarily confers holiness. The entrance of the Holy Spirit into the heart and taking up his abode there, implies a Spiritual change. It is a quickening, and the person thus affected is called a new creature.

They are called "holy," "saints," "sanctified," "disciples," "a holy nation, a peculiar people, zealous of good works," "the workmanship of God, created in Christ Jesus unto good works." These terms could not have been applied to a collection of persons of mixed character some of whom possessed the qualities, while a large portion were of the opposite character.

1. There is one text that deserves special notice in this connection, because it clearly settles the inquiry as to the character of persons who were received into the Apostolic Church. In Acts ii: 47, we read: "The Lord added unto the church daily such as should be saved (Gr. *the saved*). This furnishes a key to the whole subject.

Adam Clarke, Daniel Whitby, Doddridge, Hackett and many others who might be named, the leading commentators of various denominations, translate the text according to the Greek: "The Lord added unto the church daily THE SAVED."

Observe it is not said that the apostles did this, but that the Lord did it. As the Lord did not appear in person to receive these members, it must be understood that they were added to the church by the direction of the Lord. If any others, not included in this class, were added, the Lord did not add them. He added none but "the saved." Here then we have a rule for the reception of members. In its application we may err because we cannot discern the hearts of men; but as far as we know, we must receive only such as give evidence of being of this class. And though others, through error, may, in form, be added, they are not added in fact. They belong to that class of persons mentioned by John: "They went out from us. Because they were not of us, therefore they went out from us." Only the Lord can incorporate members into his church. It is true that he employs the disciples as his agents; but their act is only his act when done according to his will.

If then we can ascertain who are meant by "the saved," we may determine what sort of persons were admitted. Whitby, the great Episcopalian commentator, says that Christians are so styled in 1 Cor. i: 18. "To us, the saved, Christ crucified is the power of God." The persons addressed were already Christians in the proper sense of the word. They sustained the same relation to salvation before they were added that they did afterwards. This being true, the Romish doctrine that one must join the church to be saved, falls to the ground. As Hackett very well observes, "the word expresses, not a purpose but a fact—not those who in the end would be saved, as the common version implies, but those who were already saved." They were those who had complied with the terms of salvation; who by faith had accepted the crucified.

It necessarily implies that their sins were forgiven, because they could not with any kind of propriety be said to be saved, while yet the wrath of God abode upon them, and while they were yet liable to the penalty of his violated law. They were believers, because none could be saved without faith. They were regenerated persons, because an unholy person could not be said to be saved. In fine, it imports all that is implied in being fully reconciled to God in Jesus Christ; and with this agree the remarks of Adam Clarke on this passage, so singularly at variance with the practice of his brethren, and his own:

"Though many approved the life and manners of these primitive Christians, yet they did not become members of this holy church, God permitting none to be added to it but *tous sozomenous, those who were saved* from their sins and prejudices. The church of Christ was made up of *saints; sinners* were not permitted to incorporate themselves with it. * * Our translation of *tous sozomenous*, such as should be saved, is improper and insupportable. The original means simply and solely, those who were then saved. * * * * It was by embracing the gospel of Christ that they were put in a *state of salvation* and, by the grace it imparted, actually saved from the power, guilt and dominion of sin."—*Com. in loc.*

Paul lays hold of the utter incompatibility of character between the believer and the unbeliever to argue the impropriety of their association in the church, and very pertinently inquires, "How shall two walk together except they be agreed." Wherefore he commands them: "Come out from among them and be ye separate." "Be not unequally yoked together with unbelievers."

The practice of the apostolic churches to receive only "the saved" is consistent with the spiritual character of the church and the design of its institution.

Christ says: "My Kingdom is not of this world." It is a Spiritual Kingdom. Its subjects are spiritual subjects, born from above. For "Except a man be born again he cannot see the kingdom of God." The obedience of its subjects is not the result of outward force, but springs from a willing mind—from a heart renewed by grace, and moved by the indwelling Spirit. Paul declares (Eph. v: 15.) that "no unclean person hath any inheritance in the kingdom of Jesus Christ," and Christ himself said: "Except ye be converted and become as little children, ye shall not enter the kingdom of heaven."

If it should be objected that these exppressions apply to the kingdom at large, and that the church is a visible organization within the kingdom, I reply that such as the kingdom is so must the executive be. Men do not select aliens and enemies, but citizens to administer the government; and is God less wise than men, that he should entrust the execution of his laws—in part at least, to His enemies?

The kingdom of Christ is thus metaphorically described by the prophet Isaiah (xxxv: 8).

"And a highway shall be there;
And it shall be called, the way of holiness:
No unclean person shall pass through it:
But he himself shall be with them, walking in the way,
And the foolish shall not err therein;
No lion shall be there;
Nor shall the tyrant of beasts come up thither,
Neither shall he be found there;
But the redeemed shall walk in it
Yea, the redeemed of JEHOVAH shall return;
They shall come to Sion with triumph;
And perpetual gladness shall crown their heads.
Joy and gladness shall they obtain;
And sorrow and sighing shall flee away."—*Bishop Lowth's Translation.*

Jeremiah describing the Kingdom of Christ, breaks forth (xxxi: 33,) "After those days, saith the Lord, I will put my law in their inward parts, and write it in their hearts, and I will be their God and they shall be my people; and they shall teach no more every man his neighbor and every one his brother, saying, Know the Lord; for they shall all know me from the least to the greatest, saith the Lord."

In the first quotation the church is denominated "The way of holiness," and it is said "no unclean person shall pass through it." The unconverted are spiritually unclean. "No lion shall be there." The unsubdued carnal nature which is like a ferocious beast shall not be found among its members. "But the redeemed shall walk in it." This declares the kind of persons that shall compose the church, "the redeemed," "the saved." Adam Clarke remarks of this whole chapter: "The chapter shows also that no impurity should be tolerated in the church of God; for as that is the mystical body of Christ, it should be like himself without spot or wrinkle or any such thing."

In the second quotation the Lord declares. "I will put my law in their inward parts and write it in their hearts." They shall be converted and possess an affectionate love of his word, put in their hearts by God himself. Of a church composed in part of unconverted persons it could not be said that they "all know the Lord from the least unto the greatest." From the humblest layman to the highest official, all shall have an experimental knowledge of him.

If it should be urged as an objection that it is impossible to guard against the reception of unconverted persons into the church, under all circumstances, and therefore an absolutely perfect church is not practically attainable with any degree of certainty, I admit it. So, absolute perfection in holy living is no more practicable, yet implicit obedience is the standard erected by Christ: "Ye are my friends if ye do whatsoever I have cammanded you." One would scarcely justify a known and deliberately wilful sin on the ground that he is a weak and imperfect creature, and unable to reach the standard required by Christ. It is our duty to attain as nearly as possible to what is required. So in receiving members into the church the fact that we are fallible and cannot know the hearts of men, and cannot therefore keep out hypocrites and persons who are self deceived, is no excuse for deliberately introducing into the church those who are known and acknowledged to be unbelievers—unregenerate—unholy—enemies to God; for such is the character of all men until they are reconciled to God through faith in the Lord Jesus Christ. We can at least require a credible profession of faith in all who apply. It was this Philip reqired of the Eunuch: "If thou believest with all thy heart thou mayest."

To admit to membership in the church only "the saved" is in keeping with the design of its institution.

One design of the church, as we have seen, is to preserve the laws and ordinances of Christ. This only the truly converted will do. They only are interested in doing it. Unbelievers do not love the law and ordinances of Christ, because they do not give scope to their worldly ambition, and they restrain their inclinations. Hence instead of preserving, they will be disposed to alter them, so as to accommodate them to their own feelings and tastes. It would be an act of folly in any government to intrust to its subjects, who were in open rebellion, the execution of its laws—particularly those which bore upon themselves.

Another object of the church, as has been shown, is to maintain the purity of its discipline, "to keep itself unspotted from the world," and thus let its light shine. But this the unregenerated will not do. Bad men will not enforce the laws of the

State which they, violate. So unbelievers will not enforce the laws of Christ, because they are themselves the offenders. Just in proportion to the spiritual-mindedness of the church, will be the state of discipline and offenders brought to judgment. So evident is it that an unconverted membership will not enforce discipline, that those who practice the reception of unconverted members have endeavored to remedy the evil by taking the discipline out of the hands of the church, where Christ left it, and have its exercise reserved to those who are supposed to be spiritual.

But the main design of the church is to evangelize the world. This unbelievers will not do, because they do not love the cause of God, and do not feel an active interest in the salvation of men. They may possess the spirit of a party and seek to propagate the views they entertain by force, but they cannot be actuated by the love of souls and a sincere desire to extend the truth.

2. But the members of the Apostolic Churches were not only believers, but they were also baptized. "Then they that gladly received the word, were baptized; and the same day there were added unto them about three thousand souls." (Acts ii: 41). "But when they believed Philip, preaching the things concerning the kingdom of God, and the name of Jesus Christ, they were baptized, both men and women." (Acts viii: 12). The divine command was: Go ye into all the world and preach the gospel to every creature, he that believeth and is baptized shall be saved." "Go disciple all nations, baptizing them into the name of the Father and of the Son and of the Holy Spirit." It cannot be supposed that they omitted so important a command. Hence we find them baptizing their converts and organizing them into assemblies after the model of the church at Jerusalem. So important

did they regard this ordinance, that we find them on one occasion, repeating the act because it had not been properly administered. (Acts xix: 5).

I am not now inquiring what is the act of baptism, but all admit that some act, which they regard as baptism, is an essential prerequisite to church membership. It is upon this principle that Quakers, who reject water baptism, though a pious body of Christians, justly esteemed for their industrious and quiet, inoffensive lives, are not regarded by any as a church; and, indeed, they themselves lay no claim to the title, calling themselves a *society*. No baptism, no church, is the motto of all. An association of unbaptized persons is not a church of Jesus Christ, because it is not like the model church set up by Jesus Christ and his apostles. Its members have never put on the badge of Christ by openly professing Him in the manner He has prescribed. That can hardly be called a church of Christ which begins its existence by an act of disobedience to him. In the absence of baptism, none can be admitted to membership without a violation of the order of the Apostolic Church.

A loose phraseology sometimes speaks of baptism as "the door into the church," but this is not strictly correct. It is true that one must come through the water of baptism in order to enter the church. But baptism does not, *ipso facto*, introduce one into the church. He is then only fully qualified to be received. It is the act of the church receiving him into its fellowship that constitutes him a member. Without that consent, he cannot be a member.

Three qualifications then are necessary, *faith, baptism* and the *approbation of the brotherhood;* and these follow in the order here named. We read of none who were baptized until they believed; and none added until after they were baptized.

CHAPTER VII.

CHARACTERISTICS OF THE CHURCH CONTINUED.

SECTION I.—*The Basis of Association.*

It is a voluntary association. No one can rightfully be compelled to be a member of the church. Religion is a voluntary service of God. I do not mean that the obligation to serve God depends upon the will of the creature; and that His laws are binding only on those who voluntarily assume them. Every man is under obligation to become a Christian, and join the church. But it is not for man to compel the discharge of that duty. And if he could, God would not accept of it. Our service to be acceptable to Him must be a freewill offering. It is not possible to compel one to believe. One can be forced to conform to the externals of religion, but this only makes him a hypocrite—not a Christian.

This right of voluntary association is violated by those laws which prohibit ones choice, and compel him to unite with the established church under pain of the loss of civil rights. But such laws are as unwise as they are oppressive. The corruption of all established churches, from the days of Constantine to the present, prove how little is to be gained for pure Christianity by such compulsory means; and the blood of dissenters at every step has been an earnest protest against the violation of the rights of conscience. It is the glory of our times to witness a rapid advance in the recognition of these rights.

In like manner those who seek to introduce unconscious infants into the church, violate this principle of voluntary association. Infant membership is compulsory membership. It forestalls the choice of the infant, for who can tell whether he will like the association or not?

Fellowship can only exist on this voluntary principle. He who is forced into an association distasteful to himself, is debarred from that pleasurable intercourse which subsists between those who have fellowship one for another. So also if a member is forced upon an unwilling church; or if the church is compelled to retain one for whom there is no fellowship, the harmony is broken. In such cases there may be an association in form but not in reality. Force may compel a hypostatic union but never that blending of kindred souls that constitutes true Christian fellowship. That must flow from the free consent of the unbound spirit—a common will; a common purpose; a common heart. In this consists the communion of the saints.

SECTION II.—*Its Local Character*.

It is a local assembly. The idea of an organization extending over a whole province, or country, or coextensive with the world, rendering the assembly of the whole impracticable, does not comport with the scriptural idea of a church, which implies a frequent coming together. We read of the church at Jerusalem, the church at Antioch, the church at Philippi, the church at Rome, the churches of Asia, the churches of Judea, the churches of Syria, the churches of Macedonia, the churches of the Gentiles, the churches of Christ, the churches of God, but never of the church of any particular province or a church universal. If the term is ever applied to the whole body of believers, it is used, not literally, but figuratively. It is never applied to them as one visible organization, connected together as a single body; for no such visible, organic connection existed at first. It may be sometimes used to express the whole; but it is only applied to the conception of the mind, the mental grouping of the whole; not a real but an imaginary assembly. Thus we read of "the assembly of the church of the first born" where all the disciples of Jesus in all ages are concieved of as meeting together in one grand convocation in heaven.

Each local assembly was a church complete in itself, without reference to any other. The church at Jerusalem, the first formed, was a complete church. The church at Antioch was not an extension of the church at Jerusalem, but was itself a complete church. It did not require the organic connection of the two to constitute the church. Both were churches.

The local character of the church best adapted it to accomplish its mission. It could only act locally and by personal contact. Each individual became a propagator of the new faith, and each local church a nucleus around which the disciples gathered. It needed no government but such as it could provide for itself. So long as there were unbelievers in the community, there was work enough to employ it. When its members removed to other localities, where there was no church, they began a new interest, and soon a new church sprang up among them. When a church became strong enough to extend its labors beyond its own bounds, it combined with other churches similarly situated to send missionaries into the "regions beyond." But the union thus formed related solely to the work in hand, and did not respect the local government of each.

The simple character of the apostolic churches which I have been describing, and which all admit they had at first, proved eminently successful in all the great objects for which Christ established His church, viz: the maintainance of internal order and the evangelization of the world. All look back to apostolic times as the golden age of Christianity, distinguished for purity of doctrine and simplicity of manners. In no age of the church has the gospel achieved such triumphs. It was well adapted to its aggressive work. If I were going to destroy a great city, I would not rely upon one central fire growing and extending until it covered the whole. But I would run everywhere with lighted torches kindling a thousand independent fires.

The peculiar local character of the church, a government complete in itself, rendered it indestructible. Any other form could not have stood the terrible persecution of the first age. It made persecution itself subservient to the ends of its establishment. "They that were scattered abroad on the persecution that arose about Stephen, went everywhere preaching the gospel." No such organizations as have grown up in later times could have withstood the persecutions of the first century. The banishment of John and the martyrdom of the rest of the apostles would have destroyed an Episcopal organization. It would have dethroned the Pope and dispersed his cardinals. There can be no Episcocal church without its thrones and jurisdictions, but these were broken up. Destroy their conferences and their connectional superintendence, and there is no Methodist church. Synods and assemblies are an essential part of the Presbyterian organization. These destroyed, Presbyterianism falls. All those Christian organizations which embrace the idea of a union of the whole in one compact body embracing the whole, united under one governing head, must have fallen beneath the overwhelming shock of persecution which the first churches encountered.

The internal structure of the churches organized by the apostles was such that if each was severed in twain, the separate parts possessed all the elements of a complete church. Nay, if it was scattered into as many fragments as there were individual members, each possessed in himself the elements out of which a church might grow. If the church at Ephesus was persecuted and broken up and scattered, each if he found other disciples where he went, could unite with them in the formation of a church. No succession of ministers descending from the apostles, would be necessary to perpetuate the church, but they might originate a ministry by authorizing one of their number to preach and administer ordinances. Thus the few might become many. But in any other form of government it would be destroyed by being dissevered from its ecclesiastical head. Jesus Christ was the only head of his church, and from him, says Paul, " neither death, nor life, nor angels, nor principalities, nor powers, nor things present, nor things to come, nor heights, nor depths, nor any other creature, shall be able to separate us." (Rom. viii : 28).

SECTION III. *Church Independence.*

Each local assembly was independent of every other. It was a government complete in itself; or with the power to complete its organization. Its members were such as voluntarily associated together. The assembled church chose its own officers, received new members, and excluded the disorderly. In fine did every act which an independent body might do, subject only to the law of Christ. No foreign power imposed upon it either laws or rulers, or subjected its acts to revision. There was no higher judicatory. Its decisions so far as they conformed to the law of Christ, were final. No power on earth could compel it to reverse its decision.

If it should be objected to this form of government that bad men, or ignorant and prejudiced men, might get control of the church, and do injustice to individuals; a Diotrephes might cast a good man out of the church, or depose a worthy minister, I reply that the gospel theory of the qualification of church membership would preclude the kind of persons mentioned. A gospel church is a body of good men, of holy men. If such men err, as they may err, they are always ready to be set right, if the error can be made apparent. But suppose an extreme case, which is not likely to occur in a church composed of scriptural material—suppose a worthy minister is deposed from the pastorate, is the oversight of a church such a vested right that he may not be deprived of it by those who have bestowed it upon him? If a church should desire to be rid of their pastor, to withdraw that authority which they have placed in his hands, is it a greater evil that he should be dismissed, than that they should be compelled to retain a ruler who is unacceptable? Suppose some higher judicatory should compel a church to retain their pastor against their will, will he be able to benefit them?

But as no church comes fully up to the gospel theory of a church, and with the greatest possible care may have bad members, who may get the control of the church as did Diotrephes; suppose such a church should depose a preacher from the ministry wrongfully, and should accomplish the fact so far as they are concerned, it could work no irreparable injury to the man or to the cause of Christianity. Every other church being just as independent, may examine the facts for itself and govern its own conduct according to its understanding of them. The act of one church cannot bind another further than it chooses to be bound by it. Of course that comity and good fellowship that subsists between sister churches would lead each to respect the solemn acts of the other, unless manifestly wrong; for it is a part of the comity of the church that each should conform to the law of Christ. But the case we are supposing is one where the church is manifestly wrong.

In the case of a member, who under the discipline of the church has been wrongfully excluded from its fellowship—a subject we have already touched upon—how could the cause of religion be benefitted by his being forced back into a distasteful association with his brethren. Fellowship is voluntary, and when broken, whether justly or not, it cannot be restored by force. A member retained in the church by the compulsion of a higher power, would disturb the harmony of the church and paralyze its efforts. But if a higher judicatory may compel a church to retain a distasteful member, or an unacceptable minister, it may with equal right compel the church to dismiss one she loves and whom she desires to retain.

But if the church is liable to abuse this power, so is any judicatory to whom it might be entrusted. Bishops and synods have not proven to be more exempt from human frailties than local churches, the difference being that the abuse of power in the case of the church is not irremediable, but in the other case it is irreparable.

I close this section with the admission of the learned Dr. Mosheim:

"The churches in those early times were entirely independent, none of them being subject to any foreign jurisdiction; but each governed by its own rulers and by its own laws; for though the churches founded by the apostles had this particular deference shown to them, that they were consulted in difficult and doubtful cases, yet they had no juridical authority—no sort of supremacy over the others, nor the least right to enact laws for them. Nothing on the contrary is more evident than the perfect equality that reigned among primitive churches; nor does there even appear in this first century the smallest trace of that association of provincial churches from which councils and metropolitans derived their origin. It was only in the second century that the custom of holding councils commenced in Greece, when it soon spread through the other provinces."—*Ec. History, B. I. Part II., Chap. ii. Sec. 14.*)

PART II.

The Organization of the Church.

CHAPTER I.

INTRODUCTORY.

By the organization of the church I mean that form of government which it took under the guidance of the Holy Spirit; and the code of laws by which it is governed.

Many looking in vain in the history of the apostolic church for the traces of that particular form of organization to which they are attached, hastily conclude that Jesus Christ left His church in a chaotic state, to develop itself into an organized body, by gathering up the widely scattered parts and cementing them into a condition of visible unity. But who ever carefully studies the Word of God will find that what some have supposed to be an accidental state of things, is but the result of the design of the Holy Spirit, and that each of the local assemblies into which the primitive disciples were organized, is in itself a complete government sufficient for all the purposes for which the church was organized. In the New Testament we gain such glimpses of these bodies as to show clearly that they possessed all that goes to make up a government.

Here we find described the kind of persons who should compose such a body; we find persons of that character associated and calling themselves a church. The first element of government is the association of a qualified class of persons in order to erect a government. The component parts of the government are delineated; the officers required and their qualifications, rights and duties are laid down. The code of morals by which each is to be governed is given, the penalty denounced against every violation is stated; the manner of electing officers, and inflicting punishment may also be learned with reasonable certainty. These elements constitute a government. It embraces subjects and rulers, and the rights and duties of each are defined. It contains laws and the manner of administering them; and what more can any government contain?

That the form of government which the apostolic churches took was not accidental but of design, I think is evident from several considerations:

1. It is not likely that God would leave His church unprovided when He could select the form which was best adapted to the ends. The same truths were to be propagated, the same obstacle—the opposition of the carnal heart—was to be overcome, from the beginning as afterwards. No new truths were to be revealed, no contingencies likely to arise that could not easily be anticipated. That those who were under the guidance of the Holy Spirit selected a certain form is proof that the Spirit meant to select that form, or they would have indicated otherwise, as they do in many directions which they give; and that it continued during the lives of those who were thus inspired goes to confirm this view.

No supposed necessity arose after the days of the apostles for a change of form that was not known to the Holy Spirit and which did not exist during apostolic times. If a visible unity of all believers was required and an organic connection between all the assemblies necessary or desirable at any time, it was equally so during the times of the apostles. If the power of the church could better be administered by the clergy it was equally so from the beginning. There is no conceivable state of things demanding a change that did not exist from the first. Hence there can be no reason given for the selection of a certain form at first, except that God meant that form to be permanent; for He is not a God of caprices, and acting from a mere whim, but a God of purpose, of deliberation and fixed principles of action.

2. If mere expediency had governed in the selection of the form best calculated at first to meet the immediate wants of Christianity, and the circumstances of the hour had given shape to the institutions of the church, then the popular form of government would not have been chosen rather than another.

(1). The imperial and not the popular form of government was then in favor in the Roman Empire, in which the gospel was first preached. It appeared necessary to the present success of the new religion that the rulers should be conciliated —that those who had power to advance its cause should not be offended by a form hateful to them. No man could hope to gain favor with tyrants by espousing the cause of the people.

(2). It was very natural to conclude that that form of ecclesiastical government would be chosen to which the people were used. Certainly there would have been less collision, less inconvenience from the adoption of new and unfamiliar forms. The Jewish was aristocratic—being a government of elders. The Roman was pontifical and hierarchical. There must have been some design in differing from these forms to which the people were accustomed. Had mere expediency been the rule the Jewish converts would have been organized on the Presbyterial order, and the Gentiles would still have found their priests and pontiffs. But we find the case otherwise. Both Jews and Gentiles formed the same kind of government, essentially different from the kind of ecclesiastical and civil government to which they were used.

(3). If mere accidental circumstances had controlled they would never have used the popular form of government. If in the face of seemingly adverse circumstances we find them selecting this form we must conclude that there must have been some reason pertaining to the absolute fitness of things, and looking to permanent continuance. The opposition and persecution to which they were subjected, both by Jews and Gentiles, would have suggested the inconvenience of lodging the ruling power in the multitude of the disciples; for the assembling of a large number of persons was surer to attract notice than of a few; and thus their exposure was greater. There must therefore, have been some strong reason for incurring this risk.

Hence it is clear that an organization was effected under the guidance of the Holy Spirit, and that it was just such as the Spirit designed, and was meant to be adapted to all ages.

We are therefore prepared to enter upon the inquiry as to the nature of that organization.

CHAPTER II.

ITS COMPONENT PARTS.

We are now led to inquire into the constituent parts of that organization set up by Christ and His apostles and which they denominated the church. This institution we find exemplified in several organizations that existed in various countries each of which was a church, and so denominated by the sacred record. We are not compelled to comprehend all the local assemblies in the world, consolidated in visible unity, to obtain a correct idea of the church; and as they were all fashioned after the same model, the church at Jerusalem, whatever may be affirmed of one may be affirmed of all.

SECTION 1. *The Ministry.*—The principal design in the institution of the church was to propagate and establish a knowledge of the doctrines of Jesus, which he either communicated in person to his disciples, or subsequently revealed to them by the Holy Spirit, as the great instrument in the salvation of men. But while it was the duty of all who had a knowledge of the gospel to communicate it to others, and persuade them to embrace it, it is plain that this object can best be attained by having persons set apart, whose special duty it shall be to devote themselves wholly to the ministry of the word. I propose to notice this constituent part of the church considered merely as a preaching class, without reference to the incidental duties they were called upon to perform.

They were variously denominated in the Apostolic Church according to the functions they discharged; apostles, prophets, evangelists, bishops, elders and teachers. Whether deacons were preachers will be considered when I come to speak of the office of deacon.

The ministry were not designed to be a self perpetuating class, independent of the rest of the church, but they were in subordination to the church and derived their authority from it under Christ. This subordination Christ himself taught by his act in washing his disciples' feet, and in his declaration: "He that will be chief among you let him be your servant." It is also recognized in the term minister—servant—which is applied to them: "Surely the servant is not above his master."

The example of the apostles cannot be adduced as a proof that the ministry are independent of the church. It is true the first twelve were not called to ordination by the church, but they were chosen and ordained by Christ himself in person; and they were divinely inspired both to teach and to set in order. This cannot be affirmed of any other ministers. When it became necessary to select another to fill the place of the apostate Judas Iscariot, the apostles themselves recognized their subordination to the whole church by taking their voice in the selection of a successor.

While Christ continued on earth in visible association with his disciples he had no need of an executive in His kingdom, because he administered His laws in person. His recognition was a sufficient authentication of the authority of the twelve and the seventy, who were also ordained by Him to the ministry. But when He ascended He left His whole church, not a select few chosen out of it, as a depository, in a subordinate sense, of His authority.

1. The entrance into the ministry is peculiarly guarded as the importance of the office demands. Two things must concur; a divine call and a recog-

nition of that call by the church in an orderly, public manner. That recognition is ordinarily expressed by the solemn act of laying on of hands of the presbytery, called by the church for that purpose. This act is called ordination; but the imposition of hands confers nothing. It only recognizes the divine call, and furnishes the individual letters of commendation to the world. The authority is derived from God; but He has required before exercising that authority, that the called shall submit the evidence of his mission to the examination of a church, and have their concurrence as an indispensable evidence of the existence of the divine call. The Holy Spirit is harmonious in His operations and when he impresses this duty upon an individual, He also impresses the fact upon the church, and upon the ministers of his acquaintance. The concurrence of these impressions furnishes the evidence of the call.

We must distinguish between the call itself and the evidence of its existence. One is a fact, the other is a proof of that fact. But they are so inseparably connected that one cannot exist without the other. We will consider them separately.

The call is the work of the Holy Spirit, designating the office. This Paul distinctly ascribes to God. "God hath set some in the church, first apostles," etc. Said Christ: "Ye have not chosen me, but I have chosen you and ordained you." Paul begins his letter to the Romans by the recognition of this divine call: "Called to be an apostle." An instance of a special call is given Acts xvi: 10. Here Paul was directed to a special field of labor. He recognizes a general call to preach the gospel in Gal. i: 15. "When it pleased God who separated me from my mother's womb and called me by His grace to reveal His Son in me, that I might preach Him among the heathen, immediately I conferred not with flesh and blood," etc. The Holy Spirit directed the elders at Antioch: "Separate me, Barnabas and Saul for the work whereunto I have called them."

The first step in this divine call is regeneration. An experimental knowledge of Christianity is necessary before one can expound its doctrines. How can one rebuke sin and warn sinners who himself has never felt a proper sense of its guilt? Who can urge another to repent and believe who has no proper conception of these duties by himself obeying them? How can one who is an enemy to God become an embassador for God, beseeching men to be reconciled to Him?

The same Spirit which regenerates also prompts to obedience. He who has not obeyed, and has no inclination to obey the outward requirements of the gospel, cannot be under the influence of the Spirit. In the absence of baptism and church association as required by the law of Christ one can have no assurance of being called to the ministry. He is in no condition to teach obedience to Christ who himself refuses to obey him.

He also must be impressed with a strong desire for the salvation of souls. This is the great end of preaching. If he is lacking here he is wanting in the essential qualifications.

He must also love the doctrines of Christ and realize their importance as an instrumentality in the conversion of the world and the sanctification of the heart.

He must feel it to be his duty to labor for the cause of religion. He feels that he is not his own, that he is bought with a price; and that he owes it to God to consecrate all his talents to his service.

These qualifications he must possess in common with other Christians and without them there is no sufficient evidence of a divine call.

But he must also be deeply impressed with a sense of duty to labor in the line of the ministry. There must be a distinct impression that God requires this service; not simply to speak occasionally in the interest of Christianity but to devote himself entirely to this work. His choice of the ministry must not be as he would choose any other profession. He must feel: "Wo! is me if I preach not the gospel," and this must not simply be a passing impression, slight and evanescent, but it must be a fixed and settled conviction of duty.

The church must also be impressed with his fitness for the work. Those who come in contact with a man in his daily life can usually judge with tolerable accuracy whether he is called of God to preach. His manner of living will furnish the evidence of his calling. The absence of the outward manifestations of the indwelling spirit, is a sure proof of the want of a genuine work of grace in the heart. When these are wanting there is reason to believe that the party is either a pretender or at least mistaken in the nature of his impressions. The proof of his obedient spirit is equally clear. He will strive to know and do his duty in all things. He will not seek to evade obedience to even the smallest of Christ's commandments, by depreciating its binding force. He will meekly inquire: "Lord what wilt thou have me to do?" He will manifest his concern for souls by striving to win sinners to Christ. His love of the doctrines of Christ will be seen in his faithful and unprejudiced study of God's word, and his manifest desire to see all men embrace the truth. His devotion to the cause of Christ will be seen in abundant labors to build it up. In fine his whole life will be an epistle known and read of all men. Certainly he whose conduct is such as to leave any doubt upon the subject might well himself hesitate; for if be fails to impress those who are intimate with him, he can hardly impress strangers.

2. Ordinarily the imposition of hands of a presbytery is required as an additional recognition of the call. This takes place in the name of the church, and is designed to give expression to the voice of the church as well as the concurrent recognition of the members of the presbytery. I say ordinarily, for it is not certain that the presence of a presbytery was invariably the rule in apostolic times. Paul tells us that he was "not an apostle of men neither by men, but by Jesus Christ and God the Father." He also informs us: " When it pleased God to reveal his Son in me that I might preach him among the heathen, immediately I conferred not with flesh and blood, neither went I up to Jerusalem to them which were apostles before me—but I went into Arabia and returned again to Damascus." (Gal. i: 16, 17). " Then Saul was certain days with the disciples which were at Damascus, and straightway preached Christ in the Synagogues." (Acts ix: 19, 20). "Three years afterwards he went up to Jerusalem to see Peter and abode with him fifteen days." (Gal. i: 18). The occasion of his going we find in Acts xi: 30. When Paul and Barnabas returned to Antioch, having fulfilled the object of their visit, they were then ordained. (Acts xiii: 3). They had both been preaching sometime before this. As ordination is only a formal recognition, in the name of the church, of the qualifications of the minister, I can conceive of an emergency in which the church might adopt some other mode of authenticating the call, and by her own act, without interposition of a presbytery, set apart one, who gives satisfactory evidence of a divine call, to the discharge of all the functions of a minister. The opinion that a presbytery, is at all times necessary, grows out of the

belief that the imposition of hands confers some kind of mysterious gift. The true idea of an ordination is not that it imparts any quality or grace, but it is a formal recognition of existing qualification. Strictly speaking it confers no authority. The authority to preach is embraced in the divine call; but the voice of the church is an indispensable link in the chain of testimony by which one is authorized to conclude that he has been called of God. Without that concurrence he may not proceed to preach, for in its absence he may well doubt the genuineness of his call.

But while circumstances may sometimes justify a departure from the ordinary mode of authentication, as the imposition of hands by the presbytery, which was usually practiced by the apostles, where this is practicable their example should be followed.

The act of ordination is only declaratory—not communicative. It confers no gifts *per se*. It is only a solemn dedication to the work of the ministry. It is true, we read that the apostles conferred the gift of the Holy Ghost by the laying on of their hands. But this was not the object of the ordination ceremony. Some who were ordained received this gift before, and others not until after. And the gift of the Holy Spirit was sometimes conferred upon some who were not ministers. But while this form of setting apart to the ministry did not confer either the authority or the qualification, the evidence of the divine call was not usually complete without it, either as respected the called himself, or third parties.

This ordination was *presbyterial*. Such at least was the case with Paul and Barnabas. (Acts xiii: 13), and Timothy. (1 Tim. iv: 14). If sufficient in these cases it is certainly sufficient in any.

SECTION 2. *The Apostles.*—These were extraordinary ministers. They were missionary teachers peculiarly endowed by the Holy Spirit to go into regions where the gospel had not been preached; and to give instruction to the churches. They had no authority beyond their specific work, and were careful to abstain from any interference with the local churches, except to make known the will of Jesus Christ. They can hardly be classed as officers of the church, except when they departed from their general work to become the pastors of local churches. They were then officers by virtue of this relation, not by virtue of their being apostles. Under no circumstance did their functions resemble those of modern bishops and archbishops. They were confined to no jurisdictional limits and exercised their functions indiscriminately wherever they happened to be.

Some have supposed that they exercised a general authority by virtue of their office over all the churches, and that the office was perpetuated, and that their successors exercised the same general supervision.

They have nowhere said anything about their successors, or intimated that they would bequeath to others their extraordinary functions. Many of them passed away during the period of the sacred writings of the New Testament, but no mention is made of any successors.

We look in vain for those divisions into sees with jurisdictional limits. They passed through various countries exercising whatever oversight they had indiscriminately and without respect to any particular boundaries. Sometimes they became local pastors for a time, but most generally labored as missionaries. That they were often called upon to settle matters in doubt among the churches cannot be denied, but this affords no proof of their prelatical authority. Popular and well informed ministers in the churches having the congregational government, are just as frequently called upon to give their views of doctrine and discipline, and exercise just as much authority over churches which they plant. The decisions of Jesse Mercer fill a considerable part of a large volume, and one reading his biography would have the same reason to conclude that he was an Episcopal Magnate as that Paul or Peter was, because they were often appealed to in doubtful questions.

The nature of the functions of the apostolic office precludes the idea of its perpetuation. They were selected of those who had companied with Jesus from the baptism of John; who had heard all His teachings; had been eye-witnesses of His miracles; had witnessed His crucifixion and had seen Him after he had risen from the dead. They were selected mainly as witnesses of these things. They were divinely inspired to deliver the laws of Christ and under the guidance of the Holy Spirit to complete the organization of the church. This accomplished, their work was done. Their order no longer continued according to the law maxim *cessante ratione legis, cessat lex*—the reason of the law ceasing, the law itself ceases. The end for which the law was enacted having been accomplished, the law is no longer of any force.

Again they possessed extraordinary gifts, the possession of which was necessary to the discharge of their duties. They could speak with tongues. They could foretell future events. They knew by inspiration the will of God. They could work miracles. They could handle serpents and drink poisons with impunity. It was these things which distinguished them from the rest of the preachers, and gave them whatever pre-eminence they enjoyed. Take these away and the most eminent apostles became only preachers.

These gifts were not transmissible. From **their**

nature they were personal, and were bestowed only by the Holy Spirit. Therefore they could have had no successors except in that subordinate sense in which every faithful minister is their successor, holding authority not transmitted from the apostles; but conferred by the special call of Jesus Christ and formally recognized by the church. Every true minister of Jesus Christ receives his authority as directly from heaven as did Peter or Paul. Whatever rightful power any minister may exercise in the church, it is not the authority of the apostles transmitted through an unbroken line of successors, but it is as original a grant from the head of the church as any of the apostles had.

Although most of the apostles had passed away before the gospel history closes, we find no mention of any steps taken to fill their places except in the single instance of Judas Iscariot who proved unworthy of the office to which he had been chosen; and the reason assigned for choosing another in his place shows that the apostleship was for a specific purpose which precludes the possibility of its transmission.

The qualifications of an apostle were such that the office must have ceased with the first chosen. They were the witnesses of Jesus Christ and it was necessary that they should have seen the Lord, and been eye and ear witnesses to the things to which they testify. When about to fill the vacancy occasioned in the apostolic office by the apostacy and death of Judas Iscariot, Peter thus declares to the assembled multitude of the disciples: "Wherefore, of these men which have companied with us all the time that the Lord Jesus went in and out among us, beginning from the baptism of John unto that same day that He was taken up from us, must one be ordained to be a witness with us of his resurrection." Paul though not a disciple of Jesus during His stay on the earth nevertheless saw Him after His resurrection and conversed with Him; nay, was even permitted in spirit to ascend into the third heavens and to hear things not lawful to be uttered. It was necessary that they should have been chosen and sent forth by Jesus Christ himself in person. They were called apostles because they were *sent* (*apostolos* from *apostelloo* to send.) They derived their title from the fact that they were sent of Jesus Christ. Their mission ended with their own lives; and they were nowhere authorized to depute their powers. Agency is a personal trust and cannot be transferred to another without express authority.

It was a peculiar work they had to perform in setting in order the things pertaining to the kingdom, and therefore it was necessary that they should be set apart to this office by the head of the church Himself, in person. He alone could judge of their fitness for this great work. They must be infallibly inspired and endowed with the power of working miracles. Without the first, they could not have certainly known the will of Christ, and delivered his laws with unerring fidelity. Without the second, they could furnish no sufficent evidence of the genuineness of their claim to divine authority.

It was mainly upon their divine designation to the particular work to which they were assigned, and their infallible inspiration that the authority they exercised, rested. But as no subsequent minister of whatever grade can truly claim either of these and attest his claims by working miracles, he cannot claim to have succeeded to the authority of the apostles. God's will was fully made known; His church was fully set in order. There was therefore no necessity for their continuance.

CHAPTER III.

THE PRIMACY OF PETER.

I will probably not find a better occasion than in this connection to consider the primacy of Peter, upon which the Papal claim to supremacy rests. To establish this claim three things must be proven:

(1). That Christ conferred upon Peter the supremacy of authority over the rest of the disciples. (2). That he was authorized to transfer this authority to another; and (3) that he became bishop of Rome, and conferred his supremacy upon his successors in that see.

SECTION I.—*The Supremacy of Peter.*

1. To prove this claim for Peter it is not sufficient to show a pre-eminence, for pre-eminence does not necessarily imply authority. It must be an established pre-eminence of authority, asserted and exercised on all occasions. During the reign of the present Pope there have lived in the Roman Catholic church men much more eminent for learning, wisdom and piety, and whose labors have been much more abundant than his; but who in point of ecclesiastical authority fall far below him. Peter the Hermit was only an humble monk, but the luster and magnitude of his achievements obscure the fame of Urban II, his master. The most eminent men the world has ever produced have not been those who were highest in authority. So that though Peter was distinguished among his brethren, it does not follow that he had any authority over them, further than that just respect which is voluntarily conceded to eminent merit.

2. In the catalogues of the apostles the name of Peter stands at the head. (Matt. x: 2; Mark iii:

16; Luke vi: 14.) This, say the Roman Catholics, could not have been accidental, and in Matthew he is expressly called the *first*. When he went into the mount of transfiguration it is said He took with Him Peter, James and John, and the historians uniformly place the name of Peter first. The same is true when He entered into the house of Jairus, to restore his daughter, and when He was undergoing His passion in the garden of Gethsemane. But nothing can be inferred with certainty from the fact that Peter's name stands first in the list. To be of any positive value the inference from this source must be so strong as to exclude every other solution. But there were other reasons, to say the least, quite as probable, for placing his name first on the list. A sufficient explanation may be found in the fact that he was the oldest of the apostles, and that he was a man of great force of character, which always pushed him into a place of prominence. Hence it was natural that the historian should first think of him. But he was not uniformly named first, as in John i: 44, Andrew, his brother, takes precedence, and James in Gal. ii: 9.

That he was called *first* by Matthew proves nothing to the purpose. *Protos*, first, may refer not to rank but to order, as the first mentioned, or the first ordained or chosen. He must necessarily begin somewhere; but if He began at Peter it gives him no claim to superiority over others who were chosen and ordained by the same Lord.

3. It is said that in conformity with the supposed primacy of Peter we find him as the recognized leader taking the initiative, and first consulted by the disciples. The angel at the tomb told the woman to tell the disciples and Peter that Jesus went before them into Galilee. It was Peter who stood up in the midst of the disciples to propose the election of a successor to Judas Iscariot. It was Peter

who wrought the first miracle after the ascension of the Lord. It was he who undertook the explanation of the miracle, both before the people and before the assembled rulers. It was Peter at whose words Ananias and Sapphira were stricken dead. It was to Peter that the multitudes were brought that his shadow might fall upon them. It was Peter who on the day of Pentecost stood up and addressed the multitude.

The prominence thus assigned him may be readily accounted for on other grounds. His ready speech, his superior knowledge, his natural boldness, his impetuous zeal, his stronger faith and greater mental endowments, were qualities which always push men to the front, regardless of authority.

The same mode of reasoning might as easily prove the primacy of John. He was called the beloved disciple. He leaned on the Lord's breast at the supper, and even Peter, not presuming to propound a question, asked him to do it, as being more in the confidence of the Lord. It was to John that the dying Saviour commended the care of his mother. He was unmarried. He outlived all the apostles, and hence was most fit to be universal pastor.

4. The passage most frequently alleged by Roman Catholics in proof of Peter's supremacy is Matt. xvi: 18: "Thou art Peter, and upon this rock I will build my church, and the gates of hell shall not prevail against it," or as they unwarrantably render it, "thou art Peter, and upon *thee* will I build my church, and the gates of hell shall not prevail against it."

It is urged that Peter is declared to be the rock upon which the church is built. If this interpretation were conceded the conclusion does not follow that Peter had any authority which he transmitted to a long line of successors. "The words," as Barrow says in his admirable treatise on the supremacy of the Pope, are "metaphorical and thence ambiguous, or capable of divers interpretations; whence they cannot suffice to ground so main a point of doctrine, or to warrant so huge a pretence; these ought to stand upon down-right, evident and indubitable testimony." The grant of power should be so clear and distinct as to leave no ground of cavil. But what can there be in the metaphor of a *rock* that imports authority. Taking the rock as they insist, for the power of Peter, and allowing that on him the church should be built, it is far from being clear, as Bellarmine declares that government is denoted, the principate of the whole church. What resemblance is there between being a rock and a governor? What if he were declared to be the foundation of the church, are governments always and necessarily built upon their rulers; and when the foundation of a government is spoken of must we necessarily understand that its governors are meant?

Taking the person of Peter as the rock, an easier and more natural interpretation would be that by these words the Lord imported that Peter was designed as principal instrument, the first mover in the support of His truth and in the propagation of His gospel, as we may say of any good and great man, he is a pillar of the State, because he is one of its supports. Peter as the chief agent in building up the infant church might with great propriety be called a foundation stone, as all the apostles are so represented in the metaphorical language of the Apocalypse; as Ambrose says:

Petra dicitur eo quod primus in nationibus fidei fundamenta posuerit—He is called a rock because he would first lay in the nations the foundations of faith.—(*Ambr. de Sanctis. Serm. 2.*)

But even if the metaphor should import government the words do not seem to be spoken so exclusively with regard to the other apostles as to limit the authority conferred on Peter, or to import a peculiar grant to him. He might be a governing rock, so might they. He might be a foundation rock of the church, so might they. He might be a chief ruler, so might they; and all this without any violence to the words employed by the blessed Jesus.

Entirely consistent with the supposition that Peter is the rock, is the interpretation which some of the fathers have given, viz: that the confession of Peter was made by him in the name of all the rest of the disciples. He was their spokesman and in his representative capacity he is declared to be the foundation of the church; that is, the church is built upon all true disciples who make the good confession that Peter made.

But it is needless to push further into these interpretations, which, to say the least, are as clear as that given by the Papists. They serve our purpose to show that even admitting that Christ meant to declare Peter the rock upon which he was building His church, still it is not clear that He meant to found the Papacy upon him, since His words are capable of different interpretations without doing them any violence.

Again, if Peter be the foundation upon which the church is built, he cannot in the nature of things have a successor in this, unless the church is torn down and a new foundation laid every time a new Pope is elected. Besides it is usual to lay foundations at the bottom, not on the top of the building; and indeed in this thing the Papists seem to have gotten the church upside down since they put Peter and his successors in the highest place.

But to warrant this meaning of the Saviour's language, the word Peter in the first clause must be the same, or at least identical in signification with *rock* in the second clause. I am aware that Roman Catholics strive to make the impression that this is so. But an appeal to the original will readily decide the matter against them. The words are not "upon thee" as the Papists dare to give it, corrupting the pure word; nor yet "upon this Peter," but: "Thou art *Petros*, (a stone) and upon this *petra* (rock) I will build my church." *Petra* is not the accusative form of *petros* (which is *petron*) as the Romish interpretation requires, but it is a different word, though from the same root, and differs from it in signification. This difference of signification is well expressed by the English words *stone* (petros) and *rock* (petra) bearing the relation to each other which the part does to the whole.

A few examples of the scriptural usage of these words will show their relation to each other. *Petra* occurs in the New Testament in the following places, and Arius Montanus, a Roman Catholic and a member of the Council of Trent, uniformly renders it by the Latin *Petra*, a rock: Matt. vii: 24: Built his house upon a ROCK; Matt. vii: 25: For it was founded upon a ROCK; Matt. xvi: 18: Upon this ROCK I will build my church; xxvii. 51: And the ROCKS rent; 60: In his own new tomb which had been hewn out in the ROCK; Mark vi: 46: Which was hewn out of a ROCK; Luke vi: 48: Laid the foundation on a ROCK—for it was founded on a ROCK; viii: 6: And some fell on a ROCK; 13: They on the ROCK (are they) which; Rom. ix: 33: A stumbling stone (*lithon*) and a ROCK of offense; 1 Cor. x: 4: Drank of the spiritual ROCK that followed them and that ROCK was Christ; 1 Peter ii: viii: And a ROCK of offense; Rev. vi: 15: In the dens and in the ROCKS; 16: And said to the mountains and ROCKS, fall on us.

Petros occurs but once in the New Testament

except as a proper name. John i: 42: Cephas, which is by interpretation *a stone.*

In the Septuagint version of the Old Testament, it occurs but seldom. The following references will show the sense in which it is used:

2 Mac. i: 16: Casting STONES they slew the leader; iv: 41: Catching up STONES.

Accordingly the learned Trommius in his concordance of the Septuagint, gives *petra* invariably the sense of *rupes* (a rock) and *petros* the single meaning *lapis* (a stone.)

There are two other interpretations of this passage, either of which is more in accordance with the words of the Saviour. One makes *petra* refer to Christ himself, as the foundation of the church; and this does not at least contradict the declaration of Paul: "Other foundation can no man lay than is laid, Jesus Christ." The second and to my mind the more accurate, makes *petra* refer to the confession of Peter, a profession of faith in Christ being the foundation principle of the church.

The latter interpretation has the merit (if merit it be) of having received the infallible (!) approbation of more than one of Peter's supposed successors.

Gregory Maximus says: (Ep. iii: 33) *In vera fide persistete, et vitam vestram in petra ecclesiae, hoc est, in confessione Petri Apostolorum principis, solidate*— "Persist in the true faith, and establish your life upon the rock of the church, that is, the confession of the blessed Peter, the chief of the apostles."

Felix III (Ep. 5) glossing this very passage, says: *super ista confessione edificabo meam ecclesiam*— "Upon this, thy confession, I will build my church." Also vide. Nic. I, Ep. II: 6, John VIII, Ep. 76. Now every good papist must acknowledge that the church was built upon the confession of Peter, and not upon Peter himself, or else repudiate the infallibility of Gregory the Great, Felix III, Nicholas I, and John VIII. But as other Popes have been equally explicit in declaring that Christ meant to build His church not upon the confession of Peter but upon Peter himself, I am at a loss to know how the infallible teachers!! will escape the dilemma.

If the Saviour meant by this Scripture to teach so important a fact as the supremacy of Peter, it is remarkable that the other Evangelists do not mention it, and it is not elsewhere alluded to.

Elsewhere it is said the church is built upon the apostles and prophets, Christ himself being the chief corner stone; and so in Revelations, the twelve apostles are represented as the foundation stones. Whatever relation therefore Peter bore to the church it was equally shared by the rest.

5. They also allege the words of the Saviour used in the same connection: "To thee will I give the keys of the kingdom," that is, say they, "the supreme power over all the church; for he that hath the keys is master of the house."

This proof is liable to many of the same objections as the last named. The words are figurative and therefore not clear enough to prove their assertion. They admit and have received various interpretations by the highest authorities. The words, "I will give thee" are not exclusive. It is said *I will give thee*, but not, I will give *thee alone*.

But this promise was fulfilled to Peter when on the day of Pentecost, he had the distinguished honor of opening the kingdom by being the first after Christ arose to preach the gospel to men from all parts of the world, assembled in Jerusalem at the feast. To Peter it was given to open the kingdom to the Gentiles by first preaching the gospel to them.

6. It is also said that at the same time Christ gave him the power of binding and unloosing. "Whatsoever thou shalt bind on earth shall be bound in heaven, and whatever thou shalt loose on

earth shall be loosed in heaven," which clearly imports great power.

I will not now stop to inquire the import of the words "binding and unloosing." Whatever power they confer that power was not limited to Peter. But was conferred upon the disciples asssembled as a church. In the 18th chapter of Matthew the Saviour gives special directions for the treatment of personal grievances, then says to His disciples: "Verily, I say unto you, whatsoever *ye* shall bind on earth shall be bound in heaven, and whatsoever *ye* shall loose on earth shall be loosed in heaven." The same thought is afterwards expressed in somewhat different terms: (John xx: 23) "Whosoever sins *ye* remit they are remitted unto them, and whosoever sins *ye* retain they are retained."

7. The injunction to Peter: "Feed my sheep," is figurative; but clearly imports the duty to instruct, to guide, to edify in faith and obedience. But this was not the peculiar prerogative of Peter. When Christ said to him: "Feed my sheep," He did not say, *Do thou alone feed my sheep.* But the duty of instructing was made obligatory upon all. "Go *ye* into all the world and preach the gospel." "Go disciple all nations, teaching them to observe all things whatsoever I have commanded you." Hence Paul exhorts the elders at Ephesus to feed the church of God. This care of the church was not exclusively committed to Peter, but he himself, says, (1 Peter v: 1) "The elders which are among you, I exhort, which am also an elder, feed the flock which is among you." Peter could scarcely claim a monopoly in what was commonly enjoined upon all.

8. But there are positive proofs of Peter's want of supremacy. First, the Saviour himself declares that no such supremacy shall exist. (Matt. xx: 25.) They were discussing who should be chief, a

discussion which could not have taken place if **Peter** had been the recognized head. The question was referred to the Master, who promptly decided it in words that should rebuke the ambition not only of Popes, but of all those who elevate themselves above their brethren. "Ye know that the princes of the Gentiles exercise dominion over them, and they that are great exercise authority upon them. *But it shall not be so among you.* But whosoever will be great among you let him be your minister, and whosoever will be *chief* among you let him be your servant." Here is the kind of supremacy the Saviour established. It was a primacy of service. The only superiority He allows, and that to which He invites them to aspire, is not a superiority of authority, but of service. He is greatest who deserves most by being most useful to his brethren. He rebukes that unholy ambition for power and place, which characterizes men of the world, and teaches them that the only authority which they should seek is that just influence which is conferred by superior excellence in piety, knowledge and labor. They are brethren and therefore equal. He also declares this equality of His disciples (Matt. xxiii: 8: "Be ye not called *Rabbi,* for one is your master, even Christ, and all ye are brethren. And call no man father upon the earth, for one is your father which is in heaven." Here is an express declartion not only adverse to the primacy of any one of them, but declaring all equal, and forbidding them to call any man father. This injunction the papists constantly violate. They call the Bishop of Rome Pope, in the Latin *papa,* father, and they call every priest father; and if we are forbidden to call any man pope (father), every man is forbidden to be a pope, and therefore Peter could not have assumed this dignity in the face of the Lord's command.

Secondly. So far from Peter assuming or exercising

this authority over others, we read in Acts 8th chapter 14th verse, that the apostles at Jerusalem *sent* him and John to Samaria. Had he possessed the supremacy claimed for him he might have *gone* to Samaria, but could never have consented to be *sent* by others, his inferiors in office. It would be a novelty if the college of cardinals at Rome should presume to send Pius Ninth to preach the gospel to the refractory Germans.

Thirdly. When the church at Jerusalem, with the apostles and elders assembled to consider the question of circumcision, referred to them by the church at Antioch, Peter only gave his opinion like the rest; but James presided and delivered the sentence of the church. And the decree was not sent forth in the name of Peter, but in the name of all the apostles and brethren.

Fourthly. When Peter had preached the gospel to the Gentiles in the house of Cornelius, and baptized such as believed, the report of his unusual proceedings reached the ears of the apostles, and brethren in Judea, and when he was come up to Jerusalem they that were of the circumcision contended with him, and he was compelled to enter into explanation. This could not have happened if they had understood Peter to be the highest ecclesiastical authority, answerable to no earthly power. His acts would not have been called in question, if they had known him to be possessed of the infallible authority which is claimed by his pretended successor.

Fifthly. No formidable bull, issued by Peter, rivals the thunders of the Vatican, but his epistles bear the marks of a humble spirit. He entreats and exhorts, but never commands. "Dearly beloved, I beseech you as strangers and pilgrims, abstain from fleshly lusts." (1 Peter ii: 11) "The elders which are among you, I exhort, who am also an elder."

(1 Peter v: 1) No swelling words of pompous greatness escape his pen. In the only allusion he makes to his apostolic authority (2 Peter iii: 21) he includes his fellow apostles with himself, "the commandment of us the apostles," probably referring to the decree of the council at Jerusalem. He respectfully quotes: "our beloved brother Paul," referring his writings as well as his own, "to the wisdom, given unto him." What he communicated was by virtue of his inspiration, which he shared with others, and not by virtue of his office.

Sixthly. So far as the gospel history goes Paul after he became converted occupies a much more prominent position than Peter, particularly with reference to the Gentiles. Indeed it is expressly declared that Paul was the apostle to the Gentiles and Peter to the circumcision.

When Paul was called to the work of the ministry he did not wait for authority from Peter, but he informs us: "Immediately I conferred not with flesh and blood: neither went I up to Jerusalem to them who were apostles before me. But I went into Arabia and returned again into Damascus. Then after three years I went up to Jerusalem to see Peter." (Gal. i: 16).

The proceeding was indeed singular, if he recognized the voice of Peter as superior to the voice of God within him. Indeed the whole scope of this and much of the second chapter of Galatians, is to prove that his apostolic authority was derived directly from Jesus Christ, and was independent of Peter and the rest. He declares that he is "an apostle not of men, neither by man but by Jesus Christ." This he could not have truthfully declared if Peter had been constituted the sole foundation of ecclesiastical power.

Again, Paul informs us (Gal. ii: 11.) "But when Peter was come to Antioch I withstood him to the face, because he was to be blamed. For before that certain came from James, he did eat with the Gentiles; but when they were come he withdrew and separated himself, fearing them which were of the circumcision. And the other Jews dissembled likewise with them; insomuch that Barnabas was carried away with their dissimulation. But when I saw that they walked not uprightly according to the truth of the gospel, I said unto Peter before them all: If thou being a Jew, livest after the manner of the Gentiles, and not as do the Jews, why compellest thou the Gentiles to live as do the Jews?"

The papists ask us to believe that this supreme pontiff, endowed with infallibility, shrinks from the practice of the truth through fear of one of his subordinates, and then allows himself to be publicly rebuked by another because he walked not uprightly according to the truth of the gospel! *Credat Judeus Appella!* The fact is, instead of permitting Peter to exercise authority over him, Paul asserts his own authority against Peter's dissimulation.

Lastly. The mission of Peter was too circumscribed to allow him to become universal bishop. Paul declares (Gal. ii:7.) "But contrariwise when they saw that the gospel of the uncircumcision was committed unto me, as the gospel of the circumcision was unto Peter (for he that wrought effectually in Peter to the apostleship of the circumcision, the same was mighty in me towards the Gentiles) and when James, Cephas, and John who seemed to be pillars, perceived the grace that was given unto me, they gave to me and Barnabas the right hand of fellowship, that we should go unto the heathen, and they unto the circumcision." Peter's ministry was specially directed to the Jews, and therefore he could not have been bishop over all the disciples, Jews and Gentiles.

Hence we conclude that the primacy of Peter is

a fiction unknown to apostolic times; but invented afterwards to sustain the assumptions of the bishops of Rome.

SECTION II.—*The Right of Peter to Transfer his Authority.*

If it should be conceded that Peter had supreme authority in the college of apostles, and exercised a general oversight over all the churches, with power to regulate their affairs as universal bishop, it by no means follows that the necessity for such a primacy continued to exist and that he was authorized to choose his successor. On the contrary we might reasonably conclude that when the organization of the church was completed and the laws all delivered, such plenary powers, if they were ever entrusted to him, would be withdrawn as no longer required. Or if such an office was to continue in the church that Christ himself would designate the persons best fitted for it. At any rate mandate is a personal trust and an agent cannot transfer his powers to another without express authority from the principal to do so.

By a rule of the canon law "a personal privilege follows the person and is extinguished with the person." If Peter possessed this privilege at all, it was personal, because grounded on personal acts such as the readiness with which he abandoned all to follow Christ; his clear recognition of the Messiahship of Jesus, and his faithful confession of Him; or upon personal graces, such as his great faith, his devotion to the Lord, and his active zeal in His service; or upon his personal gifts and endowments, such as his boldness, his resolution, his activity, his readiness to apprehend, and his fluency of speech. These qualities are not transmissible; and as the privileges claimed for Peter were based upon these characteristics, the privilege itself was not transmissible. The qualities of mind and heart which fitted him for the high office to which he was called are not the subject of bequest; neither was the office based upon them.

The pretended grant of the primacy to him is grounded by its advocates upon words directed to his person, distinguished by personal adjuncts, such as name and parentage, and which were accomplished in the personal acts of Peter and cannot therefore be justly extended further. It was to *Simon, son of Jonas*, that Jesus said: "Thou art Peter, and upon this rock I will build my church." If this was a promise to build His church upon Peter, it was fulfilled in an eminent manner by the early success of the gospel under his labors. The keys were also promised to him by name and this promise was accomplished by his first opening the gospel to the Jews on the day of Pentecost and afterwards to the Gentiles in the house of Cornelius. Our Lord charged *Simon, son of Jonas*, to feed His sheep. This he accomplished by preaching, writing and instruction. All these things being clearly accomplished in the person of Peter, the sense of the words is exhausted and nothing can be inferred beyond.

The apostolic office itself was personal and temporary. It required peculiar gifts to qualify for its functions. It was requisite that they should be able to attest the resurrection and ascension of Christ from personal knowledge. This the twelve could do, having seen Him alive, and talked with Him after He arose, and witnessed His glorious ascension from the Mount. This Paul could do, having seen and heard the Lord speaking to him out of heaven—and being afterwards admitted to the unveiled glories of the third heaven. It was requisite that they be endowed with power to work miracles and confer the Holy Spirit; and to be infallibly inspired to know and declare the will of God. These were all personal endowments, the gift of the Holy Spirit, which they could not transmit. But these constituted all that distinguished Peter and the rest of the apostles from the humblest minister in the church. These being personal to them, died with them, and left nothing to transmit.

If so important a power as the right to confer all His authority upon a successor existed at all, a power so deeply concerning the interests of the church in all ages, where in the Record Book of Christ is it to be found? For the sake of general direction, for the satisfaction of all those who conscientiously desire to follow Christ, to relieve the mind of His disciples of all doubt, to prevent unnecessary discussion, heresy and schisms, it was very necessary that such declaration should have been made and that it should have been expressed in some authentic record, clear and unmistakable, so that we might avoid error and yield ready submission to the truth. Surely a matter of such consequence could not have escaped mention somewhere. But where is the charter for such a grant? In its absence we may justify ourselves in the conclusion that none such exists.

SECTION 3. *Peter at Rome.*—Before the claim of the papacy can be considered established not only all that is claimed for the primacy of Peter and his right to transfer his authority must be established, but also that he was bishop of Rome, and conferred upon his successors in that see all the rights pertaining to the office of universal bishop.

The Romish tradition claims that Peter was twenty-five years bishop of Rome, where he died, leaving to Linus all the rights and authority which had been conferred upon him by Jesus Christ.

It is admitted that the latter part of Peter's life

is involved in great obscurity, and the claim that he was bishop of Rome for any length of time rests solely on very uncertain tradition. It cannot be shown from any authentic history that Peter was ever in Rome, still less can it be shown that he was pastor there. But even if we accept the tradition, which I think is not at all improbable, that he came to Rome during the reign of Nero and was crucified in that city, it does not follow that he ever was bishop at Rome.

It is certain the papal account cannot be true, which is that Peter went to Rome A. D. 44, and continued as pastor there until 69, when he suffered martyrdom. Lactantius, whom Dr. Lardiner regards as the best authority on this subject, says that he came to Rome and suffered martyrdom during the reign of Nero, whose accession took place October 13th, A. D. 54, and ended the middle of June A. D. 68.

In the examination of this question I take the life of Paul which is much more conspicuous as the standard of comparison, and I am guided by the chronology of Conybeare and Howson in their admirable "Life and Epistles of St. Paul."

About the year 44 "Herod the King put forth his hand to vex certain of the church, and he killed James the brother of John with the sword, and because he saw it pleased the Jews he proceeded further to take Peter also." (Acts xii: 1–3). This is the year according to Romish tradition when Peter was inducted into the Roman see. But we find him residing at Jerusalem and afterwards shut up in prison by the command of Herod.

We next hear of him six years afterwards (A. D. 50) in the council at Jerusalem. No mention is made of his having come from Rome. But the natural inference from the narrative is that he still resided in Judea. In the speech which he made in the council he refers to the occasion of his having preached the gospel to the Gentiles in the house of Cornelius many years before. Had he been pastor of a Gentile church he could not well have omitted mention of the fact.

In 52, Claudius expelled all the Jews from Rome. Paul meets with some of these at Corinth and began an acquaintance that lasted long afterwards. It was an occasion for the historian to make mention of so prominent a Christian leader as Peter, had he been among those ordered to depart from the city.

Some time subsequent to this we find Paul withstanding him to his face on account of his dissimulation at Antioch.

It is remarkable that the Acts of the apostles which were written by Luke mainly to commemorate the leading acts in the lives of Peter and Paul, should omit so important a fact—important in the view taken by Romanists—as the residence of Peter at Rome during a large part of the time covered by the history.

Paul wrote his epistle to the Romans A. D. 58, in which he says: "I long to see you that I may impart unto you some spiritual gift, to the end that you may be established." What! enjoying the pastoral labors of the chief of the apostles, God's vicar on earth, and yet needing spiritual gifts from Paul to the end that they might be established! Incredible! The epistle to the Romans abounds in precepts and instructions that would have been unnecessary and impertinent, if they had been blest with the labors of so eminent an apostle as Peter for their pastor. In the salutatory part of this epistle Paul greets many of the church by name, some of them so obscure as never to be mentioned again, and yet has no greeting for Peter, his fellow apostle, eminent for his labors in the church. The conduct of Paul is inexplicable on the supposition that Peter was then pastor at Rome over the church to which this epistle was addressed.

After this Paul is arrested at Jerusalem and is sent a prisoner to Rome where he arrived in the spring of 61. The Roman brethren went out to meet them as far as Appii-forum; but the historian makes no mention of Peter, nor yet after they reached the city. Paul called together the chief of the Jews, and strange to say they were ignorant of the doctrine of Christ and had only remotely heard of the followers of Jesus, as a sect everywhere spoken against. Peter, the great apostle to the Jews seventeen years—preaching at Rome, according to the papists, and the best informed people of his own nation had never yet heard these things explained! Although Paul dwelt two whole years in Rome in his own hired house, receiving all who came, so far as the narrative goes, Peter never once visited the distinguished Christian prisoner!

During his confinement at Rome Paul wrote his epistles to Philemon, Colossians, Ephesians, and Philippians; and although many of the Roman brethren are mentioned by name not the slightest allusion is made to Peter.

In 68 we again find Paul a prisoner in Rome, writing his second epistle to Timothy, when he was ready to be offered up, and the time of his departure was at hand. Here again he mentions a number of Roman Christians and among them Linus, who is said to have been Peter's successor; but not a word of Peter. Here is a chain of circumstances inexplicable on the supposition that Peter was pastor at Rome. The next year, A. D. 69, the papists say he suffered martyrdom, but Lactantius says during the reign of Nero, and if so not later than A. D. 68.

A material fact in the papal proof thus fails, for if he was not pastor at Rome he could not have had a successor in that see.

But even if it could be shown that Peter was pastor at Rome for any period of time, another material fact must be shown, viz: that by some authentic act he conferred all his powers upon his successor in that see. It is not even pretended that such authentic act exists. Hence the papal claim falls to the ground for want of proof.

CHAPTER IV.

MINISTRY CONTINUED—PASTORS OR BISHOPS.

In addition to those extraordinary officers, the divinely inspired apostles, employed in setting up the kingdom of Christ, and in delivering the laws communicated by the Holy Spirit, the peculiar nature of that kingdom required others.

I have shown that the church is local in its character, composed of the organized body of baptized believers who ordinarily assemble in one place. The church propagates itself by contact, and this requires local organization. At the head of this organization stands the pastor or bishop. These names do not import two offices, but different phases of the same office. Considered as a flock the pastor leads them forth to green pastures. He feeds the weak with the sincere milk of the gospel, affording more substantial food to the strong. He watches over their spiritual welfare and guards them against ravenous wolves. Considered as an assembly the bishop presides over them, taking the oversight of them willingly and not by constraint, expounding to them the law of the kingdom, instructing the ignorant, rebuking the disorderly and exhorting the weak.

SECTION 1. *Their qualifications.*

It may be supposed that an officer of so much importance requires peculiar qualifications and that minute directions are given as to the kind of persons who are to be installed into the pastorate. These respect his *social relations*, his *capabilities*, *his moral character* and the *soundness of his faith;* and these are given at length, especially in 1 Tim. iii. chapter, and Titus i. chapter.

(1.) *His social* relations; "The husband of one wife." (1 Tim. iii: 2; Titus i: 6.). His marriage relations must be pure. He must not be a polygamist, not that he must necessarily be a married man, for we learn from apostolic example that marriage is not a necessary qualification for the ministry. Each must decide for himself whether he should be a married man or not. And this he must determine from the particular circumstances that surround him. Each state has its advantages and disadvantages. The married man is more identified with the interests of society, and therefore has a hold upon others which the unmarried cannot attain. The marriage tie and tender relationship of parentage bring us into closer sympathy with our fellowmen. We need to have our rugged natures softened and the tender and gentle elements of character developed, which can only be done by close and intimate association with the opposite sex. Without this association, calling into exercise our affections, we are apt to retreat within ourselves, and become morose and selfish, and unsympathetic. Above all, the counsel of a pure minded, sensible woman, to whom you can entrust every thought and unburden your whole heart, is of infinite value to those who watch for souls. On the other hand to provide for the wants of a family engrosses much of our time, and the cares growing out of the responsibilities incident to this relation necessarily divert our thoughts from the great work before us. Besides the increased expense of a family renders it impossible to labor in many fields for the want of adequate support.

Every man is more or less affected by the character of his wife. Therefore in setting apart a married man to this important function, due regard must be had to the companion of his labors; because she may be such a one as will wholly **destroy** his usefulness and render him, however well qualified otherwise, wholly unfit to be a bishop.

"Having faithful children not accused of riot or unruly." (Titus i: 6.) "Having believing children." (Bible Union Version.) Commonly this circumstance is too lightly considered in the selection of those who are to be set apart to the gospel ministry. I do not suppose that the apostle meant that none should be ordained but those whose children are believers. But he whose adult children are Christians is better qualified to become a pastor than one whose children are wicked, unbelievers. If riotous and defiant of law, they may so mar his usefulness as to render him unfit for the holy calling. It is a fair presumption that a man who can exercise so little influence for good over his own family will hardly be likely to benefit strangers.

"Having a good report of them without." (1 Tim. 3: 7.) It is very necessary to the success of the minister that he enjoy public confidence. He must have a reputation for sincerity, truthfulness and integrity. No man who has lived so questionably as to leave a doubt in the minds of his fellowmen as to these qualities will ever have that weight which a man of God should have. He must be so true to his principles that men will believe him to be what he pretends to be. If he has lived so inconsistently that men doubt his sincerity he can never affect them for good.

(2.) *His capabilities*: "Ruling well his own house, having his children in subjection with all gravity." (1 Tim. iii: 4;) and the apostle reasons well: "For if a man know not how to rule his own house, how shall he take care of the church of God?" A successful business man makes the best pastor. The very qualities that give him success in the management of his private affairs and in controlling his own household are required in the discharge of his pastoral duties. He who is the common counselor of his flock in the minutest affairs of life should be a man of great prudence and wisdom. In all the complications of the church over which he presides no little administrative ability is required. If he is loose and careless in the administration of his own business—if he is an impractical visionary in his domestic concerns, he will be so in the concerns of the church. His capacity for government may be discovered by the manner in which he rules his own household. If he is deficient here—if he lack the tact and will to govern his own family, he will be too careless and weak to govern the church.

"Apt to teach." (1 Tim. iii: 2.) The chief work of the pastor is to expound the word—to teach his people the great truths of the gospel. This requirement imports a faculty for imparting knowledge, and the possession of knowledge also; for how can a man teach what he does not know? The knowledge required is an experimental knowledge of religion, and an acquaintance with the Scriptures. This embraces all those branches of learning which throw light upon the sacred writings. It is a question where the standard should be fixed, and whilst I would not depreciate the valuable services of many excellent men who are deficient in literary attainments, I think I am within the meaning of the apostle when I say that the more knowledge of the right kind one possesses the better he is prepared to discharge the duties of a minister.

The aptness required embraces a knowledge of those rules of preparation and delivery which render a discourse clear, forcible and attractive. But behind these is an aptness—a facility in communicating knowledge without which the preacher is a mere artificial declaimer, without point or effectiveness. This faculty consists in an illuminated mind, an easy command of language, and a memory ready to yield up its stores of knowledge.

"Not a novice." (1 Tim. iii: 6.) There are two obvious reasons why a novice should not be put into the office of a bishop. (1.) He has not yet given proof of his stability in his profession, and (2) he who had just begun to learn is hardly in a condition to begin to teach.

(3.) *His moral qualifications*: "Blameless." (1 Tim. iii: 2. Titus i: 6.) This implies that he should not only be without blame, but that he should be undeserving censure. An irreproachable character is essentially necessary. He who is without it, whatever may be his deserts, will fail of success in the ministry. He must start with a fair name and keep it free from a just reproach.

"Vigilant." (1 Tim. iii: 2.) He watches for souls. He must be on the out-look to seize upon every favorable occasion to impress the truth. He must be watchful to prevent the ingress of false doctrine. He must guard against the wiles of the enemies of religion. He must especially be vigilant, lest he fall into temptation and bring reproach upon his office. He must be watchful over his reputation, and not allow himself to be placed in circumstances of suspicion, where he cannot clearly establish his innocence when suspected.

"Sober." (1 Tim. iii: 2. Titus i: 8.) That healthy state of mind implied in the word sober, (Gr. *sophrona*—sound minded) gives rise to a gravity of deportment, equally removed from levity on the one hand, and severity on the other. Levity is a proof of mental weakness and acerbity of perverted sentiments. Frivolity subjects the minister to a want of respect, and sternness renders him repulsive. He should possess that graceful dignity which invites the free approach of the serious, but represses the easy familiarity of the light and frivolous.

"Of good behavior." (1 Tim. iii: 1.) An ill-bred, boorish minister is a disgrace to the calling. It is absolutely necessary that a bishop should be a gentleman in the highest sense of that term. Coarseness is inexcusable in any man; it is unpardonable in a minister. The apostle does not refer so much to that acquired polish of manners which merely pertains to the external man, as to that courteous demeanor and that unselfish regard for others, which flows from a kind heart; and that delicate sense of propriety which springs from a refined and cultivated mind.

"Given to hospitality." (1 Tim. iii: 2.) "A lover of hospitality." (Titus i: 7.) Hospitality is a social virtue that was much more demanded by the circumstances of ancient times when there were fewer accommodations for strangers than now. Or rather hospitality took a differnt form then and now. Then strangers required lodging and entertainment, but the more practical civilization of modern times has provided these necessary comforts with less sacrifice of personal independence; and hospitality takes a different shape. There are many attentions to strangers fully as important as attention to their physical comfort. And in these the pastor should be conspicuous. One coming into a strange community should receive such welcome as will make him feel that he is not an intruder; and that he is among people who care for each other's wants and happiness. He should be sought out, brought to the house of God, introduced to others, and encouraged in some honest pursuit. How many young men are yearly lost in our cities for the want of proper attention. Such might often be saved to the church and to morality, if they were sought for and introduced into good society instead of being abandoned to seek social enjoyments in drinking saloons, club rooms and even worse places of resort. How grateful these attentions are to one sojourning among strangers and oppressed with a sense of loneliness; and how we are drawn to those who manifest such interest in us! In this hospitable work the pastor should be pre-eminent.

"Not given to wine." (1 Tim. iii: 3. Titus i: 7.) The wine bibber is not the man to instruct men in the duty of temperance and sobriety. If Timothy and Titus were prohibited from ordaining to the office of bishop one who was addicted to wine, how much more forcibly the prohibition applies to those who are addicted to stronger drinks! The minister must be without the slightest taint himself, if he would successfully resist the evil of intemperance. How can he rebuke a sin which he himself is guilty of. This passage is often misquoted as though the apostle said, "not given to much wine," but the apostle means not given to wine at all.

"No striker." (1 Tim. iii: 3.) (Titus i: 7.) Not quick to resent an injury—not quarrelsome—not ready to knock one down who refuses to be convinced. One should be ready to defend the truth when assailed and expose error. But not in an angry, vindictive spirit. The Christian minister should not wrangle nor manifest acrimony—but there is nothing in this passage to prohibit him from engaging in religious controversy. Paul himself was the greatest controversialist of his day, disputing daily with the enemies of truth. If there is anything wrong in religious discussion, it lies at the door of those who oppose the truth.

"Not greedy of filthy lucre." (1 Tim. iii: 3.) "Not given to filthy lucre." (Titus i: .) Aside from the sin of dishonesty, he who is intent upon acquiring dishonest gains, will be too much engaged in the pursuit to watch for souls. But while this qualification relates more particularly to the acquisition of property, it includes also the attainment by unfair and indirect means of any advantage whatever. We may not even do wrong with a good end in view. The calling of the minister requires openness, directness and candor. He who is destitute of these qualities is unfit for the office.

"Patient." (1 Tim. iii: 3.) "Not soon angry." (Titus i: 7.) There is much in the ministerial office to try one's patience. The impatient, irascible man, who loses his temper whenever he meets opposition, or finds matters not exactly to his liking, will soon find himself arrayed against a large part of the church and his influence for good destroyed. If he discovers anything wrong he must patiently set to work to correct it. But when he loses his temper he also loses his power. But perhaps the apostle by the term "patient" refers to that perseverance in well doing, that sows the seed and cultivates the soil, patiently awaiting the harvest. Those hasty persons, who abandon their work immediately unless they see results at once will make poor pioneers in the gospel.

"Not a brawler." (1 Tim. iii: 3.) Instead of being contentious, and a stirrer up of strife, he should be the peace-maker in the church. If he delights in strife and contention he is unfit to preside in the house of peace.

"Not covetous." (1 Tim. iii: 3.) There are two reasons why a covetous man is unfit for the ministry.

1. He would soon bring the office into disrepute, and lose the confidence of his fellowmen, for the world does not readily excuse a grasping disposition in a preacher.

2. The inordinate desire for gain will draw him away into secular pursuits to the neglect of the duties of the office, and thus his services be lost to the church.

Perhaps some may suppose that Paul meant to

guard the church against those who would make a gain of the church; but the scanty remuneration of ministers is an effectual guard against any temptation of this sort. The same talents are better paid in secular pursuits and therefore the covetous would not be likely to adopt the ministerial calling with the view of making it profitable.

"Not self-willed." (Titus i: 7.) If he has an obstinate will, he will be continually in conflict with others. While he should never yield a principle, he should conciliate others by proper deference to their views. He who would gain men must be ready to concede something to them. A self-willed man, bent on always having his own way, is unfit to preside over men having equal rights with himself.

He must be "just" in all his dealings with his fellowmen, that he may judge impartially and administer faithfully in all matters that come properly before him. He must be "holy" in his life that his example may incite others to like attainments; and that his own rich experience of grace may fit him as a spiritual adviser. He must be "a lover of good men" that he may gather such around him as his constant companions and by holy association keep himself unspotted from the world. He must be "temperate"—moderate in his indulgencies—that he may preserve his health and avoid bringing scandal upon the church by intemperate habits.

(4.) *The soundness of his faith:* "Holding fast the faithful word as he hath been taught, that he may be able by sound doctrine, both to exhort and to convince the gainsayers." (Titus i: 9.)

Perfect soundness in the faith is not required as a condition of church membership, but the largest tolerance consistent with the peace of the church is inculcated. Him that is weak in the faith receive ye, but not to doubtful disputations." (Rom. xiv: 1.) The church is a school of instruction in the truths of the gospel; and he is received with the hope that he may learn the way of the Lord more perfectly. But if he aspires to become himself an instructor, the church should see to it that he "holds fast the faithful word as he has been taught." This embraces several particulars.

(1.) He must give his assent to the truths of the gospel. To undertake to teach things he does not believe would be hypocritical. If he openly rejects any of these doctrines and teaches error instead, the church would be untrue to her mission to arm him with authority to overthrow the truths which she is solemnly charged to preserve. Every church is responsible for the doctrine of her ministers, for she endorses them by setting them up as teachers. Hence she should institute the closest inquiry into the religious belief of those who aspire to ordination.

(2.) But it is not enough to give a bare assent to the truth. He must be well grounded in it. He must be firmly established in the faith. His convictions of religious truth must be too deep and lasting to yield to every wind of false doctrine that blows. Says James: A double-minded man [an undecided man] is unstable in all his ways," and therefore unfit to be made a standard bearer.

(3.) Neither is it sufficient that he have a firm religious belief. That belief must be in accordance with the faithful word. It must be a belief, sustained by the Scriptures—Not what pretends to be —but what *is* the doctrine of God's word—what is really God's word—not the glosses of men upon it —not the false translations and interpretations of the word, but the faithful word which is the only infallible rule of faith and conduct.

(4.) "As he has been taught" *i. e.* according to the teachings of the inspired apostles It is not enough that he holds firmly what has been taught him for the truth, because he may have been taught wrong, unless taught by God's word. If he has been wrongly taught the more stubborn he is in his error the worse for him. But if he has been taught by God's holy word, the firmer he is, the fitter he is to be intrusted with his truth.

(5.) The reasons given are worthy of notice: "That he may by sound doctrine, exhort and convince gainsayers." Paul did not suppose that gainsayers were to be convinced by suppressing the truth; or so modifying its utterances as to make it palatable to those in error. Error must be met by the truth. Sound doctrine is the best antidote to false teachings. Some object to what they call doctrinal preaching because it is offensive to gainsayers. They declaim against upholding denominational peculiarities. Certainly no man should teach any peculiarity that is not taught in the Scriptures; but if it is embraced in the term "sound doctrine" who may dare to omit it?

(6.) There are a few corollaries that follow from the above which I desire to present.

1. If we may not set apart to the gospel ministry one who is unsound in the faith, it follows that we may not give encouragement to such, even though set apart to the ministerial office.

2. The mere form of ordination cannot make one who is lacking in this essential Scriptural qualification, a true minister of Jesus Christ.

3. No courtesy known to the Scriptures requires me to recognize one as a minister of the gospel who denies the elementary doctrines of the gospel, and teaches doctrines which subvert gospel ordinances.

4. We may no more accept a heterodox minister made by others than we may make one ourselves.

5. If this rule was strictly adhered to, less encouragement would be given to heterodoxy.

SECTION 2. *Rights.*—1. It is his right to judge of

the subjects to be presented in his pulpit administrations. While he should be open to respectful suggestions, made by pious and intelligent brethren, he must himself be the ultimate judge of the subject matter of his discourses. So long as he confines himself within the limit of Scriptural doctrine, and the spirit of the gospel, no one may interfere. If a true minister, called of God, he is more or less under the guidance of the Holy Spirit in the choice of subjects. Besides, if he does his whole duty, he is better informed what the spiritual wants of his flock require than another possibly can be. He has a right to be free from every unwarranted interference that would in any way restrict the independence of his pulpit and his freedom "to be instant in season and out of season, to rebuke, exhort, reprove with all long suffering and doctrine." He would not be a competent instructor if he were not capable of choosing proper lessons for the taught.

2. He has a right to be consulted in every matter of importance, relating to the work of the church. By the choice of the church, he is made *an* overseer, and so long as he holds that position it is his duty and his privilege to give general direction to the work. If he prove to be incompetent, or abuse his powers, it is the right of the church to depose him. But so long as he confines himself within the bounds prescribed by Christ, his voice may not be disregarded. He is styled in the Scriptures a *ruler*. A ruler without any authority to govern is an absurdity. But as one says: "He must take the oversight (the office of bishop) not by constraint, but willingly." There can be no conflict of will so long as the will of God is made the rule on the part of pastor and flock.

3. He has the right to claim the co-operation of the church in Christian labor. He is not

employed by the church to do their work in order that they may be eased. The church cannot do her work by proxy. His duties are peculiarly his own, and not such as the church can do. Each has his own work, but that work is a harmony. Pastor and people are co-workers and each must perform his own appropriate work or it goes undone.

4. He is entitled to the attendance of his flock upon his ministry. An important part of his duty is to instruct; but how can he instruct those who are absent from his lectures.

The church is always more or less responsible for the success of the pastor, and that minister whose people habitually neglect to attend upon his preaching has a double burden to bear. Their very absence is in the eyes of many a tacit reflection upon him. It is in vain that they protest that they do not mean to reflect upon him. The effect upon his usefulness is the same. They bring him into discredit the same as if they intended to do so; and the effect is as disastrous to the cause of Christ. The world very naturally concludes that he must be a very poor preacher, when his own flock will not hear him. And they go elsewhere. Even those who have heard him with pleasure and profit begin to suspect there must be something wrong in his character not known to the public, and they cease to attend. And as a climax to this injustice and injury, the very persons who have produced all this injury often justify themselves in their neglect, by the reflection that he does not appear acceptable to the people! And will God hold them guiltless for such palpable and cruel injustice to the minister and the consequent injury to the cause of Christ, from the impaired usefulness of his servant? Perhaps driven from his field of labor by such heartless neglect he seeks a new one. But he goes there with the prestige of failure to overcome. He is already prejudiced by that class, who seek for an excuse for their neglect, even at the expense of the minister; and he soon sinks again under the accumulated weight of this cruel wrong. And thus he goes on through life crippled in his usefulness and he dies at last with the sad reflection that perhaps after all he may have missed his calling. Have I not in this paragraph written the life of many a pastor?

But the effect of this treatment is soon visible in the minister himself. Finding himself unappreciated by those for whom he labors, and lacking that mental stimulus which is always to be found in an appreciative audience, he neglects his pulpit preparations and really deteriorates in his ministerial abilities. He never knows what to bring forward, and therefore cannot "feed his flock, rightly dividing the word, giving his portion to each in his season."

5. He is entitled to the protection of the church in his property, his person and his reputation. The duties of his calling deprive him of the opportunity to give that attention to secular affairs which is necessary to the proper administration of his personal estate. His brethren should at least aid him so far in this that no undue advantage shall be taken of him to the injury of his property. The faithful discharge of his duty may expose him to personal danger. As far as possible his brethren should ward off evil from him. Both the law of Christ and public opinion impose upon him such restrictions as virtually make him a non-combatant. His brethren should see to it, that advantage is not taken of this fact to abuse his person. But of nothing should they be so careful as his reputation. They should defend him when unjustly assailed, and always suggest the most favorable construction of his conduct when blamed. His worth as a man

and a preacher, should not be depreciated, but he should always be judiciously commended to the world, so far as it may truthfully be done. The apostle says: "Let them that rule well be accounted worthy of double honor."

6. His decisions in all matters that come properly before him are entitled to respect. He is no autocrat whose will is law, but as the presiding officer of the church, charged with the administration of the laws of Christ, and as the umpire of reference, unless his opinions were entitled to respect, he would be a mere dumb statue raised to the Episcopal seat for ornament rather than use. In that event the empty chair would serve as well. It is not meant that his decisions are obsolutely binding so far as to preclude any appeal; but his position supposes a higher degree of intelligence and piety; and having given his whole attention to the interests of the church, his opportunity for forming an accurate judgment is so much better than others that his decisions should not be lightly disturbed. But if they are manifestly wrong they may be reversed by the church.

7. He is entitled to the prayers of his church. It should be borne in mind that he does not triumph in his own strength. He is but an earthen vessel, to whom is committed the great treasure of the gospel. He is but an instrument in the hands of a higher power. However gifted he may be, though he may possess the burning eloquence of Isaiah; the soft pathos of Israel's sweet singer, the wisdom of Solomon, the melting strains of Jeremiah, and the impetuous vehemence of Ezekiel, it will all avail nothing without the intervention of other instrumentalities. The gospel is the power of God unto salvation only when accompanied and vitalized by the Holy Spirit. Only then it overthrows the powers of darkness and overcomes the world. Human

words are empty sounds echoing powerless through the vacant aisles of the Godless soul until animated by the spirit of God. Then every syllable sparkles with light and peoples the heart with living emotions. God is no niggard in the bestowment of this power in answer to the prayers of his people. He often chooses the weak things of this world to confound the great. The rich magazine of his grace is accessible to the humblest of his followers. Here we may come, not as haughty stipendaries claiming a thankless boon, but as poor pensioners upon his bounty, with humble boldness entreating his goodness. Prayer is the indispensable channel of God's spiritual blessings. This Paul felt when he besought the brethren at Thessalonica to pray for him "that the word of the Lord might run, have free course and be glorified." The prayer of God's people is a power. Before them obstacles to the progress of the gospel give way. A people who pray for their minister are more interested in his labors, and more heartily co-operate with him. The reflection that his flock remember him at a throne of grace, gives him boldness to declare the whole counsel of God. It requires more moral courage than most men possess to assault alone the ramparts of sin. He has mental and spiritual conflicts that require much of the grace of God to sustain him. The thought that he has an interest in the prayers of his brethren gives him renewed strength to battle for the Lord. In answer to the prayers of the church the unction of the Holy Spirit will descend upon him and divine grace will mingle in his administrations. Then every sentence that falls from his lips will be big with the Holy Spirit. Then will he be able to dip every shaft in the blood of Jesus and wound only to heal.

But how can he tread alone a rugged path over hills of snow? He must lean upon some sympathetic heart, warmed by Christian love. He will falter if left to struggle on alone and isolated in frozen solitude. Oh! who can bear the cheerless thought that no one prays for him; that no fond wish goes up to God in his behalf? It will cheer him in his humble labors to know that even one heart has a pulse for him—that the lips of even one whisper his name into the ear of the Almighty.

8. He is entitled to an adequate support, while devoting himself to the duties of the office. To become a pastor, he gives up the emoluments of secular business and it is only just that those who receive the benefits of his labors should supply what he could otherwise provide for himself. As Paul correctly reasons on this subject: (1 Cor. ix: 11) "If we have sown unto you spiritual things is it a great thing that we shall reap your carnal things?" The law of reciprocity requires it, for he who contributes to the general prosperity, is justly entitled to share in the benefits derived. Ministers are not idle drones in the social hive, fattening on the substance of others, but no class contributes more to the material prosperity of the country. Without them religion would cease to be taught, and without religion society would be destroyed. To fully appreciate the value of religion as a productive agency in society let us conceive of the state of things, if the principles of our holy religion were eliminated from society. Strike out the law, "thou shalt not steal," and who could accumulate property if it were at the mercy of every man whose rapacity might lead him to desire it? Whose reputation would be safe, if men were not taught, "thou shalt not bear false witness?" Who could live in a state of society if life and virtue were at the mercy of every man whose violence or lust might be aroused? And yet there could be no security to life or virtue, no accumulation of

property, no progress in the arts of civilized life—without the protection of that correct moral sentiment which is fostered by the institutions of our holy religion. Their instructions do more to give quiet and security to society than all the enactments of legislators and all the decrees of courts. And may not those who fill so important a part in the general welfare, claim no return at the hands of those who are benefited? Society is a partnership, and each of the co-partners is entitled to a fair division of the income. Hence the injunction: "Let him that is taught in the word communicate unto him that teacheth in all good things." (Gal. vi: 6) "Communicate" means to share, to have in common. Whatever good things you possess share them with the man who ministers to you the word of life.

But there is even a higher point of view. The duties of the pastor require all his time, talents and energies; and whatever of these is diverted to procure a livelihood, is lost to the church—is lost to the highest interests of society. The church cannot afford to allow this diversion.

9. It is sometimes disputed whether the pulpit is under the control of the church or the pastor. One party contends that the church may invite whom she pleases to hear, and that the pastor is bound to acquiesce; and the other party maintains that the pastor may invite whom he will to fill his place. Without doubt, originally the pulpit is under the control of the church. But the call of the pastor puts him in possession—that is, gives him a right to occupy it during the term of his pastorate. The church parts with the right to put another in it without his consent; but he acquires no right to substitute another in the place of himself without the consent of the church. Neither is independent of the other. To displace him by a person offensive

to him would virtually be to depose him. On the other hand the church is entitled to his services and he has no right to exchange them for those of another who is not acceptable to his brethren. Should he grossly disregard the feelings of the church by substituting a man offensive to them he might justly be deposed from the pastorate. Each is bound to respect the feelings of the other, and where this is done there is no danger of conflict.

SECTION 3. *Duties.*— 1. It is evident that the first duty of the pastor or bishop is to "preach the word, to be instant in season and out of season, to reprove, rebuke, exhort with all long suffering and doctrine." "The gospel is the power of God unto salvation to every one that believeth." Men "are chosen unto salvation through sanctification of the Spirit and the belief of the truth." The pulpit is the great instrumentality for extending a knowledge of Christ and the duties He has enjoined; and it cannot be neglected without irreparable injury to the cause. Whatever other duties may be omitted this cannot be left off without suspending the progress of the gospel.

(1). Preaching should be at regular times. Regularity secures punctuality on the part of the hearers and confirms them in the habit of attending. He is thus enabled to impart instruction more systematically and hence more intelligently. Occasional preaching is apt to be desultory, and the subjects bear little or no relation to each other. The effect of the gospel consists, in a great measure, upon presenting it as a system of harmonious doctrines. Many of the doctrines of the New Testament, dissevered from their proper connections, seem harsh and forbidding; but if considered in relation to other truths they form part of a harmonious and attractive whole.

To avoid presenting these great doctrines in

disconnected fragments the preacher must pursue a settled plan. But irregularity is utterly at war with any systematic presentation of doctrine.

(2). To derive the full benefit of connected preaching it is not only necessary that it should be regular but frequent. If long intervals come between discourses, the connection is broken and the effect destroyed. Hence the apostolic churches met weekly to hear the word. It is to be regretted that many churches in our country, in their effort to compensate for the scarcity of preachers, in the early settlement of North America, adopted the practice of dividing the service of one minister among four congregations, contenting themselves with monthly meetings. What at first seemed justified by the scarcity of preachers was afterwards perpetuated on the plea of the poverty of the country churches, and in many instances as a matter of choice. The whole practice violates the gospel theory of a church, which supposes each church to have its own bishop and each bishop the oversight of but one church. Let it not be supposed that this theory is impracticable. If any church is in the full discharge of duty, God will see that they are not without an under shepherd. There is in every church gathered by the authority of Christ, the material to supply its own wants. If the members come up to the gospel standard of piety, ministerial gifts will be sought for and found. Churches are too much in the habit of looking abroad for preachers, instead of asking and expecting God to raise them up of their own number. Then by such support as every church might give to their minister he might meet them every Lord's day. Thus the word would prosper and the church though weak would be materially strengthened. There is too much tendency for mere convenience of attendance, to break up into small congregations. This is bad economy. It requires more preachers and diminishes the support of each, and multiplies the expense of meeting houses. If the disciples over a large territory, would combine, the church would be better able to support a pastor, and as a strong body would possess a moral power that a number of feeble organizations could not attain.

(3). The frequency with which a particular subject is to be presented depends upon the state of the congregation. That which is most neglected should be most insisted upon, that which is least understood and opposed should be oftenest explained and defended. When there is no special call for a particular subject he may find a sufficient guide if he considers the frequency with which the several duties and doctrines are named and enforced in the New Testament and present them in the same proportion. It cannot be said that the inspired writers gave any undue prominence to any one doctrine, and if we follow their rule we may be sure we are following a safe precedent.

(4). To be able to present the whole truth in all its power, he must give himself to the study of the word. He must study to show himself "a workman approved of God who needeth not to be ashamed." So much of his time should be devoted to this purpose as is necessary to accumulate the best material and to arrange it to the best advantage and deliver it in the most impressive manner. If Paul thought it necessary that Timothy should give himself to reading as a preparatory exercise, even when the miraculous gifts of the Holy Spirit aided the progress of the gospel, how much more important now, when we have no such extraordinary aids, and when the intelligence of the masses requires a higher culture. It is not my design to treat of the methods of pulpit preparation, but to insist upon the duty of making the very best preparation the circumstances allow, sparing neither time nor labor to accomplish this end. I am the more inclined to insist upon this duty from the fact there is a disposition to burden the pastor with administrative duties and to exact so much pastoral visitation that he finds no time for study. I think this one reason of the great want of permanency in the pastoral relations so much complained of. His whole time is occupied in these secondary duties until he exhausts his stock of prepared sermons, and is compelled to seek a new field, or if he continues, his preaching will fall so far below the expectation of his hearers that dissatisfaction is the result.

As preaching is his principal duty it is plain that the greater part of his time should be devoted to pulpit preparation. When he is thoroughly prepared then he may consider what else he should do.

2. Among the secondary duties of the pastor is that of pastoral visitation. However effectively he may dispense the word in public, his whole duty is not discharged when he descends from the pulpit.

(1). He must follow up that word in the details of its application to the personal experience of each of his hearers. Like the apostles he must preach the word from house to house. Thus divine truth may be fastened upon the mind. An impression that otherwise might prove to be transient may become fixed and indelible by a word of private counsel. Besides there are a thousand opportunities in our daily intercourse with our fellow-men for making good impressions upon them. When the heart is torn with grief or bowed with disappointment, when prosperity seems to be drawing the mind away from Christ, or passion threatens by some rash deed to involve the life in darkness and in ruin—these are the occasions for which the pastor must be on the look out, and when he must **interpose the consolations and precepts of the gospel.**

(2). But in every flock there are some who from age or infirmity, or some other unavoidable cause, are unable to attend upon the public administrations of the word. These are by no means to be neglected, but must be diligently sought out and cared for. Indeed they should be his first care after he has made the necessary preparation for his pulpit duties.

(3). Pastoral visitation is a necessary preparation for the pulpit. Unless the pastor mingles with his flock and learns the spiritual condition of each, he will be wholly unable "rightly to divide the word, giving his portion to each in his season." There are some spiritual wants so universal that he cannot well fail to benefit all, whatever general truths he may present. But there are special ones. Peculiar difficulties arise in the personal experience of each, and these can only be known by intimate personal intercourse between pastor and flock. He may draw a bow at a venture and occasionally make a fortunate hit, but most of his arrows will spend their force in the air and fall without effect to the earth, unless he frequently reconnoiters so as to find the lurking places of sin and error and temptation.

(4). But pastoral visitation is also necessary to secure a larger attendance in the sanctuary. The pastor, if pastor he may be called, who isolates himself, is cut off from the affection and sympathy of his people, and will be a stranger among his brethren. To win their affection and confidence he must mingle with them at their firesides, and thus they will be drawn to the house of the Lord, at first perhaps from respect for the preacher; but after while from the love of the word itself.

(4). A word in conclusion as to the etiquette of pastoral visitation. No part of the pastor's duty is frequently more embarrassing. He desires to visit a particular family but he has no invitation to call, and with that delicacy of feeling that belongs to every cultivated gentleman, he shrinks from intruding himself where he is not wanted. He feels that every man's house is, in legal phrase, "his castle," within whose sacred precincts no unwelcome visitor may intrude; but he equally knows that every man's house should be open to the worthy minister. If every pastor would manifest sufficient interest in his people, and if every member of his flock would treat him with proper consideration, there could be no difficulty. None would then feel that the pastor was disposed to slight them, and he would feel that he was welcome in every house. True etiquette requires that every member should make the pastor feel that he is welcome; and the pastor should so act as to make his flock feel that he is not disposed to shun any, even the most humble. If a church member never invites the pastor to call, and never manifests any desire that he should do so, he may fairly conclude that he is not wanted there, and such a member cannot complain if his pastor never visits him.

SECTION 4. *Episcopal Jurisdiction.*—Lord King in his "Account of the Primitive Church," the range of whose inquiry embraces the first three hundred years of the Christian era, after maintaining that there was properly speaking, but one bishop to each church, continues in chapter II: "Having in the former chapter shown that there was but one bishop to a church, we shall in this evidence that there was but one church to a bishop." And this he maintains from the fact that the ancient dioceses are never said to contain churches in the plural, but only a church in the singular, and the bishop was usually designated as the bishop of this or that church."

Mosheim says:

"Let us not however, confound the bishops of this primitive and golden period of the church with those of whom we read in the following ages, for though they were both distinguished by the same name, yet they differed in many respects. A bishop during the first and second century, was a person who had the care of one Christian assembly, which at that time was generally speaking, small enough to be contained in a private house. In this assembly he acted not so much with the authority of a master as with the zeal and obligation of a faithful servant."—[*B. I. Part II, Chap. II, Section 12.*

It is evident that the term bishop was not at first so exclusively appropriated to the presiding officer in the church as afterwards. For it appears from the twentieth chapter of Acts, that there were a plurality of persons in the church at Ephesus who were called *overseers*. [Gr. *Episcopoi*.] Paul directs Titus to ordain *elders* in every city and immediately gives the qualifications of a *bishop*, thus connecting bishops and elders in the same persons. From these passages it is probable that most of the apostolic churches had a plurality of officers who were indifferently called elders or bishops.

But the local nature of the church, which we have heretofore established, requires one presiding officer, and he was especially and pre-eminently styled bishop. And although other ministers were sometimes called bishops as in Acts xx: 28, it is only in a subordinate sense for it is evident that the very same persons whom Paul calls "overseers"—*bishops*, Luke in the 17 verse calls elders.

Upon the second point, the extent of Episcopal jurisdiction, the admission of Lord King and Mosheim and numerous others who could be named, are important as refuting the claims of diocesan Episcopacy. The New Testament knows nothing of diocesan Episcopacy, in the modern sense, that is an Episcopal jurisdiction embracing all the churches in a district over whose pastors and members the bishop exercises authority. A bishop without a congregation to oversee would have been an anomaly in apostolic times. He would have been a useless appendage who could not have exercised his functions without displacing the pastor of a congregation. He was not needed for instruction and government, for each church was entrusted with the management of its own affairs, and every pastor was required to be "a workman, approved of God, that needeth not to be ashamed, rightly dividing the word of truth," (2 Tim. ii: 15) "thoroughly furnished unto all good works." There was no place for a diocesan bishop in the apostolic church government; and it was only after the simplicity of what Mosheim calls the golden age of the church was corrupted that Episcopal thrones were created, and ambitious prelates began to lord it over God's heritage.

Perhaps it may have happened in apostolic days, as it often does in our own, in churches organized after the apostolic pattern, that from a scarcity of ministers one person discharged the office of bishop or pastor to two or more congregations. But he was only pastor of each separately for the time he served them; and he possessed no higher office nor greater authority than the bishop who presided in a single church. Diocesan Episcopacy was the outgrowth of later ages. Much less were archbishops and universal bishops known to the apostles. Each bishop presided only over so many Christians as were accustomed to assemble in one place for worship.

So evident is it that the bishops of the New Testament were not diocesan that the advocates of diocesan Episcopacy ground it not upon New Testament Episcopacy but upon the authority of the apostles which they claim to have been transmitted to their order.

I have already shown that those things which distinguished the apostles, their extraordinary gifts, were personal to them, and that in this they could have no successors.

Diocesan Episcopacy requires particular limits within which each bishop exercises his functions to the exclusion of others. But whatever authority was exercised by the apostles, they exercised it indiscriminately, without regard to any jurisdictional limits.

The apostles never exerted any authority over the churches, but recognized the right of each to manage its own affairs, and whenever they made any suggestions or gave any directions they were careful to refer their interference to direct revelations of Jesus Christ. But they exercised no more direction than missionaries do in churches of their own planting.

The transmission of apostolic authority is grounded by its advocates upon Matt. xxiii: 20: "Lo! I am with you always even unto the end of the world." As the apostles did not live always it is urged that the promise could only be fulfilled by transferring to their successors the powers and authority which they exercised. If we take the words as referring to the end of time the promise may very well be referred to the church at large, or to the ministry in general as represented by the apostles, and refers not to the transmission of authority as to that influence and spiritual power which shall accompany Christ's servants in all their labors. The promise is not of authority but aid. Certainly it is a stretch of interpretation to construe the promise in reference to authority.

But does the phrase "end of the world" signify the end of time? It is *sunteleias tou aioonos*, the end of the age, and not *tou kosmou*, the material world. Hence some learned men refer it to the end of the

Jewish dispensation and the promise of His presence to the miraculous powers bestowed upon the apostles by which they were enabled to work miracles, to handle serpents and drink poison without injury. At any rates, the meaning is not sufficiently clear to ground upon this single passage so pretentious a claim; for nothing is said of any authority they possessed or any continuation of their office.

CHAPTER V.

ELDERS OR PRESBYTERS.

Much controversy has arisen as to the precise position of elders in the church. There are three principal opinions upon this subject which I propose to notice in order.

1. Some regard presbyters (elders) as an inferior order of the clergy. Such divide the clergy into three orders: 1, Bishops, who have the sole power of ordination; 2, Presbyters, who may preach and administer ordinances but cannot set apart to the ministry; and 3, Deacons who may preach and baptize.

I will consider the duties and powers of deacons under a separate head. I now address myself to the inquiry whether the New Testament recognizes any distinction in the order of bishops and elders. I think a candid examination will result in the conclusion that an elder is simply a bishop in rank without a charge. We have already seen that the term bishop and elder are indiscriminately applied to the same person. The case cited in the 20th chapter of Acts is a very clear example of this. Paul addressed his Philippian epistle "to all the saints in Christ Jesus which are at Philippi with the bishops and deacons." Here are recognized two classes of officers, bishops and deacons and we observe a plurality of bishops in the church at Philippi. Elders must have been embraced in the term, for in a strictly Episcopal sense there could have been but one bishop. Paul in Acts xiv: 23, is said to have revisited the scenes of his former labors and "ordained them elders in every church." Here no distinct reference is made to presiding bishops, because when elders were ordained the churches were supplied with pastors or bishops without further ordination; and hence no other ordination is named. The same form of expression is employed by Paul in his direction to Titus: "Ordain elders in every city as I appointed thee. If any man be blameless, &c., for a bishop must be blameless as the steward of God." Here the terms are so connected as to show that the words were used interchangeably. A very striking example of this use is to be found in 1 Peter v: 1-2: "The elders which are among you I exhort, who am also an elder—feed the flock of God which is among you, taking the oversight thereof (*Episcopountes*—bishoping) not by constraint but willingly."

The following paragraph from Chancellor King is so much to the point that I do not hesitate to transfer it entire:

"That bishops and presbyters were of the same order appears also from hence, that originally they had one and the same name, each being indifferently called bishops or presbyters. Hence we read in the sacred writ of several bishops in one particular church; as the bishops of Ephesus and Philippi; that is, the bishops and presbyters of those churches as they were afterwards distinctly called And Clemens Romanus sometimes mentions many bishops in the church at Corinth, whom at other times he calls by the name of presbyters, using those two terms as synonymous titles and appellations. You have obeyed, saith he, those that were set over you, *tois hegoumenois humoon*, and let us revere those that are set over us, *pregoumenois hemoon*, which are the usual titles of the bishops and yet these in another place he calls presbyters, describing their office by their sitting or presiding over us. Wherefore he commands the Corinthians to be subject to their presbyters, and whom in one line *Episcopoi* or bishops; the second line after he calls *presbuteroi* or presbyters. So Polycarp exhorts the Philippians to be subject to their presbyters, and deacons under the name of presbyters including both bishops and priests as we now call them"—[*Primitive Church, pp. 70, 71.*]

The next point to be noticed is the Episcopal claim *jure divino*, to exclusive ordination. If it can be shown that elders in the New Testament ordained, this arrogant assumption is overthrown. Nor need it be shown that they uniformly did it. It is enough to produce a single clear example of it.

Dr. Bangs claims the ordination of Paul and Barnabas (Acts 12th chap.) as an example of this kind, but that is not clear enough to rely on. (1) It is not certainly an ordination to the ministry, but appears to be a solemn recognition of their separation to a special work; (2) Paul and Barnabas were already in the ministry; (3) It is by no means certain that the prophets and teachers mentioned were only presbyters. To assume that they were and then adduce the example is to beg the question; (4) Paul claims his office directly from Jesus Christ. He begins his epistle to the Galatians: "Paul, an apostle (not of men, neither by man, but by Jesus Christ and God the Father who raised him from the dead.") His own account of his entry into the ministry is: "But when it pleased God who separated me from my mother's womb, and called me by His grace to reveal His son in me that I might preach Him among the heathen, immediately I conferred not with flesh and blood, neither went I up to Jerusalem to them that were apostles before me, but I went into Arabia, &c. 1 Gal. i: 15–24.

But we have a clear example in the ordination of Timothy, and that is sufficient. Paul admonishes him (1 Tim. iv: 14) "Neglect not the gift that is in thee, which was given thee by prophecy with the laying on of the hands of the PRESBYTERY."

2. Others regard elders as the senate of the church, presided over by the bishop, to whom the government of the church is committed. They maintain that the business of governing is set apart to a certain class of officers called Ruling Elders.

Says Dr. Dick:

"God has set some as governors in the church. He has

not lodged the power as the Independents suppose, in the people at large, but has ordained that a few should be invested with authority to take order that the members should walk in the ordinances and commandments of the Lord."— *Theology, vol. II, p. 500.*

I do not know a better representative of the Presbyterian view of this subject than John Dick, and I suppose he has brought forward the strongest Scriptural proofs within his knowledge. It will be enough therefore to examine the passages upon which he relies to warrant "Ruling Elders."

His first citation is Romans xii: 6-8: "Having then gifts differing according to the grace that is given to us, whether prophecy let us prophesy according to the proportion of faith; or ministry let us wait on our ministering; or he that teacheth on teaching; or he that exhorteth on exhortation; he that giveth let him do it with simplicity; he that ruleth with all diligence; he that showeth mercy with cheerfulness." Certainly nothing but the exigencies of a party could have extorted ruling elders from this passage. Somebody rules *ergo* a certain class called Ruling Elders are vested with the sole and exclusive authority to rule! Now if this passage furnishes a warrant for a separate class of persons specially set apart to rule, it equally warrants a separate class called exhorters, devoted exclusively to the business of exhortation; another class who may be styled the givers of the church, and still another to whom the office of showing mercy is specially limited. The plain and obvious meaning of the apostle is that God has bestowed peculiar capacities for doing certain things upon different individuals and the admonition is for each to give special attention to that gift with which God has endowed him, and to avail himself of the opportunities which God has placed in his reach to promote the general good of the church. If he is endowed with the prophetic gift let him use that gift for the edification of the church. Is he called to be a servant of the church? let him faithfully serve. If he is apt to teach, it is a rare endowment which he should cultivate. If he is peculiarly fitted to move others by exhortation, let him use it for good. If he is endowed with a large degree of benevolence, let him not make an ostentatious display of his liberality, but let him give as God has enabled him, with simplicity. If he is a ruler, let him diligently discharge the duties of his station. If an opportunity is offered to show mercy, let him cheerfully discharge the duty.

I remark in this connection that the word translated "ruleth" (*proistamenos*) is used in the plural in 1 Thess. v: 12, and rendered by the words "ARE OVER YOU," where the context shows unmistakably that the reference is made to the pastors of the churches: "We beseech you brethren to know them that labor among you and are over you in the Lord, and admonish you, and esteem them very highly in love for their works' sake." The Bible Union revisers properly render this word *preside* in both cases. This is the proper signification of the word and indicates very clearly that reference is made in both cases to the pastoral office. Dr. Dick thinks that *proistamenos* cannot refer to the pastor because although he rules he is here characterized by teaching or exhorting. But if ruling is equally a part of the duty of pastor with teaching and exhorting, it is merely arbitrary to assume that the pastor is referred to in two of these cases and not in the third.

The next proof passage is found 1 Cor. xii: 28: "God hath set some in the church; first, apostles, secondarily, prophets, thirdly, teachers; after that miracles, then gifts of healing, helps, governments, diversity of tongues." He argues that in the case of helps and governments, the abstract is put for the concrete, *helps* and *governments* mean helpers and governors. He then proceeds:

"The question then is: Who were the governors to whom the apostles referred? They were not the apostles, nor the prophets, nor the teachers; because they are mentioned as distinct classes. They were not helpers because they are distinguished from them also; besides, if deacons were intended they could with no propriety be called governors; for deacons have no rule over the church. There is no other class of persons to whom this title, used as it is in contradistinction to other office-bearers, will apply but the Ruling Elder of Presbyterians; and it is with obvious propriety that they are designated governors, as the sole business is to govern the congregation over which they are appointed.'— *Theology, Vol. II. p. 500.*

I will call Dr. Dick to my aid to refute his own argument. He informs us (Vol. II, p. 493) that the extraordinary office-bearers of a church are apostles, prophets and evangelists. The ordinary office-bearers, he informs us, are pastor, teacher or doctor, deacons and ruling elders. On page 497 he maintains that teachers were different officers from pastors. Now for the application. Paul in this proof text of the learned doctor is giving the different classes according to their rank. First, apostles; secondarily, prophets; thirdly, teachers; after that those who worked miracles, then those who had the power of healing, helps, governments, diversity of tongues. Now in such an enumeration of important classes, if Dr. Dick be correct, the apostle omits the important offices of evangelist and pastor and mentions instead two comparatively insignificant officers, deacons and ruling elders, and even places them in rank above the miraculous gift of tongues. Prophets cannot include evangelists and pastors, because Dr. D. has shown that they are distinct offices. Teachers cannot include pastors for they are also two distinct offices, says Dr. D. Unless the pastors and evangelists are included in the words helps and governments these important officers are omitted by Paul, and if Dr. D. be correct two inferior offices are mentioned in their stead. There must therefore be something radically wrong in this interpretation.

But if we consult the context we will discover that the apostle is discussing the extraordinary gifts of the spirit, and therefore refers probably only to those who were extraordinarily endowed, and not to the permanent and ordinary office-bearers in the church. And of this opinion is McKnight, who says:

"No mention is made of bishop, elders and deacons, the permanent standing officers in the church; the probable reason is those only are meant to whose offices spiritual gifts were necessary, and which were to be laid aside when spiritual gifts were to cease."—[*Com. in loco.*

The last passage he quotes and which he regards as a settler is 1 Tim. v: 17: "Let the elders that rule well be accounted worthy of double honor, especially they who labor in word and doctrine." The argument is thus stated:

"There are elders who although they rule well are not worthy of double honor, unless they labor in word and doctrine But there are elders who are counted worthy of double honor because they rule well, although they do not labor in word and doctrine. Therefore there are elders who are not teaching or preaching elders; that is they are ruling elders only. The premises are clearly laid down in the passage and the conclusion is therefore legitimate."—*Theology, Vol. II, p. 502.*

The construction of Dr. Dick is by no means a natural one. The injunction does not except any class of elders who rule well, but requires all elders that rule well to be accounted worthy of double honor. The latter clause by no means restrains the force of the former, but points to a particular class who especially deserve double honor. But to justify the conclusion that there were some elders who did not preach and teach we must disregard entirely the word labor and put the stress of the sentence upon the word *especially*, which is wholly gratuitous. But the phrase "labor in word and doctrine," means more than merely to preach and to teach. The Greek word translated *labor* means to toil to weariness. It is upon this word that the stress of the sentence naturally falls. The elders who rule well are deserving double honor, and especially if they *labor* (diligently employ themselves) in word and doctrine. That the stress is laid upon the word labor is evident from what follows. There could otherwise be no propriety in the application of the proverbs quoted: "*Muzzle not the ox that treadeth out the corn*," and "*The laborer is worthy of his hire.*"

It is also worthy of note that the word here translated rule is substantially the same employed in Rom. xii: 8, and 1 Thess. v: 12, and is properly translated by *preside*, as we have already seen, by the Bible Union revisers and clearly points to the office of bishop.

If the rule of interpretation invoked by Dr. Dick in these cases was applied generally it would require a separate class of persons to discharge each duty mentioned in the gospel. But the New Testament utterly fails to make a distinction between teaching elders and ruling elders. As we have seen, the term is repeatedly used interchangeably with bishops, and the solemnity with which they were set apart to the office indicates that they were important functionaries and not an inferior police to keep surveillance over the church members. They are often mentioned as preachers and pastors but never under circumstances to justify us in concluding that they were rulers and nothing more. They ruled or presided, but it was in discharge of their duties as bishops or pastors. Dr. Dick and his brethren must look to the synagogue and not to the apostolic church for the original of ruling elders.

3. The third view which I notice occupies a middle ground between the other two and is no doubt

the Scriptural one. Elders differ from bishops in no respect except they are without charge. They have the same qualifications as appears from a comparison of the first chapter of Titus and the third chapter of First Timothy. And they have an inherent right to perform all the duties of a bishop when called to the pastorate by any church. They are bishops without charges. In the apostolic churches there were often several elders or presbyters who assisted the presiding bishop, and were qualified to discharge any duty which the church or pastor might assign them. A careful consideration of the closing article of the last chapter and the opening of this, will, I think, make this apparent without the repetition of the arguments there used to show that elders and bishops are the same order, and that elders are equally vested with the power of ordaining. I mean, of course, in that limited sense in which bishops possess the power, only as responsible agents formally transmitting the authority of the church.

Evangelists were traveling elders, whose labors were not confined to any particular church. They were the gospel pioneers, the missionaries of the churches. All were elders by virtue of their ordination, but bishops by virtue of their settlement over a particular church, and ceased to be bishops as soon as the connection was dissolved.

Prophets were extraordinary officers, miraculously endowed to deliver a knowledge of divine things and were therefore like the apostles, not permanent officers.

Teachers also are mentioned, and in such a way as to make the impression that they were persons endowed with peculiar capacities for instructing the young and uninformed in the doctrines and duties of the gospel. All ministers are necessarily teachers; but these teachers are sometimes so contrasted with preachers as to lead us to the conclusion that they were a separate class. (Eph. iv: 11) "He gave some apostles, and some evangelists, and some pastors and teachers." Here they are distinguished from apostles, evangelists and pastors. Their special duty in connection with the pastors was to edify the body of Christ, (the church). This distinctive character of teacher is also borne out by 1 Cor. xii: 28: "And God hath set some in the church; first, apostles; secondarily, prophets; thirdly teachers." As Paul is here discoursing of the extraordinary gifts of the spirit the teachers here referred to were no doubt inspired. In Rom. ii: 7, Paul admonishes teachers "to wait on teaching." Perhaps these teachers sustained somewhat the same relation to the church that teachers in the Sunday School now do.

CHAPTER VI.

DEACONS.

The term deacon (*diakonos*) signifies a servant, and is used to designate the inferior officers in the church. There is less controversy about deacons than any other officers of the church, and therefore all that need be said about them may be compressed into a very small space.

SECTION 1. *The Office.*—Deacons might be classed with the ministry in the broad sense of that word, as embracing the whole class of persons who serve the church, but as that term is now applied almost exclusively to the preaching class, to prevent being misunderstood I have placed the deacons in an intermediate place, between the ministry and laity; or unofficial class of members.

1. We can best understand the office by referring to its institution. Fortunately we have a particular account of its origin. Acts vi: 1-6:

"And in those days when the number of disciples was multiplied there arose a murmuring of the Grecians against the Hebrews, because their widows were neglected in the daily ministration. Then the twelve called the multitude of the disciples unto them, and said: It is not reason that we should leave the word of God, and serve tables. Wherefore, brethren, look ye out among you seven men of honest report, full of the Holy Ghost and wisdom, whom we may appoint over this business. But we will give ourselves continually to prayer, and to the ministry of the word. And the saying pleased the whole multitude: and they chose Stephen, a man full of faith and of the Holy Ghost, and Philip, and Prochorus, and Nicanor, and Timon, and Parmenas, and Nicholas a proselyte of Antioch: whom they set before the apostles: and when they had prayed, they laid their hands on them."

2. From the account of its institution we may learn something of the nature of the office. The design was to relieve the minsitry from the incumbrance of

secular affairs, and allow them to devote their time wholly to the ministry of the word. The particular affair that gave rise to the institution does not limit the functions of the office to similar occasions. But we must look to the reason of the thing. It was not proper that the apostles should leave the word of God for any less important work. Their great work was to preach the gospel. The design therefore in the institution of deacons was to defer to them all those secular concerns of the church which were calculated to hinder the ministers in their proper work.

3. It may be said that the immediate occasion that gave rise to the appointment of deacons being temporary, the office itself was only temporary. It is true the Grecian widows soon ceased to exist, but the reason for the institution did not cease with them.

(1.) There are always more or less widows in the church requiring the attention of the church. Poverty and widowhood are incident to our race and will always continue to be so.

(2.) The church will always have more or less common property to be administered. If the members follow the apostolic rule to lay by weekly in store as the Lord hath blessed them, there will always be something on hand to be disbursed and the occasions for disbursement will not be unfrequent.

(3.) As the conversion of the world is in all ages dependent upon the preaching of the word, the ministry can never leave the word to serve tables without material injury to souls.

(4.) The command to institute them has never been repealed and may therefore be considered still in force.

(5.) That the apostolic churches regarded the institution a perpetual one is evident from the fact that other churches, copying the example of the church at Jerusalem, appointed deacons who were recognized by the apostles. Paul addressed an epistle in part, to the bishops and *deacons* at Philippi, and gives specific directions to Timothy about the qualifications of deacons.

SECTION 2. *Qualifications.*—As might be expected we have specific directions about the necessary qualifications of this important officer. These qualifications respect his *conjugal relations, his moral and religious character*, the *purity of his faith* and his *intellectual capacity*. (1 Timothy iii: 8–13:)

1. *His conjugal relations.*—"Let the deacons be the husbands of one wife." (v. 12.) Monogamy is in accordance with the original institution of marriage and is most consistent with the happiness and wellbeing of society. But Christianity in its early progress had to encounter polygamy and met it in a practical way. While the principles of the gospel were opposed to a plurality of wives, the apostles, under the guidance of the Holy Spirit, did not propose to rupture the bonds of society. When a polygamist was converted to Christianity he was not required to abandon his helpless wives and children, but he was tolerated in the relation in which he was found rather than inflict the greater injury of throwing upon the world a number of unprotected women and children. But that this practice might in the end be overthrown, and the church be vindicated in its purity, no such persons were permitted to be office-bearers.

It is sometimes disputed whether a deacon is required to be a married man? The affirmative may hardly be inferred from this passage. But it cannot be denied that it is greatly to his advantage to be married. All the reasons that can be urged why a preacher should be married apply with equal force here, while none of the reasons against it are applicable.

The character of the deacon's wife may very materially affect the usefulness of the deacon, hence we find the requirement, "Even so must their wives be grave, not slanderers, sober, faithful in all things." (v. 11.) Lightness and frivolity in his wife would lessen his respect in the public estimation. If she be a slanderer she will be continually involving him in trouble that would bring reproach upon religion. A certain degree of sobriety is becoming a Christian matron, and redounds to the influence of her husband. If she be unfaithful in anything a part of the reproach will attach to him. Thus his credit will be injured.

Dr. Howell, in his work on the deaconship, objects to the translation of 1 Tim. iii: 11, and thinks the reference is to deaconesses. But the common version is sustained by the Revised Version. Indeed to refer *gunaikas* to deaconesses would be to break the unity of the discourse to introduce a new subject before the first is finished. Besides *gunaikas* means wives as well as women, but never *servants*. As to deaconesses, while it is apparent that women often rendered important service to the church, and while so engaged were called *servants* (deaconesses) it by no means follows that these were permanent offices of the church.

2. *His Moral and Religious Character.*—"Men of honest report." (Acts vi: 3,) that they may command the confidence of the church—men tried and found blameless (v. 10.) whose character can bear the closest scrutiny.

"Grave," so as to command respect—"Not double tongued"—an untruthful man cannot be trusted in any position of responsibility and trust. "Not given to much wine." A wine bibber would soon bring reproach upon himself and scandal upon the cause of religion. "Not greedy of filthy lucre," lest he appropriate the property of the church to his own use, or in his eagerness to gain, he may overreach his neighbor and the church suffer in her unworthy member. (1 Tim. iii: 8.) "Full of the Holy Ghost." (Acts vi: 3.) He should be a pious man. He should be an example to others. Thus he will be a leader in every good work, an active, working, praying Christian.

3. The Purity of his Faith.—"Hold the mystery of the faith in a pure conscience." (v. 9.) He must be a sincere believer of the truth—no unsound heretic, using the influence of his position to propagate error. Too much care cannot be exercised in scrutinizing the religious views of those who are about to be chosen deacons; and in avoiding those who entertain loose views on any religious subject. Hence they should be those who read the Bible and familiarize themselves with its teachings, in order that they may instruct others in the truth and defend the truth when assailed.

4. His Intellectual Capacity.—"Full of wisdom." (Acts vi: 3.) The very best business men are needed as deacons; good financiers to devise proper means to sustain the finances of the church—careful and prudent men to husband its resources, and judicious men in making needed disbursements.

As a proof of his business capacity the apostle gives us a practical test that never fails— "Ruling their children and their own houses well." (1 Tim. iii: 12.) If a man has no capacity to govern his own household and manage his own private business, we may be sure that he will develope none in an office that requires these qualities.

SECTION 3. *Duties.*—The duties of the office are varied and important; and for the purpose of covering the leading questions involved, I will consider the subject *negatively,* so as to embrace some duties which are supposed by some to belong to the office but which I think do not; and *affirmatively*, so as to present their clearly defined duties

1. *Negatively.*—It is not a part of their duty to preach the gospel. They are not preachers by virtue of their office. The occasion of their institution proves this. It was that the ministers might give themselves to the word that deacons were first created. It would therefore have been a vain thing to impose upon them one duty with which another would interfere. The apostolic direction requires that they should give themselves to this business of serving the tables. If this were not the object of their creation, then the ministry were in no way relieved. It is objected that Stephen and Philip preached. Did they do so by virtue of their office as deacons? Philip was also an Evangelist and may have preached by virtue of that office. Stephen if he preached, may have done so as every layman may, if he has the ability, occasionally defend the truths of religion. The only question to be determined is, did the office of deacon confer this power.

It is not a part of their duty to baptize. It is not a question whether the church may not authorize them to do so. Philip baptized the Eunuch, but he was an evangelist. The special duties for which they were set in the church, proves that baptizing, which is a ministerial duty, was not included.

It is not a part of their prerogative to rule in the church, beyond their own particular department. We read of bishops and elders bearing rule, but deacons never. Their very name imports that they were servants—not rulers.

2. *Affirmatively.*—They were the almoners of the church. The most important duty they had to perform was to seek out the poor of the church—the widows and orphans—and dispense to them the

bounties of the church. This duty necessarily included the plans for raising funds to meet these necessary calls upon the alms of the church.

They were to serve tables. As the term is plural it no doubt embraces not only the common table at which the disciples fed daily—but also the Lord's table which was spread weekly. In the latter sense it was their duty to provide the bread and wine, the necessary vessels, and to aid in the distribution of the elements. Perhaps the word *tables* is capable of, and has received a still further extension, so as to make it the duty of the deacons to make provision for the sustenance of the pastor. Of archdeacons and subdeacons the Scriptures know nothing.

CHAPTER VII.

THE LAITY.

The word laity, derived from the Greek *laos*, signifies the people; and is used to designate the unofficial members of the church. As these compose by far the most numerous part of the church it is fair to suppose that they are endowed with important rights and owe important duties.

SECTION 1. *Their Rights.*—Having written somewhat at large upon the Rights of Laymen in a little work published years ago, while yet a Layman, I will condense somewhat from that publication, referring the reader to it for a more extended examination of the subject.

1. Laymen possess the right of voluntary association. It does not require the permission, or necessitate the participation of the clerical order to set up a valid church. But a number of laymen may meet and organize themselves into a church of Jesus Christ.

The right of voluntary association includes: (1) the right of admission, if the body of the church deems him worthy and is willing to receive him, and (2) that he shall not be compelled to become a member of the church except of his own choice. Every institution of man that debars him from this voluntary association is in violation of his rights, and equally so is every device that seeks to compel his membership either by debarring him of civil rights under a religious test or making him a member in his infancy before he is capable of exercising a choice.

2. It is the privilege of laymen to attain to as high a degree of holiness as the ministry. Grace is

not a quality imparted by priestly hands in the ceremony of consecration, but it is the free gift of God to all his dear children. "Be ye holy as I am holy," is addressed indiscriminately to all the flock. The heights of the hill of God are not reserved to a priviledged class who may say to others "stay ye in the vallies below. We are holier than ye." *Procul iste, profani.*

3. It is the right of laymen to study the word of God for themselves, and if their opportunity allow, to attain as thorough knowledge of the Holy Scriptures as the most learned doctor of divinity.

The Bible is an open book. It is the common heritage of all Christians; whose treasures are free to all, without distinction. It is a fountain whose pure waters well up in the garden of life and all are invited to drink bountifully. The Bereans were commended because they gave diligent heed to what was spoken and searched the Scriptures daily to see if these things were so. The surest safeguard against the introduction of heresy is an intelligent laity well read in the Scriptures.

4. But laymen not only have the right to inform themselves by personal examination of the Scriptures, but they have also the right to instruct others in the doctrines of the Christian religion, and this not only privately, but even publicly on proper occasions. It is said that they who were scattered abroad upon the persecution that arose about Stephen, "went everywhere preaching the word." And occasions arise in the history of almost every church where the abilities of laymen might be utilized by the church. There are numbers of laymen well informed in the Scriptures, with good speaking abilities and full of zeal for God, who do not feel called to devote their lives to the ministry, but who while engaged in some secular pursuit

would if encouraged occasionally instruct a destitute congregation.

5. Laymen are entitled to participate in the adoption of articles of faith. It is not meant that the whole church may impose a creed that is binding upon the conscience of the individual further than as it is in accordance with the Scriptures. In setting forth the declaration of principles each is entitled to be consulted. No body of men may coerce the assent of any man to the dogmas they set up without his consent. Hence the decrees of councils are only binding upon those who voluntarily assent to them.

We have a very clear example in the Scriptures where the laity participated in settling a controverted article of faith. A dispute arose in the church at Antioch, as to the duty of Gentile Christians to be circumcised. A council of the church at Jerusalem was called about this matter, and the record of their proceedings is found in the fifteenth chapter of Acts. The matter was discussed before the whole church, (v. 12,) who participated in the final action taken. (vs. 22, 23.) Here we find the laity participating in the settlement of a great question of faith and practice even in the presence of the *inspired apostles*, who might have at once settled the matter by divine authority, thus affording a strong precedent for the government of the church in all subsequent time.

It is absurd in reason to require a man to believe what he has never given his assent to, and if he may assent to a doctrine, it follows that he may, on his responsibility to God alone, dissent from the general opinion without being subjected to any civil disabilities for doing so.

6. If, as some say, the form of church government established at first may be modified according to circumstances, laymen have an equal right with

the clergy to participate in the choice of a form of church government. There is no reason or justice in one class of men imposing a form of government upon another without consulting them. It is in derogation of the natural right of all men to choose in whatever affects their interests, or happiness, and unless some authority of Scripture can be given vesting in the clergy the exclusive right to modify the form of the church, it follows that laymen possess equal rights.

Have the laity less wisdom to contrive expedients for the advancement of the interests of the church? Have they less integrity, piety and zeal? As a class they are more interested because they compose by far the larger class. Then why should they be treated as subjects rather than fellow citizens. Christ taught the most perfect equality of the members of his kingdom, and who may reverse that equality by excluding laymen from an equal share in the councils of the church?

7. It is the right of laymen to control the disbursement of the revenues which they raise for the purposes of the church. Is there anything in reason or the Scriptures that forbids laymen who contribute to the treasury of the church to determine the ultimate destination of their money? And yet if they are not admitted upon an equal footing with the clergy in those bodies which appropriate those funds they are debarred this privilege. It is vain to say that their donations are voluntary offerings to the Lord. It is their duty to give, and it is their right to see that their funds are not diverted from the purpose for which they intended them. How can they do this unless they are permitted to have a voice in their final distribution?

8. It is necessary that each local society should have a house of worship. This involves the ownership of property. But as the laws of the land do

not regard unincorporated religious societies as bodies corporate, capable of acquiring and transmitting property to their successors in the church, it becomes necessary in order to secure the right to property beyond contingencies, that there should be some body corporate that should represent the church as its Trustees or Agents. This may be done either by the incorporation of all the members of the local society or by making a limited number of persons a body corporate. In the former case the legal ownership and control of the property is vested directly in the entire membership for the time being of each local society, but in the latter case they do not possess that control of the property unless the whole society have the power to appoint and remove the corporators at pleasure. As the individual members of each society create a church property, primarily to furnish themselves a suitable and convenient place for the worship of God, it is the right of the church, acting through all its members in their collective capacity, to control the property they acquire. To maintain otherwise is to place the disposal of church property in the power of a foreign tribunal independent of the local society. Nor does it mend the matter if members of the local society are appointed corporators or trustees, when the power of appointment and removal is vested in some other body; for they are only trustees of that body which appoints them. And whenever the local society cannot exercise this supervision, their rights of property are violated.

9. Laymen have an equal right with the clergy to write and publish books and treatises on religious subjects without subjecting their productions to the censorship of the clerical order. The invention of the printing press has placed a mighty engine of power in the hands of Christians, and

the laity are entitled to a free press. The religious newspaper should be free. If it is under the absolute control of the clergy who appoint editors of their own liking and supervise what is published and forbid the publication of everything that does not suit their peculiar views, it is not free. Laymen are entitled to be heard in their denominational organs on any matter affecting their rights and interests, and where they are interdicted this privilege they are debarred a very sacred right.

10. It is the right of each local society in its collective capacity to choose its own pastor and no human power has the right to thrust upon them a preacher not of their own choosing. The right of participating in the selection of his own rulers is one of the dearest rights of a freeman. That the members of the primitive churches exercised this right is so evident from the Scriptures that candid men, even whose practice is different, are compelled to admit it. The first apostles were chosen by Christ himself before the formal organization of His executive. But the pastors and deacons were chosen by the churches or local societies. On one occasion we even find the whole church at Jerusalem participating in the election of an apostle to succeed the faithless Judas Iscariot. If the multitude participated in the selection of so important an officer as an apostle, it affords a strong presumption that they also participated in the election of inferior officers, with whom they were more intimately connected, and who were more immediately over them. The whole church elected deacons as we learn from the sixth chapter of Acts. Pastors are called ministers (*servants*) of the church, and if servants, certainly not masters. In 1 Tim. 3rd chapter the apostle gives the qualifications for bishops or elders and deacons and requires that they should first be proved "and then use the office of

deacon." To prove is to try and find worthy, which is choice. In 1 John iv: 1, and 2 John x: and many other places, the churches are warned against false prophets and teachers, and admonished to scrutinize them closely, and if they did not come up to the apostles' standard of doctrine not to receive them or bid them God speed.

Now if the churches passively received the teachers and rulers set over them by others what propriety in all this admonition? Why enjoin them to do what they had no right to do. Peter, who was himself an elder (1 Pet. v: 2) exhorts the elders to "feed the flock of God, taking the oversight of them, not by CONSTRAINT, but WILLINGLY." This affords positive proof that the pastoral relation must be voluntary.

11. Each local society in its collective capacity has the right to judge of the qualifications of those who seek admission as members. Every member is interested in the character of those who are to be associated with him, by which he is more or less affected, and for which he assumes a responsibility.

The New Testament abounds in precepts and directions addressed to the churches *as such* defining the necessary qualifications for church membership and so rigid were the apostolic churches in the exercise of their right to judge whether applicants possessed the necessary qualifications, that on one occasion the apostle Paul was constrained to interpose his apostolical authority in order to induce one of the churches to receive a certain class of persons whom they considered weak in the faith —but even *then* they were not to admit them if it gave rise to doubtful disputations, or in other words if a considerable portion of the church members doubted the propriety of doing so, they were not to receive them. (Rom. xiv: 1.)

Paul himself, on his return to Jerusalem after his

conversion *attempting to join himself to the disciples,* was denied admission until he found a suitable voucher in Barnabas. In the letter to the Romans, the apostle commends Phebe to the fellowship of the church at Rome, and requests them to receive her in the Lord, as becometh saints. Nearly all the epistles addressed to the churches contain one or more such commendations. It is to these commendatory letters that Paul alludes, when he says: "Ye are my letters of commendation, known and read of all men." Now, as these letters were addressed to the churches, and not to the bishops or preachers, it is fair to conclude that the churches were understood to be the proper parties to receive them.

Again, the right of admitting members, necessarily results from the right of exclusion, which we will presently see belonged to the whole body of the church, and was frequently exercised by them. For it is absurd to suppose that the right to exclude existed without the right to receive; when, if admitted contrary to the wish of the body, the church can at once rid itself of distasteful persons by exercising the right of exclusion.

12. Laymen had the right to participate in the exclusion of disorderly persons, and to restore them when penitent.

Christ himself, in the 18th chapter of Matthew, gives minute directions for the treatment of personal offenses, and requires the offended, as the last resort, to appeal to the church. Not to a particular order of the church, but to the whole church, composed of the clergy and laity.

In 2 Thess. iii: 6, the church is commanded to withdraw itself from every brother that walketh disorderly. In the church at Corinth was a member who was guilty of scandalous wickedness, in reference to whom Paul commanded them in the name of the Lord Jesus Christ, when they were *assembled together*, to deliver such an one to Satan for the destruction of the flesh. This, it appears they did, and with good effect on the offender, for in his second epistle, the apostle interposes in his behalf, and declares to the church, "sufficient unto such a man is this punishment which was INFLICTED OF MANY, (*apo toon pleionoon*,) literally by the majority, thus recognizing that salutary maxim of popular governments, that the majority shall rule.

13. In fine, laymen, being a part and parcel of the church, may participate in every action which the church may rightfully perform. Nothing is prohibited to the laity, except what is particularly assigned to the clergy. But every exercise of ecclesiastical power that excludes the participation of the laity on equal terms, is in violation of the rights of laymen. Christ, in the organization of his church, recognized the manhood of his humblest disciples, and the great lesson repeatedly taught, was the perfect equality of all his spiritual seed.

CHAPTER VIII.

RELATION OF WOMEN TO THE CHURCH.

As females compose a large part and often the majority of Christian communities, it becomes an important inquiry what relation they bore to the apostolic church; and we may thus learn their rights and duties in the church of to-day, since Christ has granted no new franchises, nor withdrawn any old ones since the days of the apostles. Are they constituent parts of the church, having equal rights and responsibilities with the males, or are they mere passive appendages to the church without any voice or direction in its affairs, and consequently without any responsibility for its success or failure? Whoever fairly considers this subject, I think will discover that the truth, as usual, lies between these two extremes.

Paul declares: "Nevertheless, neither is the man without the woman, neither the woman without the man in the Lord;" (1 Cor. ii : 4) that is to say, neither possesses exclusive rights. The man is not so independent of the woman in their church relations as to ignore her existence and disregard the rights and duties that pertain to her station. Nor yet is woman released from her subordinate relations to man. Women are recognized as disciples, and as such become members of the church; and as Christ taught the essential equality of His followers, women stand upon the same footing as others, except in so far as restrictions have been expressly imposed. In other words she possesses every right and duty not expressly denied to her. What others may do, she may do, unless it is expressly or by necessary implication **denied to her.** We will find in the course of our inquiry that these restrictions upon her are neither few nor unimportant; but that they do not by any means eliminate her individuality.

SECTION 1. *Her Rights and Duties.*—This section will be devoted to the elucidation of the proposition that woman has rights and duties in the church separate and distinct from the man, though limited by the subordinate relations which God has established between the sexes and especially between husband and wife.

The Great Teacher, speaking of the union between man and wife, declares that "they twain are one flesh." But this relates to the perpetuation of the race. They are a unit with respect to their offspring; but the wife still possesses a distinct and separate personality which is not merged in his. She is distinct as to body, mind and soul. Her mental operations, her emotions, her actions are essentially her own. She must for herself exercise repentance toward God and faith in the Lord Jesus Christ—for herself render obedience to all the laws and ordinances of the gospel. She is still accountable for her own conduct, which she would not be without separate individuality—a personal existence independent of her husband. But this personality necessarily imports independent duties and obligations. If this is true of a married woman it is *a fortiori* true of unmarried ones, who are affected only by the general subordination of the sex.

There can be no conflict of duty, and her obligation of obedience to her husband is subordinate to her obligation of obedience to God. God could not sanctify a relation that suspended the duties to himself. He could not surrender his own paramount authority to an inferior. The authority He has conferred upon the husband does not **supersede**

His own. She owes duties to God, therefore, which she can alone discharge and from which she is not absolved by virtue of her marriage. Her convictions are not under the control of her husband, and he has no right to coerce her in anything respecting her service to God. She is subjected to certain service to him in order to accomplish certain ends which God purposes in relation to society. In the discharge of those duties she is only obeying God. But the authority of the husband goes no further than the specific ends which God had in view. Beyond that he may not interpose between her and God.

In the administration of the domestic government his will is absolute, just as the authority of civil government is absolute within its proper sphere, but neither may coerce the conscience. Religious duties are beyond their jurisdiction. God is the sole arbiter in matters pertaining to the conscience.

As an accountable agent, acting under her sense of duty to God, she exercises repentance and faith. She renders personal obedience to Christ in baptism, in Christian association, and in all the duties that make up the round of Christian obligation. As a member of the mystical body of Christ, woman has her rights and duties. Her personality may not be ignored here. Her husband, if she has one who is a member of the church, cannot act as her proxy in the discharge of her duties as a church member. In the church we sustain a certain relationship to each other, called fellowship. It is a community of kindly feeling one toward another. In this one cannot represent another. Our likes and dislikes are not mere matters of volition, and however obedient the wife may be she cannot always conform her fellowship to the will of her husband. It is a fair deduction from these premises that she cannot be represented by her husband in the matter of fellowship; and that she must in the nature of things have a voice of her own. This conclusion involves certain particulars.

1. The selection of a pastor. Her spiritual growth and comfort depend upon him to a great extent. Without confidence in him and fellowship for him she cannot be benefited by his ministrations. To deny to the female members a voice would allow a few males to impose a distasteful pastor upon a large majority of the church, which would materially injure his influence and impede the cause. I do not think any one would desire to force an unwelcome pastor upon any considerable number of the female membership, and the only effective way to prevent this is to take the sense of the female members when the pastor is chosen. And I think there is scripture precedent for this. The *whole multitude* of disciples (which must include the women) participated in the choice of Matthias to the apostolic office; and Peter entreats the elders to feed the *flock* (women compose a part of it) taking the oversight of them, not by constraint, but willingly. To take charge of the flock without obtaining the consent of the females would be to constrain them to compliance in what was done for them.

2. In receiving members and in exercising discipline over them. The same reasoning applies here. The church is designed to be a unit in feeling as well as in faith. But if a member is received into or retained in the church in opposition to the will of any, the unity and harmony are broken and discord reigns. Therefore it is necessary that the voice of all, including the females, should be taken to ascertain whether this harmonious fellowship is being broken.

In the apostolic church it was "the many"—the

whole *assembled* church—who inflicted discipline; (2 Cor. ii: 6) and if the women had a voice in excluding, it follows that they had also in the reception of members; for it would avail but little to deny this right in the reception of a member when they could immediately vote for his exclusion.

But the extent to which she may exercise her rights in the church is limited by her subordinate relation to man. She may not do any act to disturb the relation God has himself established between the sexes, because their mutual happiness depends upon maintaining the order he has established. There is no degradation to the female in it. It imports no inferiority except in office. The duties of the relation are specific, and no woman can overthrow them under the pretext of discharging religious duty, for as I have already observed, there can be no conflict of duty. Marital obligations cannot overthrow the duties of church membership, neither can the duties of church membership overthrow domestic duties. God has so adjusted them that they are in perfect harmony.

The field of woman's duties in the church, is wide and varied. She may serve usefully on committees in peculiar cases of discipline of her own sex, when it would be indelicate for males to act. They may serve in works of mercy and charity, in labors of love, in caring for the sick and ministering to the needy. Some such office Phebe and others filled in the apostolic church. In female prayer meetings she may lead and thus encourage and strengthen others of her sex. It may not comport with that modesty and delicacy prescribed for her to lead in public prayer before a miscellaneous assembly (and even this seems to be allowed by Paul, provided her head be covered, 1 Cor. xi: 5). But there can be no indelicacy in her praying in a company of her own sex. She may also be useful in giving private instructions in the doctrines and duties of the gospel, by exemplifying the beauties of Christianity by her walk and conversation.

SECTION 2. *Her Subordination in the Church.*—I have all the while admitted that she sustained a relation in the church subordinate to man, but only in those particulars which are expressly revealed. Christianity has this peculiarity about it that it does not disturb social relations but only heightens and enforces their obligations. Hence no duty or office is assigned to woman which is incompatible with her social status, or which would be considered indelicate by the world.

1. She may not remain uncovered in the church, but must be veiled. (1 Cor. xi: 56.) There is a delicacy and sensibility in the female character which makes her shrink from observation and the loss of which deprives her of her chief attraction. The rule in this case seems to be founded in sound reason. She should veil herself: (1.) To avoid the temptation to make a vain display of her personal charms. The desire to please the opposite sex is natural to her. The possession of that beauty of face which captivates and enchains man, tends to render her vain of an attraction which gives her so much the advantage over her less favored sisters—and the thought of the effect of her beauty upon others is calculated to divert her thoughts from the worship of God. (2.) To avoid throwing off that modest reserve which is the charm of the sex. She who can stand without a blush the gaze of a promiscuous assembly is one degree removed from virtue. But in proportion to the exposure of her face to that gaze does she become hardened to it. (3.) That Christians may not be depreciated in the estimation of the people by tolerating an act that according to their sense of propriety is deemed indelicate.

2. She may not sustain any official relation, that places her in authority over man. (1 Tim. ii: 12.) In prohibiting her to *teach* the apostle no doubt had reference to public teaching or preaching; and there is no conflict between this passage and 1 Cor. xi: 5. The latter text seems to imply that a woman may prophesy in the church, provided her head be covered; but to prophesy was to exercise an extraordinary gift imparted by the Holy Spirit and is quite different from the regular and public ministry of the word.

The only two permanent offices in the Apostolic Church were those of bishop or elder, and deacon and the qualifications for these as given at large in the epistle to Timothy and Titus, require males. The prohibition to usurp authority of the man includes the prohibition of the pastorate—or even the public ministry, which involves some degree of authority. The requirement to keep silent in the church precludes her from preaching. The reasons for this restriction—not upon her rights—but upon her duties, will appear from a careful consideration of the subject. (1.) Paul gives as one reason (1 Tim. ii: 14,) that women are more liable to be deceived than men. Their confiding nature makes them peculiarly liable to be imposed upon, and he clearly intimates that the part woman played in the transgression has much to do with her subordination to man. (2.) She is not fitted to the hardships and privations of a minister's life. It requires sterner stuff than woman is made of to meet its requirements. Her delicate nature is wanting in that rugged spirit which is necessary to meet the conflicts in propagating and upholding a faith that is opposed by the world. (3.) She could not perform its duties without neglecting her home duties. The world cannot dispense with her labors at home as wife and mother. Her peculiar mission is in the domestic and social circle. For this work God has especially qualified her, and society would be vastly loser if she abandoned it for a mission not less divine but unlike in its requirements. To be a minister or other public servant, she must leave these more important duties undone. Every effort of woman to thrust herself into public life, either in the pulpit or otherwise, is in open rebellion against that order which God has established and in neglect of those equally honorable and equally indispensable duties He has assigned her.

CHAPTER IX.

THE SOVEREIGNTY OF THE CHURCH—THE RIGHTS OF MINORITIES.

I have already discussed incidentally many of the questions that relate to the subject of this chapter which will render an extended discussion unnecessary.

I use the term sovereignty in an extremely limited sense, to express the highest power which the church may exercise. Strictly speaking the church possesses no sovereignty whatever—not even in the sense in which we say that a State is sovereign, implying the power to choose its form of government, alter or abolish the same at pleasure, and to enact laws and regulations under its own constitution. I have shown in the course of this treatise that God himself, in the exercise of his sovereign power, has chosen that form of government best adapted to the interests and happiness of his people; and has himself enacted all the laws necessary for them. The Christian church is not less a theocracy than was the Jewish government. God is equally the author of both. The command to baptize is as explicit as that to circumcise. The ordinance of the Lord's Supper is as well defined as the Passover. The duties of both officers and people respectively are as clearly stated under the new as under the old dispensation. Were all things to be made by Moses according to the pattern shown him in the mount, so that no daring innovator in subsequent times could set aside the institutions given to the Jews through him? So Christ and his apostles set up "an everlasting kingdom" whose laws and institutions are as unalterable as the rites and ceremonies of the Jews. The church has no more power to change its laws and institutions than had the congregation of Israel to change theirs. The idea of sovereignty, therefore, when applied to the church is subject to this restriction. It is an executive government only, and sovereignty is the proper exercise of its executive power. The subject of the present inquiry is: What department of the church is charged with the preservation and execution of the laws of Christ? The Scriptures do not assign this power to any co-ordinate part of the church. Neither the clergy nor laity exercise this power exclusively and independent of the other. But the highest power was lodged in the assembled whole. Peter stood up in the midst of the disciples and proposed to elect a successor to the faithless Judas Iscariot, and they all participated in the election of Matthias. (Acts 1st chapter.) The multitude of disciples were called together to elect deacons. The proposition pleased the "whole multitude," who chose seven deacons. (Acts 6th chapter.) The apostles and brethren called upon Peter for an explanation of his conduct in preaching to the Gentiles, and when they heard the account of Peter they held their peace and glorified God. (Acts 11th chapter.) When Paul and Barnabas returned from their missionary tour they gathered together the church at Antioch, and rehearsed all that God had accomplished through them. (Acts xiv: 27.) This was entirely proper, because it was this church which had sent them forth on their mission. It was the *brethren* at Antioch who determined to send messengers to Jerusalem about the question of circumcising the Gentiles. (Acts, chapter 15.) The whole church participated in the consideration of this question, (Acts xv: 22,) and the decree was sent forth in the name of the apostles, elders and brethren. (v. 23.) When the messengers returned to

Antioch, they delivered the epistle to the multitude. (v. 30.) Paul instructed the Corinthians when they were *assembled together* to exercise discipline upon an offending brother. (1 Cor. v: 4.) And afterwards he entreats them to confirm their love to the offender because the punishment which had been "inflicted by many," was sufficient for his correction. (2 Cor. ii: 6.) The epistles which contain directions for the transaction of business and administering all the affairs of the church are addressed to the whole body of the church. (Rom. i: 7: 1 Cor. i: 2; 2 Cor. i: 1; Gal. i: 2; Eph. i: 1; Phil. i: 1; Col. i 2; 1 Thes. i: 1; 2 Thes. i: 1.) It would have been a useless work to give the whole church minute instruction, involving the whole range of Christian duty and discipline, if they were not allowed to obey them.

I think it is clear, therefore, that the whole church, assembled, received members and exercised discipline over them; chose officers to preside over them; judged in matters of faith; in fine, did whatever the church might do. Mosheim says:

"It was, therefore, the assembly of the people which chose rulers and teachers or received them by a free and authoritative consent when recommended by others. The same people rejected or confirmed by their suffrages the laws that were proposed by their rulers to their assembly; excommunicated, profligate and unworthy members of the church; restored the penitent to their forfeited privileges; passed judgment upon the different subjects of controversy and dissension that rose in their community; examined and decided the disputes which happend between the elders and deacons, and in a word, exercised all the authority which belongs to such as are invested with sovereign power."—*McClaine's Mosheim Vol. 1, p 37.*

So long as there was an entire unanimity of opinion, no difficulty could arise. But as men widely differ in their views and habits of thought this could but seldom happen. What rule, then, was adopted in the Apostolic Church? The law of fellowship certainly requires unanimity; for a single person dissenting, the fellowship is broken. This applies to the reception and retention of members —for certainly no one should be introduced into the church against the reasonable objection of any member; for this would be to gain members at the expense of harmony. If a member should unreasonably and factiously oppose the admission of an applicant, or refuse to fellowship another member, he is himself liable to discipline and should be cut off for his contumacy, that the harmony and fellowship of the church may remain unbroken. In the expulsion of members and in the determination of all other questions the majority rule. This seems to have been the rule in the case of discipline referred to by the apostle Paul in his epistle to the Corinthians, "The punishment inflicted by many." (Gr. *toon pleionoon,*) might be properly translated *by the majority.* (2 Cor. ii: 6.)

But the question arises in this connection, is the voice of the majority so absolutely binding that the minority must in all cases submit under pain of schism and disorder? This brings us to consider the rights of minorities. If the majority decide a matter according to the law of Christ, then the minority have no option but to submit. But if on the other hand they decide contrary to the law of Christ the minority is not bound thereby. Any other rule would place the truth at the mercy of a numerical majority, and innovations could not be resisted; and would justify all the corruptions that have been introduced into the church; and those noble martyrs and confessors who put their lives into the scale against them, become mere heretics and schismatics, and we have no option but to return with repentance and confession to the "Mother of Harlots."

To the faithful few who have dissented in all ages we are indebted for the pure gospel to-day.

If any separate, therefore, from the disorderly majority they are guilty of no schism, for schism is a separation from the truth, whether by the few or the many. In the case supposed, the majority are the schismatics and may no longer claim the prerogative of government which they have forfeited. Good order would manifestly require that the minority should not disturb the decision of the majority unless it is clearly in violation of the law of Christ, and then it becomes their imperative duty to resist, first by kindly persuading their erring brethren to change their determination, but if this fails, to call a council of neighboring churches to advise in the matter, and if all prove unavailing then to separate from them according to the apostolic rule: "Withdraw yourselves from every brother that walketh disorderly, and not according to the traditions received of us."

But I am constrained to add, by way of caution, that if the matter in dispute be only a question of policy or a difference of opinion about a matter of fact, the minority should always acquiesce. Nothing but a clear violation of some acknowledged law of Christ can justify such separation.

CHAPTER X.

THE LAWS OF THE CHURCH.

The code of the church is embraced in two divisions, *Moral Law* and *Positive Law*. The apostolic church knew nothing of Canon Law, or that code which in subsequent times was adopted for the government of the church. No such power was conferred by Christ, and its exercise is presumptuous and wicked, because it assumes that God's work is imperfect and must therefore be mended by man in order to adapt it to times and circumstances.

SECTION 1. *Moral Law.*—The Moral Law is that part of Divine Law that is founded in the nature of things. It commands that which is right in itself and prohibits that which is wrong in itself. If we had never received any law to love God and our neighbor, it would nevertheless be only right to do so. And if we never had been forbidden to take the life of a fellow-being, it would have been wrong to kill. The Moral Law is embodied in that code which was given by God to Moses on Mt. Sinai, as expounded by Jesus Christ. It was written on tables of stone to indicate that its obligation is permanent, and was sanctioned by the thunders of Sinai. The whole has been epitomized in this comprehensive sentence: "Thou shalt love the Lord thy God with all thy soul, mind and strength, and thy neighbor as thyself." This code is contained in the Decalogue recorded in the 20th chapter of Exodus.

1. Thou shalt have no other gods before me.

This requires us to recognize God as supreme; as more entitled to our obedience than all other beings;

to make His will the great law of our being, and to love Him more than all else. The Saviour illustrates this law by the declaration: "If ye love me, keep my commandments;" or, as elsewhere expressed: "If ye love me ye will keep my commandments." "He that loveth father or mother more than me is not worthy of me." "Ye are my friends if ye do whatsoever I have commanded you." John says: "Hereby we know that we know Him if we keep His commandments. He that saith, I know Him, and keepeth not His commandments is a liar, and the truth is not in him. But whoso keepeth His word, in him verily is the love of God perfected, and hereby we know that we are in Him." Hence the only recognition of His supreme authority, and the only proof of our perfect love of Him is to be found in implicit obedience.

2. *Thou shalt not make unto thee any graven image or any likeness of anything that is in heaven above, or that is in the earth beneath, or that is in the water under the earth. Thou shalt not bow down thyself to them nor serve them.*"

The first part of the commandment was intended to prevent idolatry by prohibiting every kind of images in connection with the worship of God; and obliges us to worship Him in the manner He has prescribed. It prohibits us from fashioning any law or ceremony which God has not established, and requires us to keep the laws and ordinances of His house just as He has given them. Christ charged the Scribes and Pharisees with having made void the commandments of God by their traditions.

The second part of the commandment forbids idolatry which is the worship of anything but God. To love anything more than God is idolatry. Hence Paul tells us that the inordinate love of property (covetousness) is idolatry.

3. Thou shalt not take the name of the Lord thy God in vain.

This command forbids any but the most reverent use of the name of God, such as its use as a mere expletive, or when invoking a curse, or appealing to His arbitration in games of chance, or calling lightly upon His name to attest our affirmation. Christ has extended this law to swearing by any object, because it profanes the name of God: "Swear not at all; neither by heaven, for it is God's throne; nor by the earth, for it is His footstool; neither by Jerusalem, for it is the city of the great king. Neither shalt thou swear by thy head, because thou canst not make one hair white or black. But let your communications be yea, yea, nay, nay: for whatsoever is more than these cometh of evil." (Matt. v: 34-37).

4. Remember the Sabbath day to keep it holy. Six days shalt thou labor and do all thy work, but the seventh is the Sabbath of the Lord thy God; in it thou shalt not do any work, thou nor thy son, nor thy daughter, nor thy manservant, nor thy maidservant, nor thy cattle, nor thy stranger that is in thy gates.

Experience has shown that one day in seven is needed to rest and restore the exhausted physical energies. It is necessary also to allow us an opportunity to turn aside from the cares of business and devote a part of our time exclusively to the public worship of God, and to meditation and prayer. It is necessary also that all men in the same place should observe the same day in order to obtain the full benefit of the Sabbath. Hence God has appointed a particular day; but it is evident from the form and motion of the earth that it cannot be the same absolute period of time, but only the seventh day in any particular spot which will be later or earlier with respect to an absolute period of time as we go east or west. Two travelers setting out from the same place, one going east and the other west, and observing the seventh day, would find when they met on the opposite side of the earth that the Sabbath of the one occurred one day earlier than the other. It is the seventh day to each place that is to be observed. The original Sabbath was kept on the seventh day of the week. But after the resurrection of Christ, which occurred on the following day, the first day of the week was observed by Christians and called the Lord's day. As Christ declared himself to be Lord of the Sabbath, the change must be supposed to have been made by His authority as it was recognized by His inspired apostles. He also expounded the law of the Sabbath to allow works of necessity and mercy.

5. *Honor thy father and thy mother.*

This inculcates that respect and obedience which we owe to our natural parents. It also includes that veneration and respect which is due to those who are superior in point of age, or of official or social position.

6. *Thou shalt not kill.*

This prohibits every species of willful and unlawful killing of any human being *in esse*. And the Saviour, quoting this law, applies it to every murderous desire and revengeful passion. It is opposed to the law of retaliation and requires us to do good to those who do us wrong.

7. *Thou shalt not commit adultery.*

This prohibits not only every actual violation of the marriage vow, but every illicit and impure practice, and even desire. And hence requires us to avoid everything that tends to provoke these evil desires.

8. *Thou shalt not steal.*

This prohibits every act of dishonesty and injustice, either in purpose or action; the unjust privation of another of that which belongs to him. Honesty requires us to give every man his own; to pay a just equivalent for what we buy and to receive only a just equivalent for what we sell; to keep just weights and measures, and to correctly and truthfully declare the qualities of what we propose to sell; to render unto the government also its just dues—in a word "to do unto others as we would they should do unto us," in all our transactions. This law obliges every man to be diligently engaged in some lawful employment that he may not be a burden to others.

9. *Thou shalt not bear false witness against thy neighbor.*

This is done by swearing falsely against him in a court of justice or procuring others to do it; by concealing the truth to his injury; by spiriting away witnesses in his favor; by bringing any false accusation against him; by circulating false tales to his injury; by encouraging those who slander him; by unjustly attributing bad motives to him; by backbiting and detraction; in fine, by the use of any language, signs or writing, calculated to prejudice him unjustly in the estimation of others.

10. *Thou shalt not covet.*

This law prohibits envy at the good fortune of another; the inordinate desire for what belongs to him and the desire to get it wrongfully.

The first four of these commandments relate to our duty to God and the rest contain our duty to our fellow-men. All the moral precepts of the gospel can be reduced to one or the other of these.

SECTION 2. *Positive Laws.*—By Positive Laws I mean those commandments of God which embrace things which in themselves have no moral quality, but which take their obligation alone from the authority of God. These are not less binding than the moral law, because they rest upon the same authority and their violation is a grave sin, because it sets aside the will of God and rebels against His government.

It does not follow that because the things to be done possess no moral quality, that their performance is left to our discretion, or that they are necessarily merely arbitrary and without fitness or utility.

Literal obedience is essential to the performance of a positive law. Anything short of this is no obedience at all. The whole thing depends upon the authority of God, and one part can be no more essential than another, and any omission is a neglect of God's authority. While we may not set aside one of them because we cannot discover its fitness or expediency, they are always adapted to the purpose intended and are the most appropriate that can be devised.

The ordinances or positive laws of the church are its *external forms, Baptism* and the *Lord's Supper*. Of the first I have already treated. It remains to inquire what is the law of Baptism and the Lord's Supper. I will discuss these subjects in subsequent chapters, and close this chapter with some remarks upon the *sacramental efficacy* of the church and its ordinances, upon which a large class of professing Christians rely for hope and salvation. Having passed the water of baptism they suppose they have entered the charmed circle of the church where sin can never penetrate, and that by feeding upon the consecrated loaf their spiritual life is renewed from time to time. There are two phases of this opinion, the Catholic and Protestant. The Catholics maintain that the ordinances in themselves contain and communicate grace. The Council of Florence thus states the doctrine:

"*Hæc nostra* [*sacramenta*] *et continent gratiam, et eam digne suscipientibus conferunt* "These our sacraments both

contain grace and confer it upon those receiving it **worthily.**"
—*Decr. Eugen. ap. Concil t. xiii, p. 534.*

The Council of Trent (sess. vii, *de sacramentis* Canon vi) enacted:

Si quis dixerit, sacramenta novae legis non continere gratiam quam significant, aut gratiam ipsam non ponentibus obicem non conferre; quasi signa tantum externa sint acceptae per fidem, gratiae vel justiciae et notae quaedem Christianae professionis, quibus apud homines discernuntur fideles ab infidelibus anathema esto, &c.

"If any one should say that the sacraments of the new law do not contain the grace of which they are the signs; or do not confer grace itself upon those who do not interpose a barrier, as if they were only to be received as external signs through faith of grace and justification, and certain marks of the Christian profession by which the faithful are distinguished among men from infidels, let him be accursed, &c."

Some Protestants, while they deny that the ordinances contain and confer grace of themselves, *opus operatum*, nevertheless hold that they are the media through which the Holy Spirit confers grace to those worthily receiving them, and that without them there is no salvation. I quote from the learned Richard Hooker:

"The church is to us that very mother of our new birth, in whose bowels we are all bred, at whose breast we all receive nourishment. As many therefore as are apparently to our judgment born of God, they have the seat of their regeneration by the ministry of the church which useth to that end and purpose not only the word but the sacraments; both having regenerative force and virtue."—[*Hooker's Works, b. 5, c. l. s. 1.*

"They pretend that to *sacraments* we ascribe no efficacy; but make them bare signs of instruction or admonition; which is utterly false. For sacraments with us are signs effectual; they are the instruments of God whereby to bestow grace; howbeit grace not proceeding from the visible sign, but His invisible power."—*Ib. b. V, Append. No. 1, p. 37.*

"For so hath God instituted and ordained that together with due administration and receipt of sacramental signs, there should proceed from himself grace effectual to sanctify, to cure, to comfort, and whatsoever else is for the good of the soul."—*Ib. b. VI, Chap. 6, Sec. 10.*

"Our Saviour instructed Nicodemus that *no man can enter the kingdom of God* (that is, become a Christian, or subject of God's spiritual kingdom) *without being regenerated by water and by Spirit, i. e.*, without baptism and the spiritual **grace** attending it."—*Barrow's Works, Vol. II, p. 41.*

The sacramental efficacy of Baptism and the Lord's Supper is also taught in the Methodist Discipline, Art. XVI:

"Sacraments ordained of Christ are not only badges or tokens of Christian men's profession, but rather they are certain signs of grace and God's good will towards us, by the which He doth work invisibly in us and doth not only quicken but also strengthen and confirm our faith in Him."

Do the church and its ordinances, *opus operatum*, confer grace according to the Roman Catholic view? Paul answers that question very emphatically when he says: "Other foundation can no man lay than that is laid, which is Jesus Christ." Faith in Christ is the medium of God's grace. "By grace are ye saved, through faith." They who build upon any other foundation are like the foolish man who built his house upon the sand.

1. They vainly believe that baptism is a real cleansing; that it regenerates the soul and washes away sin. How delusive! Water may cleanse the body, but sin is a stain upon the soul. If water could wash it away, as you may cleanse your soiled hands, the vilest sinner would have nothing to do but plunge into the water and come out pure as an angel of light. But how can water cleanse the soul? It is a material, physical substance, while the soul is an immaterial, spiritual essence. If the soul were corporeal and could be brought into contact with the water, then possibly its stains might be washed out. But how is this contact to be brought about; and how came water to possess this wonderful efficacy? If it possesses it naturally as it does the property of dissolving material substances, how comes it that all sin is not washed away, since men in all ages have practiced daily ablutions? If this wonderful virtue is imparted by the mummery of the priest, how remiss in duty they must be not by one stupendous consecration to impart this efficacy to all the water on the globe,

that all the world may wash and be free from sin.

2. Equally vain is the hope that the bosom of the church can shelter men from the claims of God's offended justice. By the common law of England, if an offender, pursued by the officers of justice, should take refuge in a church, they could pursue him no further, and so long as he continued within those sacred and inviolable precincts he was secure from arrest. This was called the privilege of sanctuary. But in God's economy there is no such thing known as the privilege of sanctuary. The ministers of God's justice do not pursue the guilty to the door of the church, and turn away in disappointed rage; but no spot in the universe, save the bosom of Jesus, is too sacred to admit the pursuing vengeance of God, to reach the unbelieving sinner. If the church possesses this wonderful efficacy what a pity it does not extend its arms like seas and grasp in all the shore. Acting upon this theory whole nations have in name been brought into the church. The lowest, the vilest, the most corrupt, revel about her altars and pollute her sanctuaries while they laugh at God's vengeance, whose justice if this be true, is thus cheated of its proper victims.

3. But notwithstanding the pretended efficacy of the laver of regeneration, the washing away of sins in baptism and the security of the church, lest there may be some crevice through which God's vengeance may enter in pursuit of the guilty, in the vain hope of outwitting His justice, they have invented the dogma of the sacramental efficacy of the eucharist in which they pretend to invoke the real presence of the body and blood of Jesus Christ; upon which feeding the soul is sanctified, thus making cannibals of Christians that they may become the sons of God! A mortal man, clad in holy vestments, mumbling a few syllables of priestly

jargon converts the bread and wine into the real body and blood of Jesus! Man becomes a creator and makes God! And men black with crimes eat God! Away with such impiety!

But how does the bread and wine operate to sanctify the soul? The nutricious part of the food we eat enters into the body and forms a part of it. Bear in mind it is the body of Christ upon which we are said to feed, and not the soul; and that it is a literal, not a spiritual feeding. The body and not the soul therefore is nourished. The soul, the seat of sin, is not purified—even if the body should be; and after all it is only the cleansing of the outside of the platter; whitewashing the exterior of the sepulchre, while within it is full of rottenness and dead men's bones. If, therefore, the eucharist, on the supposition of the real presence can have no sacramental efficacy, much less can it have it, if we consider the elements unchanged.

No less untenable is the Protestant view of the subject. God has never suspended His grace upon a mere physical act, in the performance of which a third person must concur. He has not entrusted the dispensation of His grace to priestly hands, at whose will it may be administered or withheld. The soul thirsting for salvation is not compelled to wait in the vestibule of God's temple until some lordly prelate vouchsafes to unlock the stores of God's mercy.

We are nowhere informed that these ordinances are the instruments by which the Holy Spirit effects the regeneration of the soul, and by which the sins are remitted. On the contrary the word is represented as the ordinary instrument. "The sword of the spirit which is the word of God." (Eph. vi: 17). That word of God is represented as "quick and powerful, sharper than a two-edged sword, piercing to the dividing asunder of soul and spirit and joints and marrow." (Heb. iv: 12). "Being born again, not of corruptible seed, but incorruptible, by the word of God." (1 Pet. i: 23). The gospel is the power of God unto salvation to every one that believeth." (Rom. i: 16). " Whosoever believeth upon Him shall not perish but have eternal life." (John iii: 6). When the Philippian jailor asked Paul the momentous question: "What shall I do to be saved?" the answer was, "Believe on the Lord Jesus and thou shalt be saved." And throughout the Scriptures, faith is represented as the condition of salvation. That the operation of the Holy Spirit is independent of baptism and may precede it, is evident from the events recorded in the tenth chapter of Acts. Peter tells the Gentiles in the house of Cornelius, that "whosoever believeth upon Him (Jesus) shall receive the remission of sins." (v. 43). And while Peter yet spake these words the Holy Ghost fell on them. When Peter perceived this he exclaimed: "Can any man forbid water, that these should be baptized, who have received the Holy Ghost as well as we?" (v. 47).

I will renew the discussion of this subject in connection with the design of the ordinances.

CHAPTER XI.

BAPTISM—ACTION OF BAPTISM.

I will treat of this ordinance under four divisions, the *Action*, the *Subject*, the *Design* and the *Administrator of Baptism*. The present chapter will be devoted to the Action of Baptism. I prefer this term to the expression "Mode of Baptism," because it divests the subject of all extraneous matters and the true inquiry is not how a certain act is to be performed, but what is the act itself. To ascertain what act is commanded we must have recourse to the law of baptism. We find that commandment expressed in three different forms, *first* as a general recognition of the ordinance: "He that believeth and is baptized shall be saved." *Secondly* in the authority conferred upon the apostles: "Go make disciples of all nations, baptizing them," etc, and *thirdly* in the requirement addressed to the subject of it: "Repent and be baptized every one of you." The act thus commanded is illustrated by examples and allusions to it.

I take it for granted that the Lawgiver of the church meant to be understood, and that he was capable of selecting language exactly suited to convey his precise meaning, and, therefore, that his commandments are given in terms which can be understood. The Greek language, which is the vehicle of the law, possesses a wonderful capacity for expressing shades of thought and was no doubt selected on this account. From the time of the conquest of the world by Alexander the Great to the dissemination of the gospel throughout the Roman Empire it was the language of common intercourse among civilized nations and was on that account suited to convey a gospel in which all were interested. It is fair to suppose that he employed words in their common signification as they would be understood by those who spoke the Greek language, or if the sparseness of the language compelled him to use words in a new sense he would give notice of the change. Now if he meant that the act to be performed was to sprinkle or pour he had *rantizo* and *echeo* at hand which exactly convey those ideas. If he meant to wash *louo* was at his command. If he meant to cleanse without respect to the manner of doing it he had *cathurizo*. But it is significant that he employed *baptizo*, the word in common use among the Greeks, to express the act of dipping or immersion; and as we find no intimation that he meant to use the word in a new sense, it follows that he has commanded immersion as the act to be performed in baptism. *Baptizo* is the word uniformly used in the Scriptures to express the action of baptism—*rantizo* and *echeo* are never so used.

It is sufficient for our purpose to show that the ordinary meaning of the word *baptizo* is to dip, to immerse; for the rule of interpretation requires that words shall be understood in their ordinary sense unless the context forbids it. I think it will be clear from the authorities produced that *baptizo* means ordinarily *to dip, to immerse*, and that what are called its secondary meanings involve the same idea.

I will now proceed to produce the testimony in a condensed form to establish the proposition above stated.

SECTION 1. *Testimony of the Lexicons.*—That the weight of this testimony may be appreciated by the unlearned. I state what will not be disputed, that the first meaning which is given to the word is the sense in which it is most commonly used. The writers of a language are consulted, and from the frequency with which a word is used in any sense they determine what is the primary, or most general meaning, and what is the secondary. The last meanings give the sense in which it is less frequently used. If we wish to know what a word signifies in a particular passage we look at the first meaning given in the Lexicon. If it agrees with the context the law of translation requires it to be taken. If not, we look at the second meaning, and so on until a meaning is found that does agree with the context. Again, although a word may be defined by a number of terms, it must not be understood that it has all these meanings at the same time. A word, though used in different senses, means but one thing at a time. The want of proper attention to this rule has produced a great deal of false reasoning. Generic words are defined by generic terms and specific words by specific terms. No Lexicon defines *baptizo* to mean "the application of water in any manner," but all give specific meanings. Of the large number of standard Lexicons quoted below, all give the primary meaning to be to *dip, to immerse, to plunge,* and none of them give sprinkle or pour as one of its meanings.

In the course of my reading I have collected the following definitions most of which I have verified by personal inspection of the authors quoted.

The following were quoted or referred to in the great debate between Campbell and Rice in Lexington, Ky., in 1843:

(Quoted by Mr. C.)

1. *Scapula.* (1579.) *Mergo, seu immergo, item submergo, item abluo, lavo.*

To dip or immerse, also to submerge or overwhelm; also to wash, to cleanse.

(A different edition of the same author quoted by Mr. R.)

Mergo, seu immergo, item tingo ut quae tingendi, aut abluendi gratia immergimus. Item mergo, submergo, obruo aqua; item abluo, lavo.—*Mark 7. Luke 11.*

To dip, or immerse; also to dye, as we immerse things for the purpose of coloring or washing them. Also to plunge, to submerge, to cover with water, to cleanse, to wash.—*Mark 7. Luke 11.*

Baptismos—Mersio, lotio, ablutio, ipsi immergendi, item lavendi, seu abluendi actus.—*Mark 7.*

Immersion, washing, cleansing; the act of immersing, also of washing or cleansing one's self.

2. Henricus Stephanus. (1572—Mergo, seu immergo, ut quae tingendi, aut abluendi gratia in aqua immergimus; mergo, submergo, obruo aqua, abluo, lavo.

To dip, immerse; as we immerse things for the purpose of coloring or washing them; to merge, to submerge, to cover with water, to cleanse, to wash.

3. Thesaurus of Robinson. (1676,) otherwise called *Schrivilius' Lexicon*

Mergo, lavo—to immerse, to wash.

(*Schrivilius* as quoted by Mr. R., late edition.)

Baptizo, *Mergo, abluo, lavo—To baptize, to immerse, to cleanse, to wash.

4. Pasor—(London Ed., 1650.)

Bapto et Baptizo—Mergo, immergo, tingo, quod sit immergendo. Differt a *du ai*, quod est profundum petere; est penitus submergi. Comparantur afflictiones gurgitibus aquarum, quibus, veluti merguntur, qui miseris et culamitatibus hujus vitae conflictantur, ita tamen merguntur ut rursus emergant.

To dip, to immerse, to dye because it is done by immersing. It differs from *dunai* which means to sink to the bottom; to be thoroughly submerged. Afflictions are compared to a flood of waters in which they seem to be immersed who are overwhelmed with the misfortunes and miseries of life, yet only so overwhelmed as to emerge again.

5. Schleusner. (Glasgow Ed. 1824.)

1 Proprie immergo, ac intingo, in aquam immergo—Properly I immerse, I dip, I immerse in water.

2. Abluo, lavo, in aquam, quia haud raro aliquid immergi, ac intingi in aquam solet ut lavetur.

I wash, I cleanse in water because generally a thing is dipped or plunged in water that it may be washed.

---

*I have the editio quoted by Mr R , the Glasgo , 1799. which is described as 'Editio xvii, prioribus auctior et emendatior." 'The xvii edition, enlarged and amended from former editions," The Latin word *baptizo* upon which Mr. R. relies does not rest upon the authority of Schrivilius, but of some one of the many subsequent editors he same edition defines *baptisma, immersio,* tinctio, baptisma—immersion, dipping, baptism.

(The same author quoted from a different edition by Mr. R.)

Mergo, immergo, abluo, lavo, aqua purgo.

To plunge, to immerse, to cleanse, to wash, to purify with water.

(My copy is the 2nd Leipsic edition, 1801, supervised by Schleusner himself.)

1. Proprie immergo ac intingo, in aquam mergo.

2. Abluo, lavo, aqua purgo quia haud raro aliquid immergi ac intingi, in aquam solet ut lavetur.

3. Baptizo, baptizmum administro, actum baptismi exerceo, seu baptismi ritu obstringo aliquem professionis religionis christianae.

4. Metaphorice, imbuo, large et copiose do ac suppedito, largitur profundo.—*Matt. iii: 11.*

5. Per metaphorem *baptizesthai* significant calamitatum fluctibus obrui, mergi, miseris, mala perferre, etiam, sponte se periculis vitae offerre, mortem adeo ipsam sibi inferri pati.

1. Properly to immerse, to dip, to plunge in water.

2. To cleanse, to wash, to purify with water, because a thing is usually immersed or dipped in water that it may be washed.

3. (As applied to the solemn rite of baptism.) To baptize, to administer baptism, to perform the act of baptism, to bind any one by the rite of baptism to the profession of the Christian religion.

4. Metaphorically To imbue, to give and supply largely and abundantly, to pour out profusely —*Matt. iii; 11.*

5 By metaphor *baptizesthai* signifies to be overwhelmed by the waves of misfortune, to be sunk in sufferings, to bear evils; also to offer one's self voluntarily to the dangers of life, so to suffer even death to be inflicted on one's self.

Baptisma.—1. Proprie, immersio, intinctio in aquam, lotio, hinc transfertur:

2. Ad ritum sacrum, qui *kat' exochein* baptismus dicitur quo baptizandi olim in aquam immergibantur ut verae religioni divinae obstringerentur.

3 Per metaphoram gravissimae afflictiones et calamitates ob religionem perferendae, quibus, qui eas sustinent, quasi submerguntur.

Baptisma.—1. Properly immersion, dipping in water, washing. Hence it is transferred:

2. To the sacred rite, which *kat' exocheen* (by eminence) is called baptism, in which those to be baptized were formerly immersed in water that they might be bound to the true divine religion.

3. By metaphor, the severest afflictions and calamities to be borne on account of religion, in which they who bear them are as it were submerged.

6. Parkhurst.—(Lexicon N. T.)

Baptizo first and primarily means to dip, to immerse, to plunge in water; but in the New Testament it occurs not strictly in this sense unless so far as this is included in "to wash one's self" to be washed, wash the hands by immersion, or dipping them in water. (Mark vii: 4; Luke xi: 38.) To immerse in water or with water in token of purification from sin and from spiritual pollution; figuratively to be immersed or plunged into a flood or sea, as it were of grievous affliction and suffering.

[The same author quoted by Mr. R.] To immerse, or wash with water in token of purification.

[My copy is the Second Edition, London, 1795. Supervised by Parkhurst himself.]

1. To dip, immerse or plunge in water. But in N. T. it occurs not strictly in this sense unless so far as this is included in the sense 2 and 3 below.

2. Mid. To wash one's self, be washed, wash, *i. e.* the hands by immersion or by dipping in water.

3. To baptize, to immerse in or wash with water in token of purification from sin, and spiritual pollution.

4. To baptize as the Israelites into Moses in the cloud and in the sea.

5. In a figurative sense, to baptize with the Holy Ghost.

6. Figuratatively, to be immersed or plunged in a flood or sea as it were of grievous afflictions and sufferings

7. Donnegan.—To immerse repeatedly into a liquid, to submerge, to soak thoroughly, to saturate; metaphorically, to drench with wine, to dip in a vessel and draw.

Baptismos—Immersion, submersion, the act of washing or bathing.

8. Rev. Dr. John Jones, of England—I plunge, I plunge in water, dip, baptize, bury, overwhelm.

9. Greenfield. (Also quoted by Rice)—To immerse, immerge, submerge, sink, in N. T. to wash, to perform ablution, to cleanse, to immerse, baptize, and perform the rite of baptism.

10. Bretschneider.—Proprie, sepius intingo, sepius lavo, etc.

Properly to dip repeatedly, to wash repeatedly. This is the meaning of the word, for in *baptizo* is contained the idea of a complete immersion under water; at least so is *baptisma* in the N T.

[The same author quoted by Mr. R.] Proprie, sepius intingo, sepius lavo, deinde lavo, abluo simpliciter, med. lavo me, abluo me.

Properly, often to dip, often to wash, then simply to wash, to cleanse, mid. I wash or cleanse myself

11. *Bass.*—To dip, immerse, plunge in water, to bathe one's self, to be immersed in sufferings and afflictions.

12. *Pickering*—*Baptisma*, immersion, dipping, plunging, metaphorically, misery or calamity with which one is overwhelmed

13. *Stokius* (*Leipsic 1752*).—1. Generatim, ac vi vocis, intinctionis ac immersionis *baptizo* notionem obtinet. 2. Speciatim (A) proprie, est immergere ac intingere in aquam. 3. (B) proprie, per metalepsin, lavire, abluere, quia aliquid intingi ac immergi, solet in aquam ut lavetur vel abluatur.

1. Generally, and by the force of the word, *baptizo* obtains the sense of dipping and immersion. 2. (A) Specially and properly it signifies to immerse and to dip in water. 3. (B) Tropically, by metalepsis, it means to wash, to cleanse; because a thing is usually dipped or immersed in water that it may be washed or cleansed.

Lexicons referred to, but not quoted by Mr. Campbell.

14. *Wilson's Church Dictionary*, 1678; 15. *Baily*, 1772; 16. *Robertson*; 17. *Hedericus*, 1778; 18. *Ashe*, 1775; 19. *Charles Richardson*; 20. *Calmet*; 21. *Schoetgenius*, 1765; 22. *Suicerus*; 23. *Schilhornius*; 24 *Cliznetus*, 1661; 25. *Leigh's Critca Sacra*; 26 *Trommius' Concordance.* All concur with Suicerus in defining *baptizo* as properly denoting immersion or dipping into.

Quoted by Dr. Rice.

Hedericus (referred to by Mr C).—1. Mergo, immergo, aqua abruo. 2. Abluo, lavo. 3. *Baptizo* significatu sacro.

1. To dip, immerse; to cover with water. 2. To cleanse; to wash. 3. To baptize in a sacred sense.

27. *Robinson.*—To immerse; to sink; for example, spoken of ships and galleys, etc. In N T., to wash; to cleanse by washing; to wash one's self; to bathe; to perform ablution, etc.

28. *Groves.*—To dip, immerse, immerge, plunge; to wash, cleanse, purify. Mid To wash one's self; to bathe, etc

29. *Suidas.*—To sink; to plunge; to immerse; to wet; to wash; to cleanse, purify, etc.

30. *Wahl*—1. To wash; to perform ablution; to cleanse. 2. To immerse, etc.

Examined by me in addition to many of the above.

31. *Andrew Hoffman* (Leipsic, 1708).—Immergo, to immerse.

32. Liddell and Scott.—1. To dip repeatedly; of ships, to sink them. Pass., To bathe. 2. To draw water. 3. To baptize, N. T.

Quoted by J. W. D Creath in his work on baptism.

33. Basser.—To dip, immerse, plunge, bathe.

34. A'stedius —To baptize signifies only to immerse, except by consequence.

Wilson (referred to by Mr. Campbell).—To baptize; to dip into water, or plunge one into water.

35. Schwarzius —To baptize; to plunge; to overwhelm; to dip into, to wash by plunging.

36. Mintert.—To baptize properly, indeed, signifies to plunge; to immerse; to dip into water: but, because it is common to plunge or dip a thing that it may be washed, hence it also signifies to wash; to wash away.

Quoted by B. H. Carroll in a recent debate in Texas.

37 Stourdza.—Literally and always it means to plunge; baptism and immersion are therefore identical.

38. Sophocles.—1. To dip; to sink. Tropically, afflicted, soaked in liquor, intoxicated. 2. Mid. voice, To perform ablution; to wash one's self. 3. To plunge a knife. 4. Corresponding Latin words, mergo, mergito, tingo, to baptize. There is no evidence that Luke and Paul and the other writers of the New Testament put upon this word meanings not recognized by the Greeks.

39. Passow.—To dip; to immerse; to dye; because it is done by immersing. It differs from *dunai*, which means to sink to the bottom, and to be thoroughly immerged. Afflictions are compared to a flood of waters, in which they seem to be immersed who are overwhelmed with the misfortunes and miseries of life; yet, so overwhelmed as to emerge again.

Section 2.— *Testimony of Critics, Commentators and Historians*

Under this head I will group the admissions of eminent scholars, whose ecclesiastical relations forbid the suspicion that they meant to favor the Baptists. These embrace selections from a great mass, collected from the authors themselves or from undoubted authorities who have examined them, and of whose labors I avail myself.

Martin Luther.—Baptism is a Greek word, and may be translated immersion, as when we immerse something in water that it may be wholly covered: and, although it is almost wholly abolished (for they do not dip the whole children, but only pour a little water on them), they ought nevertheless to be wholly immersed and immediately drawn out; for that the etymology of the word seems to demand. * * * Washing of sins is attributed to baptism It is truly, indeed, attributed, but the signification is softer and slower than it can express baptism, which is rather a sign both of death and resurrection. Being moved by this reason, I would have those that are to be baptized to be altogether dipped into water, as the word doth sound and the mystery doth signify — *Opera vol. i. 336.*

Calvin. — The word *baptizo* signifies to immerse, and it is certain that immersion was the practice of the ancient church. — *Institutes b. iv. sec. 15.*

Grotius. — That this rite was wont to be performed by immersion, and not by perfusion, appears both by the propriety of the word and the places chosen for its administration.

Dyonisius Petavius — And indeed immersion is properly styled *baptismos*, though at present we content ourselves with pouring water on the head, which, in Greek, is called *perichusis*; that is perichysm (if I may so Anglicise), but not baptism.

Casaubon. — The manner of baptizing was to plunge or to dip them into the water, as even the word *baptizein* itself plainly shows.

Vetringa. The act of baptizing is the immersion of believers in water. This expresses the force of the word. — *Aphor. Sanc. Theol., Aphorism 884.*

Salmasius. — Baptism is immersion, and was administered in former times according to the force and meaning of the word. — *De Caesarie Virorum p. 669.*

Hospinianus. — Christ commanded us to be baptized, by which, it is certain, immersion is signified — *Hist. Sacrum. b. ii. ch. i. sec. 30.*

Zanchius. — The proper signification of the word *baptizo* is to immerse, plunge under water; to overwhelm in water

Alstedius. — To baptize signifies only to immerse; not to wash, except by consequence

Witsius. — It cannot be denied that the native signification of the words *baptein* and *baptizein* is to plunge; to dip. — *Hist. Ecc. p. 128.*

Gutlerus. — To baptize among the Greeks is undoubtedly to immerse; to dip; and baptism is immersion, dipping. — *Inst. Theol. ch. 33.*

Buddæus. — The words *baptizein* and *baptismos* are not to be interpreted of aspersion, but always of immersion. — *Theol. Dogmat.* b. iv. ch i. sec. 5.

Ewing, of Glasgow. — *Baptizo* in its primary and radical sense, I cover with water. It is used to denote, 1. I plunge or completely sink under water.

Leigh. — The native and proper signification of it [*baptizo*] is to dip into water; to plunge under water.

Bossuet. — To baptize signifies to plunge, as is granted by all the world.

Vossius. — *Bapto* and *baptizo* are rendered by *mergo* and *mergito* and *tingo*, yet they properly signify *mergo* (to immerse) and *tingo* (to dye) only by metalepsis; *i. e.*, as *tingo* implies *mergo*; as tinging follows an immersion, and is done by it.

Venema. — The word *baptizein*, to baptize, is nowhere used in the Scriptures for sprinkling. — *Vol.* v. p. 5.

Bloomfield. — There is here (Rom. vi. 4) plainly a reference to the ancient mode of baptizing by immersion; and I agree with Koppe and Rosenmuller, that there is reason to regret that it should have been abandoned in most Christian churches, especially as it has so evident a reference to the mystic sense of baptism.

Scholz — Baptism consists in the immersion of the whole body in water — *Com. Matt:* iii 6.

Augusti. — The word baptism, according to the etymology and usage, signifies to immerse, submerge, etc.; and the choice of the word betrays an age in which the later custom of sprinkling had not been introduced.

Dr. George Campbell. — Some words they [the translators] have transferred into their languages; others they have translated. But it would not always be easy to find a reason for this difference Thus the word *Peritomia* they have translated *circumcisio* which exactly corresponds in etymology but the word *baptisma* they have retained, changing only the letters from Greek to Roman. Yet the latter was just as susceptible of a literal version into Latin as the former. *Immersio tinctio* answers as exactly in the one case as *circumcisio* in the other.—*Prelim Dissert. viii, Part iii, Sec. 2.*

Neander — In respect to the form of baptism it was in conformity with the original institution and the original import of the symbol performed by immersion as a sign of entire baptism into the Holy Spirit; of being entirely penetrated by the same.—*Church Hist. Vol. I, p. 310.*

Dr. Charles Anthon — The primary meaning of the word is to dip, or immerse; and its secondary meanings, if it ever had any, all refer in some way or other to the same leading idea. Sprinkling, etc., are entirely out of the question.—*Letter to Dr. Parmly.*

Prof. Stewart, of Andover.—Bapto, baptizo mean to dip, plunge or immerse into any liquid. All lexicographers and critics of any note are agreed in this.—*Bib. Repos. 1833, p. 298.*

Dr. Chalmers—The original meaning of the word *baptisma* is immersion, and though we regard it a point of indifference whether the ordinances so named be performed in this way or by sprinkling, yet we doubt not the prevalent style of the administration in the apostle's days was by an actual submerging of the whole body under water.—*Lecture on Romans.*

Daniel Whitby—The observation of the Greek church is this, that he who ascended out of the water must first descend down into it; baptism therefore is to be performed not by sprinkling but by washing of the body. And indeed it can only be from ignorance of the Jewish rites in baptism that this is questioned; for they, to the due performance of this rite, so superstitiously required the immersion of the whole body in water that if any dirt hindered the water from coming to any part of it the baptism was not right; and if any one held the baptized by the arm when he was led down into the water, another must dip after him holding him by the other arm that was dipped before; because his hand would not suffer the water to come to his whole body.—*Com. Matt. iii: 16.*

Barrow—The action is baptizing or immersing in water.—*Works Vol. III, p. 45.*

Maldonatus—For in Greek to be baptized is the same as to be submerged.—*Com. on Gospels.*

Arnoldi—*Baptizein*, to immerse, to submerge. It was as being an entire submersion under water—since washings were already a confession of impurity—and a symbol of purification, the confession of entire impurity and a symbol of entire purification.—*Com. Matt iii: 16.*

Bishop Tayler—Straightway *Jesus went up out of the water* (saith the gospel). He came up, therefore He went down. Behold an immersion, not an aspersion! And the ancient churches following this example of the gospel did not in their baptism sprinkle water with their hands but immerged the catechumen or the infant.—*Rule of Conscience B. iii. chap. iv, Rule xv. 13.*

Towerson—As touching the outward and visible sign of baptism there is no doubt it was the element of water as is evident from the native signification of the word baptism, which signifies an immersion or dipping into some liquid.—*On Sacrament, p. 18.*

Conybeare and Howson—The ordinary use of *baptizein, baptisma, baptismos* in connection with the passages respecting baptism adduced in the text the clear testimonies of antiquity, and the present prevailing usage of the oriental churches puts it beyond all doubt, that entire or partial immersion was the general rule of Christian antiquity, from which certainly nothing but urgent outward circumstances caused a deviation. Respecting the form of baptism, therefore, (quite otherwise with the much more important difference respecting the subjects of baptism, or infant baptism) the impartial historian is compelled by exegesis and history substantially to yield the point to the Baptists, as is done in fact (perhaps somewhat too decidedly and without due regard to the arguments just stated for the other practice) by most German scholars *e. g. Neander Apostelgesh, 1. p. 276   Knapp Vorlesungen uber die Christliche Glaubenslehoe II p. 453; Hofling 1. C i. p 47 sqq.—Life St Paul 1. 471.*

Phil Schaff—Immersion and not sprinkling was unquestionably the original normal form. This is shown by the very meaning of the Greek words *baptizo, baptisma, baptismos*, used to designate the rite —*History Apostolic Church p 568.*

SECTION 3. *Testimony of the Classics.*—It must be apparent to every candid inquirer that the highest tribunal to which we can appeal in controversies concerning the meaning of words is the usage of the language to which they belong. It is asking too much of our credulity to admit without any evidence that Christ and His apostles used the word baptize in a sense in which no Greek writer before or afterwards used it.

The patient and careful labors of Dr. T. J. Conant, one of the most distinguished scholars of the present age has collected in a little volume which he calls "Baptizein" all the passages in which the word occurs in Greek literature from the earliest times down to the latest of the Christian Fathers who wrote in Greek. This work which can be had for a trifle is so arranged that the reader, though unacquainted with Greek, may fully appreciate the array of facts presented and judge of the meaning of the word from the connection as well as the reader of the original Greek.

A careful and impartial examination of these passages establishes the following facts:

1. No passage occurs in which the context requires it to be translated sprinkle or pour.

2. The Greater part of the examples necessarily involve the idea of immersion, either literally or figuratively.

3. No passage occurs in which the context is inconsistent with the idea of an immersion either literally or figuratively.

I present a few specimen quotations referring my readers to the work itself which is very accessible. My citations will be from writers near the time of Christ and His apostles.

Strabo (born about 60 years before Christ) Geography Book XII Ch. ii. 4. Speaking of the underground channel through which the waters of the Pyramus (a river of Cilicia in Asia Minor) force their way he says:

"And to one who hurls down a dart from above into the channel, the force of the water makes so much resistance, that it is hardly IMMERSED (baptized)."

The same work Book VI, Chap. ii, 9:

"And around Acragas [*Agrigentum in Sicily*] are marsh lakes, having the taste indeed of sea water, but a different nature, for even those who cannot swim are not IMMERSED (baptized), floating like pieces of wood."

The same work, Book XIV, Chap. iii, 9, speaking of the march of Alexander's army along the narrow beach (flooded in stormy weather) between the mountain called Climax and the Pamphillian sea, he says:

"Alexander happening to be there at the stormy season, and accustomed to trust for the most part to fortune, set forward before the swell subsided and they marched the whole day in water IMMERSED [baptized] as far as to the waist."

Diodorus Siculus, (who wrote his history about 60–30, before Christ) Historical Library Book XVI, Ch. 80, in his account of Timeleon's defeat of the

Carthagenian army on the bank of the river **Crimissus** in Sicily, many of the fugitives perishing in the stream, swollen by a violent storm, he says:

"The river rushing down with the current increased in violence SUBMERGED [baptized] many, and destroyed them attempting to swim through with their armor."

The same work, Book 1, Ch. 36, describing the effects of the rapid rise of the water during the annual inundation of the Nile, he says:

"Most of the wild land animals are surrounded by the stream and perish, being SUBMERGED [baptized] but some escaping to the high grounds are saved."

Josephus, (a Jewish writer, born in the year 37, after Christ) Jewish Antiquities Book XV, Ch. iii, 3, describing the murder of the boy Aristobulus, who (by Herod's command) was drowned by his companions in a swimming bath, he says:

"Continually pressing down, and IMMERSING [baptizing] him while swimming, as if in sport they did not desist until they had entirely suffocated him."

Plutarch, (born in the year 50, after Christ) **Life of Theseus XXIV**, quotes the following oracle of the Sybil respecting the city of Athens:

"A bladder, thou mayest be IMMERSED [baptized] but it is not possible for thee to sink."

Hippocrates, on epidemics, Book V: describing the respiration of a patient affected with inflammation and swelling of the throat (*cyanthe*) and oppression about the heart, he says:

"And she breathed as persons breathe after having been IMMERSED [baptized] and emitted a low sound from the chest like the so-called ventriloquists."

Strabo (born about 60 years before Christ) Book XII, 5, 4, speaking of the Lake Tatta in Phrygia, (which he calls a natural salt pit) he says:

"The water solidifies so readily around everything that is IMMERSED [baptized] into it that they draw up salt crowns when they let down a circle of rushes."

SECTION 4. *Testimony of Versions and the Usage of the Latin Fathers.*—1. The versions of the New Testament both ancient and modern, especially the former, afford important testimony upon this subject. These prove that when *baptizo* is translated and not transferred, the translators employ a word that signifies to immerse except in a few modern versions. They never translate it by sprinkle or pour.

I copy the following table from Campbell and Rice's Debate, page 120. It was prepared by Mr. Gotch, of Trinity College, Dublin:

TRANSLATIONS.

VERSION.	DATE.	WORD EMPLOYED.	MEANING.
Syriac..............			
Peschito............	2nd c'y	amad............	immerse......
Philoxenian	6th c'y.	amad	immerse ......
Arabic.............			
Polyglott.........	7th c'y.	amada 47 times..	immerse.
Propaganda.......	1671......	amada	immerse......
Sabat.............	1816	amada..........	immerse......
Persic.............	8th c'y	shustan shuyid n..	wash
Ethiopic...........	4th c'y.	shustan..........	immerse.......
Amharic..........	1822......	shustan	immerse......
Egyptian..........			
Coptic............	3rd c'y	tamaka..........	immerse, plunge.
Sahidic...........	2nd c'y. }	baptizo.........	immerse......
Basmuric.........	3rd c'y. }		
Armenian.........	5th c'y.	mogridil........	immerse ..
Sclavonic.........	9th c'y.	krestiti.........	cross........
Russian...........	579......)		
Polish............	1 85.....		
Bohemian.........	1593......		
Lithuanian........	1660......	same root........	cross........
Livonian..........)			
or .... }	1685......		
Lettish ....)			
Dorpat Eston an &c.	1827......)	daupjan.........	dip........
Gothic............	4 h c'y.		
German...........	1522......	taufen...........	dip........
Danish...........	1524......	dobe	dip........
Swedish..........	1534......	dopa............	dip........
Dutch, etc. etc. ..	1560......	doopen..........	dip........
Icelandic.........	1584......	skira............	cleanse ....
Anglo Saxon......	8th c'y.	dyppan fullian ..	dip, cleanse....
Latin.............			
Early Fathers.....	8th c'y	tingo............	immerse.....
Anti-Hieronym i n..	3 d c'y	baptizo..........	
Vulgate...........	4 h c'y	baptizo..........	
French............	15 5 ...	baptiser	
Spanish...........	1556 ..	baptizar.........	
Italian etc........	1562	baptizzare	
English, Wicklif..	1380	wash christen baptize....	
Tyndal............	1526 ..	baptize	
Welsh.............	1567	bedyddio	bathe........
Irish	1602	baisdim..........	
Gaelic.............	1650......	baisdeam.........	

2. The early Latin Fathers when they translate *baptizo* employ the word *tingo*, to immerse. The learned Grotius says: "Nor should we wonder that the old Latin Fathers use *tingere* for *baptizare* seeing the Latin word *tingo* does properly and generally signify the same thing as *mersare*, to immerse or plunge."

My leisure has not permitted me, nor do I think it at all necessary, to collate all the passages in the Latin Fathers where they employ *tingo* to translate *baptizo*.

The following passages taken at random will illustrate this usage:

Tertullian, De Baptismo Cap xviii, "If Philip baptized (*tinxit*) the eunuch on the spot, let us recollect it was done under the immediate direction of the Lord. * * * But Paul, you say, was baptized (*tinctus est*) immediately. True, because Simon, in whose house he was, instantly knew that he was a vessel of mercy."

Tertullian de Vel and Virg. Cap. ix, "It is not permitted to a woman in the church to speak nor to teach, nor to baptize (*tingere*)."

Tertullian de Prescript, adv. Heriticos, speaking of the devil who apes the service of God's house, says: "He also baptizes [*tingit*] some as his faithful and believing servants."

Tertullian, [advers. Prax.] Not once, but three times we are dipped [*tingimur*] at the naming of each Person.

Tertullian [Exhort. ad Castitc 7.] "When there is no assembly of the ecclesiastical order the priest, who is alone, may officiate there and baptize [*tingit*].

Cyprian, [A. D. 250]. "Those who are thus baptized [*tincti*] * * * when they come to us and unto the church, which is but one, they are to be baptized."

Caecilius. Bp. Billa in Mauritania in Concil.Carthage. A. D. 250. "I know no baptism but one, and that in the church only; none without the church. This is the only baptism where is true hope and certain faith. For thus it is written: "One Faith, one Hope, one Baptism," not among heretics where there is no hope and a false faith, where all things are done through falsehood; where * * * Antichrist baptizes [*tingit*] in the name of Christ."

Eusebius Emis. de Epiphan, Hom iii. "Although a man by the water of baptism seems to be the same in his outward person, yet within he is entirely changed * * * The person is baptized [*tingitur*] and the nature is changed."

The Apostolic Church.

Section 5. *Monumental Testimony.* I BAPTISTERIES.

1 *Baptistery of the church at St. Sophia.*—This was an immense and beautiful structure founded by Constantine the Great in Byzantium, (Constantinople) early in the fourth century, and adorned by his successors. In it Chrysostom preached and administered the rite to thousands The building surrounding it was so large that Councils were often held in it. In the center was the font supplied with water by means of pipes and sufficiently large for the immersion of numerous candidates following close upon each other.—*Robert Turnbull; Benedict's History Baptists, p. 209.*

2. *Baptistery at Pisa.*—This was built in the eleventh century. The font is quite capacious; from three to four feet deep and sufficiently wide to admit of the immersion of the largest persons.—*Ib.*

3. *Baptistery of the church of St. John de Lateran.*—It was built by Constantine the Great. It is an octagonal building. The baptismal font consists of an immense porphyry vase occupying a great part of the floor and "evidently intended for immersion," says Murray, in "Hand Book for Italy." Three steps lead down into it. Its depth is somewhat over three feet. "It was in this vase," says Murray, "that Rienzi bathed on the night of August 1347, the night before he appeared with his insignia of knighthood and summoned by Clement XII, and the electors of Germany to appear before them.—*Ib.*

4. *The Baptistery of Parma*—Adjoining the old gothic Cathedral at Parma is an antique baptistery probably of the eleventh century with a capacious font of marble in the center for immersion. Its depth is about four feet and its diameter five or six.—*Ib. 291.*

5. *Baptistery of S. Giovanni in fonte at Ravena.*—"The ancient baptistery, called also "S. Giovanni in fonte," now separated from the Cathedral by a street, is supposed to have been founded by St. Orso. It was repaired in 451 by the Archbishop Neo and dedicated to St. John the Baptist. It is like most of the baptisteries of the early Christians—an octagonal building. The interior has two circles each of eight arcades, the lower resting on eight columns with different capitals placed in each angle of the building; the upper are twenty four in number, dissimilar in form as in the capitals. The lower columns are considerably sunk, and both these are supposed to have belonged to some ancient temple. The cupola is adorned with well preserved mosaics of the fifth century, representing Christ baptized in Jordan, and in the circumference the twelve apostles with their ornaments. The grand vase which was formerly used for baptism by immersion is composed of Greek marble and porphyry. * * *

The ancient metal cross on the summit of the baptistery merits notice on account of its antiquity It bears an inscription recording that it was erected in 688 by Archbishop Theodorus."—*Murray's Hand Book for Italy.*

II. THE PRACTICE OF THE GREEK CHURCH.

Moses Stewart, of Andover, says:

'The mode of baptism by immersion, the Oriental Church has always continued to preserve even down to the present time. The members of this church are accustomed to call the members of the western churches *sprinkled* Christians by way of ridicule and contempt. They maintain that *baptizo* can mean nothing but immerge; and that baptism by sprinkling is as great a solecism as *immersion by aspersion.*"

Now it must be supposed that the Greeks themselves understood their own language, and when they exemplified the meaning of *baptizo* by the action of immersion they afford testimony of a very high order as to the import of the commandment. The gospel was preached to them by the apostles, the Scriptures of the New Testament were written in their language, and they understood immersion to be the thing commanded and practiced accordingly; and shall their understanding be gainsayed by men who rise up at this late day?

The modern Greek continues to bear the same testimony to-day that his ancestors have done for eighteen hundred years and more. And he uses *baptizo* to express the idea of an immersion though usually in a sacred sense. Nor can it be said that the present meaning attached to the word is due to a radical change in the language. Competent witnesses testify that there is a striking resemblance between the ancient and modern Greek. Indeed, this resemblance is so great that any one with only a knowledge of the ancient language can read a modern Greek author with as much ease as an Englishman can read Burns.

Prof. Sophocles, of Howard University, a native of Greece, says:

"The modern dialect is so intimately connected with the

ancient that a critical knowledge of the former without a corresponding knowledge of the latter is wholly out of the question. In fact a Greek's mastery of his native tongue is just in proportion to his acquaintance with ancient Greek."

Negris, a modern Greek by birth and education, and well versed in the ancient language says that the modern Greek "contains valuable remains of the ancient idiom which will throw light upon the sense of authors that often appears obscure, on account of the incorrect interpretation of words, the true signification of which is still retained in the modern language."

Rev. R. T. Buel, a learned missionary, who spent several years in Greece, says:

"So far as my own observation has extended, whether in Greece or in this country the striking resemblance between the ancient and modern Greek, have been the delight and surprise of all travelers of classical scholarship, who have visited Athens. The modern so far as it goes, has but few exceptions, the same vocabulary as the ancient, and that is the main thing constituting similarity between languages and dialects of the same language."

Dr. John A. Broadus says:

"Now, the Greek is not really a dead language: scholars in Germany, England and America are every day seeing this fact more clearly, and recognizing more freely its importance. I remember when at Athens a few years ago, a Scottish gentleman who spent most of his life in Greece, and had given very close attention to the language, told me of his own accord that although a Presbyterian, he thought the Baptists were quite right about the meaning of *baptizo;* and he hunted up a book in modern Greek on Natural Philosophy, in which I found the word repeatedly employed. The Greeks usually leave this as the sacred word and take other words for common actions. But this writer, in describing the mode of determining specific gravity, explained that we first weigh a body in air and then immerse it in water and weigh it thus, being suspended by a cord, and this action of immersion he constantly and naturally describes by *baptizo.*"

SECTION 6. *Scripture Usage.*—I propose to present only a brief statement of the argument under this head.

1. The practice of John the Baptist illustrates the meaning of the word. This is generally ad-

mitted to be immersion. But it is urged that John's baptism is not Christian baptism. It matters not so far as the action is concerned, whether it is or not. The evangelists employ the word *baptizo* to express the action he performed and if he immersed we have here an inspired interpretation, a conformity by the inspired writers to the classic usage of the word. That John immersed is evident not only from the word employed but from the places selected to perform the rite and the circumstances attending the performance. Mark says he baptized in the *river* Jordan, and the oldest and most authentic copies of Matthew, as Adam Clarke admits, have the same reading. He is represented as baptizing in Enon near Salem, because there was "much water there." Much water is not required for aspersion, nor do men go into rivers for its performance.

In the account of the baptism of Christ he is described as coming up straightway out of the water, and as the Greeks well say he could not come up out of the water without first having gone down into it.

2. That the practice of the disciples of Christ was the same as that of John, at least so far as the action of baptism is concerned, is evident from the use of the same, the word as descriptive of the act, without any intimation of a change of meaning. Indeed the numbers baptized by Christ and John are so contrasted as to leave no doubt that the same action was performed by each. In the eighth chapter of Acts we have a particular account of the baptism of the eunuch by Philip. As they journeyed and Philip expounded the Scriptures to him they came to a certain water. On the road they were traveling, from Jerusalem to Gaza, were many small streams, affording abundant water for immersion. It is said that they "went down both into the

water, both Philip and the eunuch, and he baptized him, and when they were come up out of the water the spirit of the Lord caught away Philip," &c. This description could only apply to an immersion.

3. The figurative allusions to baptism require the act of immersion. In Rom. vi: 3–5, and Col. ii: 12, it is compared to a burial and resurrection. The ablest commentators concede that the allusion is here to immersion.

Adam Clarke: "It is probable that the apostle here alludes to the mode of administering baptism by immersion."—*Com. Rom. vi: 4.*

Wesley: "*Buried with Him,*" &c., alluding to the ancient manner of baptizing by immersion."—*Notes Rom. vi: 3.*

Albert Barnes: "It is altogether probable that the apostle in this place had allusion to the custom of baptizing by immersion."—*Com Rom. vi: 4.*

Sam Clarke: In primitive times the manner of baptizing was by immersion or dipping the whole body into the water And this manner of doing it was a very significant emblem of the dying and resurrection referred to by St. Paul in the above mentioned similitude."—*Com. in loc.*

Doddridge: "It seems the part of candor to confess that here is an allusion to the manner of baptizing by immersion."—*Com. in loc*

Whitby: "It being so expressly declared here (Rom. vi: 4) and Col. ii: 12 that we are buried by Christ in baptism—by being buried under water and the argument too, obliges us to a conformity to His death, by dying to sin, being taken thence; and this immersion being religiously observed by all Christians for thirteen centuries, and approved by our church and the change of it into sprinkling even without any allowances from the author of the institution, or any license from any council of the church, being that which the Romanist still urgeth to justify his refusal of the cup to the laity, it were to be wished that this custom might be again of general use; and aspersion only permitted as of old as in the case of clinics or in present danger of death."

This figurative application of the emblem furnishes the only satisfactory explanation of 1 Cor. xv: 29: "Else what shall they do which are baptized for the dead if the dead rise not at all? Why are they baptized for the dead!" Paul was enforcing the doctrine of the resurrection of the dead, and his argument is that there would be no significancy in baptism if there were no resurrection. Why are they buried in baptism to represent that they are dead to sin, and raised again to walk in newness of life, if the buried dead rise no more? If the dead rise not the emblem has no application.

4. In the last place I propose to consider briefly some of the objections urged by anti-Baptists.

(1). It is said that there "went out to him Jerusalem and all Judea and all the region round about Jordan and were baptized of him in Jordan, confessing their sins," and that such multitudes could not have been immersed. But even if it could be demonstrated that the entire population of these regions were baptized, who shall say that in the whole course of his ministry he could not have immersed every man, woman and child in Jerusalem and all Judea, and all the region round about Jordan, for the declaration does not confine the action to a particular day, month or year. But the truth is, if immersion were impossible, aspersion was also, for it takes just as long to sprinkle or pour a subject, including the formula which occupies the principal time, as to immerse him; unless we adopt the shrewd conjecture of some ingenious aspersionist that John employed a *squirt* or some such instrument by which he sprinkled the whole multitude at once. But how could he be sure that the scattered drops fell upon every individual that ought to have received them, and none of them upon the scoffing Pharisees and Sadducees whom he denounced as a generation of vipers, is more than I can conjecture. But does the evangelist mean that every individual was baptized? Clearly not, for he tells us that the baptized confessed their sins. There could have therefore been no infants in the number, for they could not confess. But he required repentance in connection with his baptism, and indeed confession implies previous repentance, but as all did not repent all were not baptized. To many of the Pharisees and Sadducees who came to his baptism, he said: "O generation of vipers, who hath warned you to flee from the wrath to come? Bring forth therefore fruits meet for repentance." (Matt. iii: 7-8.

But in truth the writer employs a figure of speech called Synecdoche, common to all languages, by which the whole is put for a part, and he means only to say that large numbers resorted to the baptism of John from the countries named.

(2). The figurative baptisms of the New Testament it is said, are not immersions but aspersions. The Holy Ghost is "poured out" and "shed forth" and this they say is the baptism of the Holy Ghost. But if the pouring out of the Spirit were expressly called a baptism of the Holy Ghost (no instance of which can be found) it is not in accordance with the principles of sound criticism to determine the literal meaning of a word by its figurative usage but *vice versa.* The very idea of a trope involves the *turning* (*tropeo*—to turn) of the word from its common literal usage, or rather applying the literal idea to a conception of the mind, rather than to a physical fact. The force of the figure consists in the resemblance between the two things thus compared. The literal sense gives all the force that the figurative has. The baptism of the Holy Ghost is the conception of one so thoroughly pervaded by the influence of the Holy Spirit as to resemble one immersed in water. How is the force of this figure weakened by conceiving of it as a mere aspersion in which the man is only partially under the influence of the spirit! The same is true of the baptism of fire. Whether we refer this to the fire of hell, or the fiery persecutions of the church it was no mere sprinkling but a fearful overwhelming—an entire immersion. So the blessed Saviour speaks of His coming sorrows as a baptism. Whoever forms a just conception of His agony when He sweat as it were great drops of blood, can easily recognize an immersion in sorrows.

It is said that Christ referring to the events of the day of Pentecost told the disciples they should be "baptized with the Holy Ghost not many days hence;" and that the Holy Ghost is said to have been poured out on the occasion. So it is also said that they were *filled* with the Holy Ghost. The coming of the Spirit is represented like the sound of a rushing mighty wind, and it filled the whole house, where they were sitting. Here are two immersions spoken of. It is true that the prophet describing the scene says the spirit was poured out, but the pouring is nowhere called a baptism, and forms no more a part of it than the preparations on a baptismal occasion constitute a part of the baptism.

(3). It is objected that three thousand could not have been immersed on the day of Pentecost, for want of time and the insufficiency of water. This takes for granted three things, that it takes longer to immerse a subject than to sprinkle one, that the whole were baptized in one day, and that Peter was the only administrator. As already remarked it takes no longer to immerse one than to sprinkle him. And it is not certain that they were all baptized in one day. It is said that they that believed were baptized, but when? But "the same day there were added about three thousand souls." True, but *tee heemera ekeinee* (that day) often refers to a period of time as in John xvi: 23--26, and *prosetetheesan* (added too) also means to *agree with,* and may refer to the number who were convinced. As to the want of water this objection could only have originated in ignorance of the facts. There were a great many pools amply sufficient for the purpose. We read 2 Kings xviii: 19 of the "Upper Pool;" 2 Kings xx: 20 of the "Pool of Hezekiah;" Isaiah xxii: 9 of the waters of the "Lower Pool;" John v: 2 of the "Pool of Bethesda;" John ix: 7 of the "Pool of Siloam;" &c., &c.

Robinson says:

"There are on the north side of the city outside of the walls two very large reservoirs, one of which is three hundred feet long and more than two hundred feet wide, and the other nearly six hundred feet long by over two hundred and fifty feet wide." He also mentions the pool of Siloam and two others outside of the walls. Within the walls he mentions the pool of Bathsheba, the pool of Hezekiah, and the pool of Bethesda. The pool of Hezekiah was, he says, two hundred and forty feet long by one hundred and forty four feet broad, and the pool of Bethesda three hundred and sixty feet long by one hundred and thirty wide."—*Robinson's Researches in Palestine, pp. 480 to 516.*

Surely here was water enough to satisfy the staunchest Baptist.

As to the administrators, upon what authority is it assumed that Peter alone did the baptizing? This is simply a question of arithmetic. If the whole number of disciples (one hundred and twenty) officiated there were just twenty-five apiece, and they could have baptized them in less than twenty-five minutes. But there were in the number eighty-two ordained ministers, and the number to be baptized less than thirty-seven apiece, and the baptism could have been performed in as many minutes without any hurry. I once witnessed as many baptized in fifteen minutes by an old, feeble man. If the twelve only baptized they could have performed the service in four hours and two minutes, allowing one to the minute.

Peter began to preach at the third hour, or nine o'clock A. M. Allowing three hours to be occupied by Peter in preaching, &c., six hours remained until night. If the one hundred and twenty baptized there was fifteen minutes to each candidate; if the eighty-two, ten minutes to each; if only the twelve at two hundred and fifty apiece nearly one and a half minutes to each.

But there are other historical parallels to the baptism on the day of Pentecost. On the great Sabbath of the Easter festival April 16th, 404, Chrysostom with the assistance of the clergy of his own church baptized by immersion three thousand.—*Neander, Vit. Chrysostom, Vol. 2, 325.—Augusti. Ec. Antiq. Vol. 2. 207.*

Remegius, Bishop of Rheims, in one day baptized Clovis, the French King and three thousand of his subjects, and as to the mode the early writers place it beyond question by saying that the bishop raised the king up out of the water. This was in 496.

Otho in the 12th century is said to have baptized in a single day about four thousand.

(4). It is urged that the Philippian jailer, (Acts xvi: 23–35) could not have been immersed. I answer that the facts detailed must exclude every reasonable presumption of immersion before it can be assumed that the immersion was impossible. If they were cast into the "inner prison" they were also brought "without" ($exoo$). V. 32, shows that he carried them from the prison into his house, for otherwise they could not have preached the word to all that were in his house. Verse 33, *And he took them* (*paralaboon autous*) taking them along, implies a change of place. He evidently took them out of the house for in the next verse we read "when he brought them into the house." If they had never gone out of the house there would have been no propriety in saying "when he brought them into it." But what occurred in the meantime before they were brought in? He *washed* their stripes. This occurred out of doors. *Elousen* translated *washed*, says Robinson, signifies to wash the whole body, not merely a part of it like *niptoo*. Trench makes the same distinction. If they found water enough to wash the entire bodies of Paul and Silas they found water enough to baptize the jailer and his family, which they did straightway.

It is merely captious to talk of the want of water for the purpose of immersion. The facilities for furnishing a considerable city with water for daily use would necessarily supply it in quantities for immersion. The river Gaugas flowed by the city—to which reference is made in verse 13—beside baths were necessary appurtenances to ancient houses. So says Griesbach, Rosenmuller and Kuinoel. There were also many public baths. In Rome there were eight hundred.—*Adams' Antiq. p. 480.*

(5). The baptism of Paul is urged by the opponents of immersion. (Acts ix: 18) "And he arose and was baptized." One criticism renders the participle *anastas* (arose) *standing*, as if he were baptized standing. It is a sufficient answer to this that *anastas* is a past not a present participle. Besides, if *anastas* means standing then Lot's daughter laid down standing, for the same word is used Gen. xix: 35. It would immortalize some zealous artist to represent Lot's daughter in that upright recumbent posture!!

But this construction is a very common one and *anastas* does not limit the subsequent action further than to express that the subject begins to do what follows.

(6). "Baptized unto Moses in the cloud and in the sea." (1 Cor. x: 2) furnishes nothing contrary to immersion. The objectors say they were sprinkled by the spray of the sea and rain drops from the cloud. Do the facts of history justify this conclusion. The waters stood up on either side and the

Israelites passed over dry shod. Then there was no spray. The cloud was not a rain cloud, and therefore there could have been no rain drops. But the walls of water on either side and the cloud above entirely concealing them was a complete immersion.

CHAPTER XII.

BAPTISM—THE PROPER SUBJECT.

The Scriptural subject of baptism is a believer, and none others may be admitted to this rite. In discussing the qualifications for church membership, I necessarily touched upon this question, and the same reasons apply with equal force here. The very nature and design of baptism preclude any other than believers. Unconscious infants cannot assume the personal vows which baptism imports; and unregenerate sinners will not sincerely do so. Baptism is said to be an outward sign of an inward grace, but if the grace is wanting there is no sufficiency in the outward sign. It declares a thing to exist which does not exist. If baptism is a ceremonial cleansing, typical of a real moral cleansing, in the absence of the latter, it is a false type. If it is a symbol of our death to sin and our resurrection to walk in newness of life without this radical change, it is a shadow without a substance to reflect it. Hence all the precepts of the gospel requiring baptism are associated with faith. "He that believeth and is baptized;" "Make disciples of all nations, baptizing them;" "Repent, and be baptized;" "See, here is water, what doth hinder me to be baptized?" "If thou believest with all thy heart, thou mayest;" "As many as believed were baptized." These are the expressions of the Scriptures. But there are those who think that believing parents and their infant children are proper subjects and this leads me to consider

INFANT BAPTISM.

SECTION 1. *Infant Baptism is not an institution of Christ and His Apostles.*—Eminent pedobaptists admit that there is no positive precept or plain example of it in the New Testament, and the reasons for it are so various and conflicting that the advocates of each theory successfully overthrow all the rest and leave the institution without a foundation. So in those passages of the New Testament which are claimed as supporting infant baptism, their commentators are at variance, and mutually overthrow each other. No single passage is agreed upon by all as referring to infant baptism.

I will not encumber these pages with the usual quotations to prove what I have stated above, as those admissions have long been before the public and are accessible. But I cannot resist the following extract from the Southern Methodist Review, for April 1874, in an able article from the learned editor, A. T. Bledsoe, LL. D.:

"It is an article of our faith, that the baptism of young children (infants) is in any wise to be retained in the church, *as most agreeable to the institution of Christ*. But yet with all our searchings we have been unable to find, in the New Testament, a single express declaration or word, in favor of infant baptism. We justify the rite, therefore, solely on the ground of logical inference, and not on any express word of Christ or His apostles. This may, perhaps, be deemed by some of our readers, a strange position for a pedobaptist. It is by no means, however, a singular opinion. Hundreds of learned pedobaptists have come to the same conclusion; especially since the New Testament has been subjected to a closer, more conscientious and more candid exegesis than was formerly practiced by controversialists.

In Knapp's Theology, for example it is said: "There is no decisive example of this practice, in the New Testament; for it may be objected against those passages where the baptism of whole families is mentioned, viz: Acts x: 42–48; xvi: 15–33; 1 Cor. i: 16, that it is doubtful whether there were any children in these families, and if there were, whether they were then baptized. From the passage, Matt. xxviii: 19, it does not necessarily follow that Christ commanded infant baptism (the *matheteuein* is neither for nor against) nor does this follow any more from John iii: 5, and Mark x: 14–16. There is, therefore, no express command for infant baptism found in the New Testament as Morus (p. 215, § 12) justly concedes" (Vol. II, p. 524.)

Dr. Jacobs also says

"However reasonably we may be convinced that we find in the Christian Scriptures 'the fundamental idea from which infant baptism was afterward developed,' and by which it may now be justified, *it ought to be distinctly acknowledged, that it is not an apostolic orainanee"* (p 271).

In like manner, or to the same effect, Neander says:

"Originally, baptism was administered to adults, nor is the general spread of infant baptism, at a later period any proof to the contrary; for' even after infant baptism has been set forth as an apostolic institution, its introduction into the general practice of the church was but slow. Had it rested on apostolic authority, there would have been a difficulty in explaining its approval, and that even in the third century it was opposed by at least one eminent father in the church." (p. 229). We quote this passage not because its logic does, in any respect, carry conviction to our minds, but simply to show how completely Neander concedes the point, that infant baptism is not an apostolic ordinance. We might, if necessary, adduce the admission of many other profoundly learned pedobaptists, that their doctrine is not found in the New Testament, either in express terms, or by implication from any portion of its language."

That we may see the justice of these strong admissions I propose to examine the passages, commonly supposed by pedobaptists to refer to infant baptism:

1. Children were brought to Christ, and when His disciples would have sent them away, He said: "Suffer little children to come unto me, and forbid them not, for of such is the kingdom of heaven;" and some have supposed here was an allusion to infant baptism. But it may be answered: (1) They were not brought to be baptized but to be blest. (2) They were not baptized by Him. (3) "Of such" does not mean that the church is composed of children; for that would exclude all others. It means that the kingdom of heaven is composed of persons like these. He elsewhere illustrates this idea by saying: "Except ye be converted and become as little children, ye shall in no wise enter the kingdom of heaven." (4) If this passage proves infant

baptism at all, it proves too much for pedobaptists—for children in general are spoken of and not the children of believing parents.

2. Some derive infant baptism from the commission (Matt. xxviii: 19) "Make disciples of all nations, baptizing them, &c., teaching them, &c." "Make disciples by baptizing and teaching them," N. L. Rice. (1) If this be the proper construction, the same process must be followed with adults and this is exactly what St Xavier did when he assembled the Indians and with a squirt sprinkled holy water upon a whole tribe at once. (2) It is a sufficient answer to this lame criticism that in Greek, instrumentality is expressed by the dative case, not by the nominative which is employed here. (3) The proper construction is: Go make disciples out of all nations, baptizing them (the disciples.) But who are disciples? He tells us: "Whosoever doth not bear his cross and come after me, he cannot be my disciple." It requires a voluntary consecration to His service to constitute one a disciple: "Herein is my Father glorified that ye bring forth much fruit: so shall ye be my disciples." (John xv: 18.)

The word disciple (*matheetees*) is used in the New Testament two hundred and sixty-four times always in reference to adults—never in reference to unconscious infants.

3. "The promise is unto you and your children, &c." (Acts ii: 37.) (1) What promise? Not of baptism, but of the Holy Spirit, as is plainly seen by the preceding verse: "Repent and be baptized every one of you, in the name of the Lord Jesus Christ, for the remission of sins; and ye shall receive the gift of the Holy Ghost. For the promise, &c." The promise itself had already been quoted by Peter from the prophet Joel, and that was the promise of the Holy Spirit. Whitby says:

"These words will not prove a right of infants to receive

baptism; the promise here mentioned being only of the Holy Ghost, mentioned 16–18 and so relating only to the times of the miraculous affusion of the Holy Ghost, and to those who by age were made capable of these extraordinary gifts."

(2). Peter says the promise is to you (the Jews whom he addressed and whom he had just exhorted to repent,) and to your children (the children of you Jews who hear me). Were all those Jews and their children entitled to baptism, in need of repentance as they were?

(3). The promise was equally to all that are afar off—to the Gentiles, as the commentators agree. If this authorized the baptism of children it also authorized the baptism of ALL the Gentiles.

(4). The term "children" does not mean infants, but descendants. It is often thus used particularly in the Scriptures.

(5). But the promise is limited to "even as many as the Lord your God shall call." The passage cannot be fairly construed without this limitation, but with it the passage teaches that the blessings of God's grace are bestowed upon His elect, and if baptism is included in the promise then it is the baptism of the called—believers.

4. Household baptisms are referred to as proofs of infant baptism; especially does Lydia figure in this argument. We will therefore consider her case. To obtain infant baptism out of this, five things must be proven: (1). That Lydia was a married woman; (2). That she had children; (3). That they were infant children; (4). That they were with her at Philippi; (5). That they were baptized in the faith of their mother. Was Lydia a married woman? The pedobaptist replies yes, because she had a household. But the proof fails in this, that many households are presided over by maiden ladies. The proof fails on the second and third points because there are many households without any children; and still more without infant chil-

dren. As the term household may only include servants, the proof fails to show that her children, if she had any, were at Philippi; and lastly, the proof that the household was baptized is not proof that they were baptized on the faith of Lydia. They may have been baptized on their own faith.

5. The favorite theory of many pedobaptists is that the children of Christian parents are in some sense holy, and that on this account they ought to be baptized. And they adduce as a proof text 1 Cor. vii: 14: "For the unbelieving husband is sanctified by the wife, and the unbelieving wife is sanctified by the husband, else were your children unclean but now are they holy."

But the passage proves too much for those who invoke it.

(1). The terms "holy" (*hagia*) applied to the children, and "sanctified" (*heegiastai*) used in reference to the unbelieving husband and wife, are from the same root, the former being the adjective, and the latter the verbal form; and they both convey the same idea. Whatever fitness for baptism therefore, the children possessed, the parents also possessed, though unbelieving.

(2). These terms signify that they are either *morally* or *legally pure*. If the relation of children to believing parents renders them pure in either sense then, the relation of an unbelieving husband or wife to a believer accomplishes the same result. It cannot be that the children of believing parents are morally pure, because that is contrary to the teaching of the Scriptures in regard to natural depravity. The spiritual condition of the children of believers is the same as those of unbelievers. The children of Christians are not born Christians. Like others they are conceived in sin and brought forth in iniquity. David, who was born of pious parents says this of himself. Spiritual life is not transmitted by natural descent. "That which is born of the flesh is flesh." And if the child is morally depraved much more the adult unbeliever who has added years of actual sin to his natural depravity. The apostle, therefore, cannot mean that they are morally clean by virtue of this relationship and the purity or cleanness, which he means to express by the terms "holy" and "sanctified," is of a legal or ceremonial kind.

(5). And this leads us to inquire in the last place what kind of *cleanness* he means. If we consider the subject of the apostle's discourse we will see that he is discussing not the relation of parents and children to the church, but to each other. The question raised is whether a believer and an unbeliever may live in the relationship of marriage and this gives us a clue to the meaning of the words holy and sanctified. The apostle decides that the relation is a lawful one. A believing wife or husband is not bound to put away an unbelieving companion any more than believing parents are required to put away their unbelieving children. The relationship is as lawful in one case as in the other. If the unbeliever is unclean (*unlawful*) to his believing companion equally so are your children —*your*, not *their*—unclean (*unlawful*) to you and you may no longer continue the association. But as the children are recognized by all as lawful, so the marriage must be lawful.

SECTION 2. *We cannot find the original of Infant Baptism in the Old Testament Dispensation.*—I. Baptism is not a substitute for circumcision.

1. If this could be shown it does not prove infant baptism. None were circumcised until after they were *born*. So none should be baptized until they are spiritually born. As circumcision was administered of right only to the natural seed of Abraham, so baptism should be administered only

to his spiritual seed. Paul tells us: "If ye be Christ's then are ye Abraham's seed and heirs according to the promise." (Gal. iii. 29). "Those who are of faith, they are the children of Abraham." (Gal. iii: 7).

2. But circumcision bears no resemblance to baptism. (1). Only males were circumcised. (2). Infant males were circumcised the eighth day. (3). Adult males circumcised themselves, while infant males were circumcised by their parents. (4). The infant and adult servants were circumcised as property. (5). It was not an initiatory rite. (6). The qualifications for it were flesh and property—not faith. (7). It was not a dedicatory rite. (8). Circumcision required no moral qualification. (9). It was a visible appreciable sign. (10). The right of a child to circumcision did not depend upon the faith, piety or morality of the parents. (11). It was the guaranty of certain temporal blessings. (12). It was not to be performed in the name of God or any other being. (13). The subject of circumcision was debtor to do the whole law. (14). No sponsors were required in circumcision, as pedobaptists require in baptizing infants.

3. It could not have been understood by the apostles to come in the room of circumcision, because (1) they baptized Jewish converts who had been circumcised. (2) Jewish Christians continued to circumcise their children. (Acts xxi). (3) Paul, to satisfy the Jews, even circumcised Timothy, who had already been baptized. (4) A dispute arose about circumcising Gentile converts, which could not have taken place if it had been understood that baptism came in the room of circumcision. (Acts xv).

II. But it is urged that the church was the same under both dispensations and that the covenant confers upon the children of Christians the same privileges which were accorded to the children of the Jews. I will in a subsequent chapter discuss the identity of the church under both dispensations. At present, I will only inquire whether the children of Christian parents sustain the same relation to the Christian church that the children of Jews did to the Jewish institution.

1. The Christian church is a spiritual institution; but the spiritual condition of the children of believers is the same as others. Spiritual life is not transmitted by natural descent. That which is born of the flesh is flesh. They are conceived in sin and brought forth in iniquity even as others. But not so with the Jew. His child was a Jew by birth. He sustained a different relation to the law from the Gentile child. He was not circumcised to make him a Jew, but because he was a Jew.

2. In the Jewish child was that of which circumcision could be the outward sign and seal. He was really a Jew and only needed the outward sign as the proof and seal of his rights and privileges. But there is no inward grace in the child of a believer of which baptism may become the sign and seal, and if they have not this grace it is wrong to say so by the outward sign. It is like labeling a casket "PEARLS" when there are no pearls in it, and Christ could never tolerate such a misrepresentation.

3. But it is urged that God by covenant has conferred upon the children of believers the legal fitness to be admitted to church membership by baptism. This is what is meant by *federal holiness*. Federal is from the Latin *foedus*, covenant, and federal holiness is covenanted holiness. By holiness the advocates of this doctrine do not mean moral purity but legal fitness.

But where is the covenant that secures this privilege to the children of believers? We are referred to Gen. xvii: 4-14: "As for me, behold my covenant is with thee, and thou shalt be the father of many nations. Neither shall thy name any longer be called Abram, but thy name shall be Abraham, for a father of many nations have I made thee. And I will make thee exceeding fruitful, and I will make nations of thee, and kings shall come out of thee. And I will establish my covenant between me and thee and thy seed after thee, in their generations for an everlasting covenant, to be a God unto thee and to thy seed after thee. And I will give unto thee and thy seed after thee the land wherein thou art a stranger, all the land of Canaan, for an everlasting possession, and I will be their God. And God said unto Abraham: Thou shalt keep my covenant therefore, thou and thy seed after thee in their generations. This is my covenant which ye shall keep between me and thee and thy seed after thee. Every man child among you shall be circumcised, and ye shall circumcise the flesh of your foreskin, and it shall be a token of the covenant betwixt me and thee. And he that is eight days old shall be circumcised among you, every man child in your generations, he that is born in the house, or bought with money of the stranger, which is not thy seed. He that is born in thy house, and he that is bought with thy money must needs be circumcised, and my covenant shall be in your flesh for an everlasting covenant. And the uncircumcised man child whose flesh of his foreskin is not circumcised that soul shall be cut off from my people, he hath broken my covenant."

Here we certainly find liberal promises made to Abraham and to his natural descendants, and an injunction to circumcise his children. But I am not a Jew and my children are not the children of Abraham, and circumcision is not baptism. By fair interpretation the unbelieving Jew was entitled —nay, it was his duty to have his child circumcised; so that if this covenant entitles children to baptism it is not the exclusive privilege of believers.

If it should be said that this covenant is a covenant of grace and also includes the spiritual seed of Abraham, then only his spiritual seed are entitled to the benefits of this extension. But who are his spiritual seed? Those that believe "That he might be the father of all them that believe." "Therefore, it is of faith, that it may be by grace, to the end that the promise might be sure to all the seed; not to that only which is of the law, but to that also which is of the faith of Abraham who is the father of us all."

The widest interpretation of this covenant is that temporal blessings were promised to the natural seed, and spiritual blessings to the spiritual seed of Abraham. But the children of Gentile Christians are not the natural seed of Abraham, nor yet his spiritual seed until they believe, and are therefore not in the terms of the covenant.

SECTION 3. *Historical View.*—I propose briefly to examine the question of Infant Baptism historically and inquire what evidence of it exists in the early ages of the church. If such a practice existed certainly some traces of it can be found.

1. *Proselyte Baptism.*—Dr. Wall in his History of Infant Baptism, and Dr. Lightfoot, eminent defenders of the rite, rely mainly upon this custom of the Jews to prove the origin of infant baptism. It is said that there existed long before Christ, a custom among the Jews to baptize proselytes. When one from the heathen wished to profess the Jewish religion, if a male he was initiated by circumcision, immersion and bringing a sacrifice; if a female by immersion and bringing a sacrifice. The rule in relation to infants was: "Any male child of such a proselyte, that was under thirteen years and a day, and females that were under twelve years and a

day, they baptized as infants at the **request and by the assent of the father;** or the authority of the court, because such a one was not yet the son of assent, as they phrase it, *i. e.*, not capable to give assent for himself, but the thing is for his good. If they were above that age they consented for themselves."

It is urged that this custom prevailed and was well understood in the times of John the Baptist and Christ, and explains the law of baptism; that when the command was given to baptize, it could not be understood otherwise than to include infants. It is not pretended that this custom had its origin in divine authority, and Christ has nowhere adopted it as the rule in Christian baptism. But so far from this tradition being the origin of baptism, as practiced by John and perpetuated by Christ and His disciples, it bore no resemblance to it except in the act of immersion. Certainly John never practiced it, for he baptized only Jews, who were not the subjects of proselyte baptism. Christ and His disciples, until long after His ascension, baptized only Jews, who could not be lawfully baptized by the law of proselytes. So far then from confirming and adopting this custom, they constantly and repeatedly violated it.

If the custom without any express command authorized infant baptism it equally authorized adult baptism, and no command was necessary to baptize any. "And why should we construe the law by this custom to favor infant baptism only? We should take the whole custom or none. Why then baptize children of baptized parents, or whose ancestors had been baptized, seeing that this custom of the Jews positively forbids their baptism? And why dispense with the sacrifice required of male and female? Surely these were as much parts of the custom, as sacred and obligatory as that of the baptism of infants."—*Waller's Hist. Inf. Bap.*, *p. 17*

But there is no proof that such a custom existed until long after Christ. This is admitted by Moses Stewart, in his work on Baptism. He says:

"In fine, we are destitute of any early testimony to the practice of proselyte baptism antecedently to the Christian era. The original institution of admitting Jews to the covenant and strangers to the same, prescribed no other rite than that of circumcision. No account of any other is found in the Old Testament; none in the Apochrypha, New Testament, Targums of Onkelos, Jonathan, Joseph the Blind, or in the work of any other Targumist, except Pseudo-Johnathan, whose work belongs to the seventh or eighth century. No evidence is found in Philo, Josephus, or any of the early Christian writers. How could an allusion to such a rite have escaped them if it were as common and as much required by usage as circumcision." (p. 69.)

2. *Catechumens.*—Mosheim says:

"In the earliest times of the church, all who professed to believe that Jesus was the only redeemer of the world, and who in consequence of this profession, promised to live in a manner conformable to the purity of His holy religion, were immediately received among the disciples of Christ. This was all the preparation for baptism then required, and a more accurate instruction in the doctrines of Christianity was to be administered to them after their reception of this sacrament. But when Christianity had acquired more consistence, and churches rose to the true God and His eternal Son almost in every nation, this custom was changed for the wisest and most solid reasons. Then baptism was administered to none but such as had been previously instructed in the principal points of Christianity, and had also given satisfactory proofs of pious dispositions and upright intentions. Hence arose the distinction between *catechumens* who were in a state of probation and under the instruction of persons appointed for that purpose, and *believers* who were consecrated by baptism and thus initiated into all the mysteries of the Christian faith."—*Ec. Hist*, b. 1, Part II, Ch. iii, Sec. 5.

This institution began very near the times of the apostles, and continued until the beginning of the fifth century. Its decline marks the triumph of Infant Baptism. As long as it was practiced it effectually excluded Infant Baptism, for the two could not exist at the same time.

3. *The Apostolic Fathers.*—These embrace those Christian writers who were cotemporary with the

apostles, and wrote in the age immediately succeeding them. They were Barnabas, Hermas, Clement, of Rome, Ignatius and Polycarp; to whom some add Papias. We find in their writings the same silence on the subject of Infant Baptism that is found in the Scriptures. Had the rite existed it could hardly have escaped mention, especially as they enforce the duty of parents to bring up their children in the nurture and admonition of the Lord; or as Clement, of Rome, expresses it, "bred up in the instruction of Christ."—[Ep. I ad Cor. x: 12.

Says Barnabas:

"Thou shalt not withdraw thy hand from thy son or thy daughter, but teach them from their youth the fear of the Lord."—*Barnab. Ch. xiv: 12.*

They usually couple faith and baptism. Clement mentions baptism but once, and that in his second epistle to the Corinthians, sec. 6: "If we do not keep the baptism pure and undefiled, with what confidence shall we enter the kingdom of God."

Says Barnabas:

"Consider how He has joined both the cross and the water together. For He saith: 'Blessed are they who put their trust in the cross and descend into the water.' * * * We go down into the water full of sins and pollutions, but come up again bringing forth fruit, having in our hearts the fear and hope which is in Jesus by the Spirit."—*Barnabas, Ch. x*

Hermas, Vision III, 27, describing the church under the figure of a tower built upon the water says, alluding to baptism:

"As for those stones which were drawn out of the deep, they put them all into the building; for they were polished and their squares exactly answered one another, and so one was joined in such wise to the other that there was no space to be seen where they joined insomuch that the whole tower appeared to be built as it were of one stone"

Ignatius says: "Let your baptism continue as a shield, faith as a helmet, love as a spear." Polycarp and Papias make no allusion to baptism.

4. Later Fathers.—1. JUSTIN MARTYR, A. D. 150,

gives the following account of baptism as practiced in his day:

"As many as are persuaded and believe what we teach is true, and undertake to conform their lives to our doctrine, are instructed to fast and pray, and entreat from God the remission of their past sins, we fasting and praying together with them. They are then conducted by us to a place where there is water and are regenerated in the same manner in which we ourselves were regenerated, for they are then washed in the name of God the Father, and Lord of the universe and of our Saviour Jesus Christ, and of the Holy Spirit."(sec. 79)

The following passage used to be quoted from this Father in favor of infant baptism, but modern critics have confessed that it affords no support to it:

"Many men and many women, sixty and seventy years old, who from children have been disciples of Christ, preserve their continence. (Apol. I. Sec. 18.)

All that Justin Martyr affirms in this passage is that he knew many persons who had been disciples from early life, and he elsewhere connects choice and knowledge with baptism of which infants are incapable. But as it was the duty of parents to instruct their children in the truths of religion, it does not follow that because they were thus instructed that they were baptized. If Justin used the word "disciples" in its higher sense he meant those who were Christians by personal faith, but if he used it only in the sense of learners in Christ, then it does not follow that they had been baptized; for the catechumens, whatever their age, might properly be called disciples or learners of Christ.

(2.) *Irenaeus* (A. D., 177–202) is often quoted by pedobaptists: though this passage is also now abandoned by their best critics. These are his words: " He came to save all persons by himself; all I say, who are regenerated [*qui renascuntur*] by Him unto God—infants, and children and boys, and young men and old men." Mosheim and Neander find no infant baptism in this. Hagenbach, a

German pedobaptist, says that this language of *Irenaeus:* "Merely expresses a beautiful idea, that Jesus was redeemer *in* every stage of life and *for* every stage of life: but does not say He became a redeemer for children by water baptism." Those who are saved in infancy must be regenerated; for "except a man (Gr. *tis*—any one) is born again [regenerated] he cannot see the kingdom of God." The idea of Irenaeus seems to be that Christ assumed the different stages of human life, in order that he might represent each in the great work of atonement. Pedobaptists to get infant baptism out of this passage assume that Irenaeus believed that regeneration is effected by baptism and that he uses *renascor* as the synonym of *baptizo* which is assuming more than can be proven.

(3.) *Clement of Alexandria*—(A. D., 190,) says: "The baptized ought to be children in malice—but not in understanding; even such children, who as the children of God, have put off the old man, with the garments of wickedness, and have put on the new mind."

(4.) *Dyonisius of Alexandria*, (A. D., 247,) writing to Sixtus, Bishop of Rome, testifies that it was their custom to baptize upon a profession of faith.

(5.) *Tertullian*, (A. D., 216,) makes the first certain mention of infant baptism when he appears as the zealous opponent of the practice which is proof that it had just then began to be practiced in Africa where he lived. Eminent scholars, however, even among pedobaptists are of the opinion that Tertullian does not refer to infant baptism—but to child baptism. Of this number is the learned Chevelier Bunsen, Christianity and Mankind vol. 2, p. 115.

Parvulos is the word Tertullian uses and it is, to say the least, susceptible of the translation given it by Bunsen. The following is the passage: "It is therefore most expedient to defer baptism and to regulate the administration of it according to the condition, the disposition and the age of the person to be baptized; and especially in the case of children (parvulos.) * * * Let them come when they are grown, let them come and learn; let them be instructed whither they are coming, and when they know Christ let them profess themselves Christians. Debaptismo c. 18.

(6.) *Origen*, (A. D., 203–254,) is quoted as having said that the baptism of infants was derived from the apostles by tradition. It is important in estimating the weight of this testimony to know that the works of Origen with the single exception of a small treatise are not extant in the original Greek, in which they were written; but are only preserved in the Latin Translation of Rufinus made more than a hundred years afterward. The quotation is not taken from the Greek, but from the Latin of Rufinus. Jerome, Anastasius, and others, the contemporaries of Rufinus wrote several pieces to expose the forgeries and corruptions of which Rufinus was guilty in handling the works of Origen. He was a man of base character and the Magdeburg Centuriators relate many scandalous things of him. Scaliges calls him illiterate. Mr. Daille observes that Rufinus had " so slightly mangled and so licentiously confounded the writings of Origen, etc., which he translated into Latin that you will hardly find a page where he has not re-touched or altered or added something." Mr. DuPin says: They were translated with so much liberty that it is a difficult matter to discern what is Origen's own, from what has been foisted in by the interpreter." The forgeries that have been proven upon him render him wholly unworthy of credit—so that we do not know **whether Origen ever said what Rufinus has attrib-**

uted to him. But I present as an offsett to this doubtful passage from Rufinus another taken from the work of Origen *Contra Celsum* which is preserved in the original Greek, and therefore free from the suspicions that attach to the Latin translations. Celsus who wrote against Christianity after stating that intelligent and respectable persons were admitted to initiation into the heathen mysteries he says "And now let us hear what persons the Christians invite. Whoever they say is a sinner, whoever is unintelligent, whoever is a mere child, in short whoever is a miserable contemptible creature, the kingdom of God shall receive him." Origen thus replies: " In reply to these accusations we say it is one thing to invite those who are diseased in soul to a healing and it is another to invite the healthy to a knowledge and discernment of things more divine. And we knowing the difference first call men to be healed. We exhort sinners to come to the instruction that teaches them not to sin, and the unintelligent to that which produces in them understanding; *and the little children to rise in elevation of thought to the man*, and the miserable to come to a more fortunate state—or what is more proper to say—a state of happiness. But when those of the exhorted that make progress, show that they have been cleansed by the word and as much as possible have lived a better life, then we invite them to be initiated among us."

We have now reached an age when infant baptism began to be practiced, for we find Cyprian in Africa appearing as its zealous champion in the Council of Carthage composed of 64 Bishops, A. D., 252. But that it did not generally prevail until much later, is evident from the number of eminent persons, the children of Christian parents, who were not baptized until adult age. Of these were **Basil, Bishop of Nicene, and his wife Eumile;**

Chrysostom, Jerome of Strydon; Theodore, the Emperor; Gregory Nazianzen, Augustine, Ambrose, Polycrates, and the Emperor Constantine. The first recorded case of infant baptism occurred A. D. 370. Galetes, the son of the Emperor Valens, was dying and his father demanded baptism for him at the hands of Basil, Bp. of Cesarea, who stoutly refused and the Emperor at last procured an Arian Bishop who consented to baptize him. Would any pedobaptist have refused the request?

SECTION 4. *Evils of Infant Baptism.*—I will give only a brief summary of the evils which the introduction of this rite entailed upon the church.

1. It destroyed the significance of the symbol. Baptism properly symbolizes the death to sin and the resurrection to holiness. But the administration to infants can have no such significance. As the intelligent profession of Christian faith, it is lost upon the infant with whom it is wholly involuntary—not to say compulsory. As a personal recognition of the resurrection of Christ it is worthless for the same reason.

2. It destroyed the spiritual character of the church. Whilst some who are thus introduced may be afterward converted, the great majority become Christians in name only, and the more the practice is extended, the more unconverted persons are introduced, until the church ceases to be "a holy nation." The line of distinction between the church and the world is thus obliterated and in process of time the church embraced the entire community and ceased to be separate from the world.

3. This change gave license to every species of innovation. If councils or usage, might change a fundamental law, the very basis of membership in the kingdom of Christ, there was no change which might not thus be introduced. Hence we find that

the prolific age which gave birth to Infant Baptism was fruitful in a thousand other innovations upon the simple institutions of the gospel.

4. The unconverted persons thus introduced into the church brought with them all their worldly notions. Hence the church was governed by worldly motives and exhibited all the passions that distinguish men of the world. Its offices became the objects of ambition and its rulers sought to rule the world.

5. It introduced ritualism. Men who know nothing of the work of the spirit by personal experience are apt to attach an undue importance to the externals of religion and to suppose that the worship of God is an outward act and that the rites and ceremonies are the sure vehicles of God's grace.

6. It brought about the union of church and State. Having rejected the effectual working of the Holy Spirit, as the great power to enforce the persuasions of the gospel it was natural that the church should look to the adjuncts of human government to sustain and support it.

7. It gave rise to priestly assumption. Those who believed that they held in their hands the keys that unlocked the grace of God and whose hearts were inflamed by wordly ambition were not slow to use this power to their own aggrandizement.

8. It led to persecution. The religion that did not spring from the love of God shed abroad in the heart knew nothing of that charity which suffereth long and is kind. It could not brook opposition and therefore brought its power to bear to crush all dissent. The bloody annals of pedobaptism are proofs of its intolerant Spirit.

9. The ground upon which infant baptism is

administered is ruinous to the soul. He who believes that the grace of God was conferred upon him by the "water of regeneration" will seek no other and will die unregenerated. He who is taught that he is the better for having been baptized will be tempted to rest content with the blessings it promises and thus the soul be lulled into a fatal security.

CHAPTER XIII.

THE DESIGN OF BAPTISM.

There are different views in regard to the design of this institution.

1. One party teaches that it is the instrument by which, *opus operatum*, regeneration is effected. This view I have already sufficiently considered in the general discussion of the sacramental efficacy of the church and its ordinances.

2. Another view considers baptism as the means through which regeneration is effected by the Holy Spirit. This has already been considered and I need only add that the Scriptures do not so associate baptism and regeneration as to justify this doctrine. On the contrary we find that faith is continually represented as the effect of the operation of the Holy Spirit and faith is demanded as a condition precedent to baptism. Thus when the eunuch demanded baptism at the hands of Philip, he said: "If thou believest with all thy heart, thou mayest." When Peter was preaching to the household of Cornelius, the Gentiles who were present became the recipients of God's Holy Spirit; and when Peter saw it he said: "Can any man forbid water that these should not be baptized who have received the Holy Ghost as well as we?" (Acts x: 47.) Here the work of the Spirit preceded baptism and that very fact is assigned by Peter as a reason why they might be baptized. He certainly did not understand that they were to be baptized in order to receive the Holy Ghost. Again Paul represents the Thessalonians as "chosen unto salvation through the sanctification of the Spirit and the belief of the truth." (2 Thes. ii: 13.) Here

is certainly regeneration but no baptism connected with it. Peter says (1 Pet. i: 2). "Elect according to the foreknowledge of God through sanctification of the spirit unto obedience." Here regeneration is represented as the direct effect of the Holy Spirit, and as leading to obedience and baptism is only an act of obedience. God never suspended the accomplishment of his purpose in the salvation of the believer upon a mere outward act to be performed by another; for this would involve the monstrous proposition that one might be damned who was in the exercise of faith and was ready and willing to comply with the terms, but could not from the absence or disinclination of another over whom he had no control.

3. Still another party represent baptism as the outward sign of an inward grace. But they violate this very principle in administering the sign when the thing signified does not exist. Nor can it be referred to the future, for there is no certainty that the thing signified will ever exist. It depends upon other contingencies in no way dependent upon baptism.

But the same party holds that it is not only the sign but the seal of our grafting into Christ. The seal of a covenant is that which gives validity to it. It is designed to authenticate it and give it legal effect. A seal therefore to be of any value must make a visible impression and one that is durable. Unless it leaves an impression that may be clearly perceived it affords no proof. If it is only transient the authentication is gone as soon as the impression is removed. But baptism produces no visible change in the person baptized. As soon as he changes his dripping clothes he is just as he was before and no one looking on him could discern that he had been sealed as an heir of the promise. Sovereigns in the times of the New Testament were accustomed to impress their own images upon what was sealed, and it was from this custom that this figure was applied to Christians. But the baptized man is on that account no more like Christ than he was before.

But there is a seal which answers all these requirements, and it will be found on examination that this is the only thing that seals to us the covenanted blessings of God. Baptism is no sure guaranty of this, for thousands who have been baptized die in their sins. There is a sure guaranty of our inheritance. Regeneration or the new birth, by which I mean that change which is wrought in us by the Holy Spirit, is an earnest of our inheritance. It is a visible mark impressing itself upon the character with such distinctness that the true Christian is readily distinguished from the man of the world. There is a marked change in the man easily discerned by his orderly walk and conversation. The impression is not a transient one, disappearing like the wounds inflicted upon the waves in baptism, which close again and leave no scar behind to mark the place. He is "born not of corruptible but incorruptible seed." This seal also leaves the image of Christ impressed upon the soul, thus sealing the blessings of the gospel to the believer. In the New Testament sealing is never used in connection with baptism, but frequently with the work of the Holy Spirit. Paul says to the Ephesians i: 13. "In whom also after that ye believed ye were sealed with that Holy Spirit of promise which is the earnest of our inheritance until the redemption of our purchased possession." Again he admonishes the same church (iv: 30): "Grieve not the Holy Spirit of God whereby ye are sealed unto the day of redemption."

4. Another view supposes that baptism is the appointed means to procure the remission of sins;

while it is not itself a cleansing ordinance, they say that it is in obedience to this command that remission of sins is obtained. This is only a modification of the doctrine of baptismal regeneration. That we find baptism and the remission of sins connected is no proof that baptism precedes, or necessarily accompanies the latter. John's baptism is called the baptism of repentance for the remission of sins. Here the remission is associated with repentance and we find that the Harbinger requires a confession of sins and fruits meet for repentance before he administered baptism. Confession has the promise of forgiveness, for if we confess our sins he is faithful to forgive our sins. Therefore forgiveness preceded the baptism of John and was not procured by it. In Luke xxiv: 47, repentance and remission of sins are connected without any reference to baptism. Again in Acts v: 31, they are thus associated. In Acts x: 34, it is declared that whosoever believeth upon him shall receive remission of sins. Faith and remission of sins are also associated in Rom. iii: 25, where Paul is discussing justification by the grace of God without the deeds of the law. In Col. ii: 11, Paul says: "In whom also ye were circumcised with the circumcision made without hands in putting off the body of the sins of the flesh by the circumcision of Christ." What is the circumcision made without hands? Not baptism certainly for that is made with hands. It is evident the apostle refers to the regeneration effected by the Holy Spirit, which embraces repentance and faith as the fruit of it and it is worthy of remark that baptism is placed after this circumcision—this putting off the sins of the flesh. Peter admonishes his hearers at Jerusalem. "Repent and be converted that your sins may be blotted out," and surely Peter did not understand this process of remission by baptism or he would not have omitted so important a particular. But we are reminded that Peter exhorted the people on the day of Pentecost to "repent and be baptized in the name of Jesus Christ for the remission of sins," and Ananias said to Paul: "Arise and be baptized and wash away thy sins."

It is admitted that these passages taken alone seem to teach this doctrine; but even that is doubtful, for it is not certain that the speaker in the first place did not mean to connect repentance and remission as is elsewhere done. And this is the more probable because Peter is answering the question what we shall DO, and if *eis* (for) expresses purpose it is most natural to refer that purpose to the principal action; or it may be a typical and not a literal—real remission—and this is exactly what Peter declares in 1 Pet. iii: 21. "The like figure whereunto baptism doth now save us (not the putting away of the filth of the flesh, but the answer of a good conscience toward God) by the resurrection of Jesus Christ."

But the circumstances attending the baptism on the day of Pentecost and that of Paul explain these expressions to some extent. Those baptized on the day of Pentecost are called the saved. But men are not saved in their sins. Therefore their sins must have been forgiven before they were baptized. The history of Paul's conversion shows that he was converted before his baptism. The scales had fallen from his eyes. His Spiritual blindness was gone. He was illuminated by the Holy Spirit. God had already selected him for his great life work. This very designation to an important work in Christ's Kingdom imports that he was reconciled to God—his sins were forgiven, for he would not trust such a mission to an enemy. And the washing away of his sins was not the putting away of the filth of the flesh, but the answer of a good conscience.

But these passages must be construed with other passages bearing on the same subject according to the rule of interpretation that doubtful passages are to be construed with those whose meaning is plain. In the passage already quoted that baptism is not to put away the filth of the flesh, salvation is expressly promised to every one that believeth. No other condition is imposed. Forgiveness is the gracious gift of God—not of works lest any man should boast. But if remission of sins is predicated on baptism then we should be baptized every day—nay, every hour of the day for so often do we sin and need forgiveness. Why should it require baptism in one instance and not in all?

5. We come now to consider what is the true design of baptism, as revealed in the Scriptures. It is not designed to be effective—but instructive. It is a species of object teaching—a symbol selected to impart instruction—this and nothing more. The Saviour knew that precepts addressed to the eye make the deepest impression upon the mind; hence he has left two symbols, in which are imbedded and preserved the fundamental doctrines that underlie the plan of salvation. The design of baptism is to teach certain great truths. Let us then inquire into the symbolism of baptism.

(1.) It teaches the great doctrine of the resurrection without which all our hopes are vain. Paul teaches that we are buried with Christ by baptism, that like as he was raised from the dead so we shall walk in newness of life. As he was buried so we are buried in baptism. As he rose from the dead so we rise from the watery grave. Rom. vi: 4. Hence Paul agues that if there is no resurrection from the dead our baptism has no significance: "Else what shall they do which are baptized for the dead if the dead rise not at all. Why then are they baptized for the dead?" Our baptism teaches a falsehood if the

the dead rise not. Thus it is evident that baptism symbolizes the resurrection of the body.

(2.) It also symbolizes a moral resurrection equally important to our salvation. It teaches that we must die to a life of sin and be raised to a life of holiness, and in this sense may be considered the outward sign of an inward resurrection. (Rom. vi: 4, 5, 6.)

(3.) It also incidentally teaches the forgiveness of sins, for as the body leaves its corruption behind in the grave so in the spiritual resurrection symbolized in baptism, we leave behind our sins and rise to walk in newness of life; and it is in this view of the subject that remission of sins is connected with baptism, "in a figure," as Peter says.

(4.) It is also used as the badge of the Christian profession. In the act of baptism we declare that we have passed from death unto life. We renounce the devil and all his works and undertake to live a life as different from the former as the life to come is different from the present. At the same time by this act we profess our faith in the great doctrine of the resurrection.

Beautiful and instructive emblem! how tame it becomes when shorn of its lessons. But how impressive when testifying to the great truths it symbolizes!

CHAPTER XIV.

THE ADMINISTRATOR OF BAPTISM.

All denominations of Christians are agreed upon one thing, viz: that baptism is not to be administered indiscriminately by all the professors of Christianity. All agree that the administrator of this ordinance must be qualified. But what those qualifications are and whence the authority is derived is a subject of much difference of opinion. Some make a distinction between regular and irregular baptisms, and tolerate the latter in extreme cases. Others maintain that irregular baptism is no baptism at all, as Tertullian says: *Quem rite non habent, sine dubio non habent.* "Those who do not have it rightly without doubt do not have it at all;" and that baptism being a positive ordinance must be administered just as it was appointed, and by persons duly qualified; that strict observance in every particular of the law of baptism is essential to its performance; literal obedience being of the essence of a positive law. But the greater part suppose that Christ conferred the right to baptize upon the ministerial order exclusively; but attaching a superstitious reverence to the ordinance they accept it at the hands of heretics and even of women. But did Christ commit this ordinance to the clergy alone? Under Christ the church is recognized as the fountain of authority. If any exercised authority in the apostolic church, he did not take it upon himself but the authority was conferred by the church. A divine call was not all that was required, and no one felt at liberty to use this ministry unless by the direction of the church.

We may therefore define the proper administra

tor of baptism to be one who is duly authorized by an orderly church of Jesus Christ. This implies that the person authorized be himself an orderly member of the church; for to confer this authority upon a person not a member of the church, or whose outward life is scandalous, would render the body disorderly. Therefore it could not be a representative of the body of Christ. It is the authority of the church and not his being a minister, which gives him the right to baptize; and therefore this authority may be conferred upon a layman and he may, under the direction of the church, confer valid baptism upon one who voluntarily professes faith in the Lord Jesus Christ. Although in the ordination of a minister a general authority to baptize is conferred, it is subordinate to the church; and he acquires no right in the presence of the church to baptize any without its special consent and direction. But when he is sent by the church into regions beyond, he carries with him the authority to make disciples and baptize them. Indeed a number of orderly disciples in fellowship with each other, in a place where there is no organized church, might meet and confer upon one of their number, even though a layman, the authority; because they would be the highest ecclesiastical authority in the place. Nay, I will go further and say that the Christian church is so constructed by the wisdom of its author that it can never be destroyed. Let it be divided and scattered into remote parts, each part has in itself all the elements of a church and those who happen to come to the same place may assemble and they form a complete church or have the power of completing their organization by choosing and ordaining a pastor. Thus it was impossible to destroy the church because it became self-perpetuating. It needed not to await the coming of an ordained minister in order to receive its ordinances in due form. But it could authorize one of its own members to represent it in conferring baptism. No succession of ministers deriving ordination from one another was necessary to complete the claim of succession. Churches and not ministers constitute the link in such a chain, and authority conferred by the church is all the connection required. It was thus that the gospel was propagated during the first ages. It was thus when persecution scattered abroad the disciples that "they went every where preaching the gospel," and thus Christianity was carried throughout the world.

But I said the authority must emanate from an *orderly* church. No other can be the repository of the authority of Christ. No other can confer the authority to baptize. An orderly church of Christ is one that is organized according to the law of Christ; and preserves the ordinances as they were delivered. What right has any other to exercise his authority, having renounced it in departing from that order which He has established. Can an embassador abroad who renounces his allegiance to his country, and sets up for himself continue to represent the government? In renouncing his allegiance he renounces his authority also. So those who depart from the gospel order withdraw from Christ and cease to represent Him in the administration of His government.

This brings us to consider the subject of "alien immersion" as it is denominated; by which is meant the immersion of a believer by a person not authorized by an orderly church. The question frequently arises in the reception of members: Should they be received upon a baptism admitted to be irregular; or be baptized by the authority of the church? Or, can the consent of the church in receiving such members have a retroactive effect so as to authorize it? This last question is sufficiently answered by the inquiry whether the church has this authority in the present? May she transfer the authority of Christ to any not qualified as He requires? May she employ those who have renounced the order of God's house to do God's work? And if not in the present, certainly not in the past.

There are two things which invalidate such baptism; one relating to the subject and the other to the administrator. (1). It is a disorderly act on the part of the recipient. It is not the case of one who has no option; for if it were possible that he could nowhere find a proper administrator he might well inquire whether he is not excused from obeying when it is impossible for him to obey properly? But such an extreme case rarely if ever presents itself, and it is not upon such grounds that the question should be settled; for no one can plead such a lack of qualified administrators. In practice it is simply a question whether a person who might have found a proper administrator, but has of choice received baptism at the hands of an unauthorized person, should be received. Those who receive such do it through sympathy, upon the ground that the person meant to obey Christ, and the intention must be taken for the deed. But the person who receives aspersion for baptism is equally sincere, and if the intention is to be taken he should be received also. But did he really mean to obey Christ by cleaving to those who walk disorderly in rejecting the authority of Christ by encouraging organized opposition to His laws, and by thus despising His visible church? In all such cases it will be found that those persons were led by some other motive than a sincere desire to do just what Christ commanded, and in the way He commanded. They walk disorderly and the church is required to withdraw from every one that walketh disorderly.

But (2). Such baptisms cannot be received because the person administering is in disorder. He refuses to obey Christ. He rejects His laws. He despises the order of God's house, and sets up a different order. He has no authority to confer baptism and therefore cannot do it. If the church should withdraw fellowship from one for grave errors, would any one be willing to receive his baptism? If not, how is his authority improved by associating with others who hold the same errors? But in what respect are those in a better condition for whom the church has no fellowship, and who are virtually excommunicated, and who have entered into an organized opposition to the authority of Christ and His earthly representative, His visible church.

It is not plain that these false teachers have any ecclesiastical authority to baptize any more than their laymen, or even a pious person of no connection; for what advantage have they over the latter? They are no more baptized than he, and as baptism is an essential prerequisite to church membership they are no more members of the church than he. The only thing that can be said of the former is that they perhaps have sincerely intended to comply with the law of baptism and the order of God's house. And those who would receive such baptisms place it upon the ground that these ministers are sincere, pious men, and give evidence of being called of God to preach the gospel. I do not question their sincerity or piety; nor do I doubt that many of them are called to preach the gospel. But they have not fully obeyed the call, for it embraces as prerequisites obedience to His ordinances and a recognition of the authority which He has set up in His church. They may be called, but so far as they propagate error and neglect the Scriptural qualifications they disobey the call. So far as they preach the gospel it is well enough, but they may not disregard the order of God's house by taking upon themselves to baptize without being first baptized themselves, and without the authority of an orderly church. It will not avail to say that they have been authorized by their societies; for these based upon a rejection of Scriptural baptism both in the action, subject and design, have no authority to confer. It is impossible to obey the injunction to withdraw from every brother that walketh disorderly and yet receive such baptisms.

CHAPTER XV.

THE LORD'S SUPPER.

This ordinance has not been more fortunate than that of baptism in the controversies in respect to the design and proper administration and the qualifications necessary to a participation in it. To these I now address myself.

SECTION 1. *The Nature and Design of the Lord's Supper.*—A mistake in regard to the design of this ordinance has led to many errors. We will, therefore, consider this first.

1. It is not designed as a social meal. The participants should not partake of it with reference to each other. While the utmost fellowship and good feeling should prevail among them, the Supper is not meant to be an expression of that fellowship. Hospitality is inculcated as a Christian duty, but this is not meant as an occasion for it. A mistake in this regard often makes people feel uncomfortable, because they cannot invite some dear friend or relative to participate in the Supper. From their stand point it looks unsociable, inhospitable and exclusive, because they suppose the ordinance was designed to show forth our kindly feeling towards each other, and that exclusion from it imports social inferiority, or at least an inferiority of Christian standing. But this is a perversion of the ordinance from its original design.

2. Its design is not sacramental. Even those who have correct views on this subject sometimes improperly employ the term sacrament to designate the Lord's Supper, thereby perpetuating the erroneous idea of the Papists that the ordinance has in itself the power of imparting grace. It is not

denied that it may be a means of grace as the discharge of any other duty may be a means of grace. But that grace is not derived from the bread and wine. It may be imparted by the Holy Spirit during the participation; but this is only an incident, and not the main design of the ordinance, which I will hereafter show. But I have already considered the question of the sacramental efficacy of the ordinances and need not repeat the arguments here.

3. It is not an act of worship. Worship is paying divine honors to God, such as adoration, confession, prayer, thanksgiving and the like. It is not a sacrificial offering to God. But there are those who so regard it and teach, that, by the prayer of consecration, the bread and wine really become the body and blood of Jesus Christ, and that the officiating priest offers him in this form for the sins of the people. This transformation is called transubstantiation, and gives rise to the idolatrous worship of the host. (1). To this doctrine the evidence of our senses is opposed. We can see no apparent change in the elements. They appear to be the same before and after consecration. They look like bread and wine, they feel like bread and wine, and they taste like bread and wine. (2). The closest chemical analysis cannot detect any change in them. Chemically they are unchanged. (3). The apostles could not have understood Him literally when He said: *This is my body and this is my blood*, for they saw Him standing there beside them in person. It was impossible for Him to be two different things at the same time. (4). The body of Christ is a material substance and therefore can occupy but one place at a time. It cannot be in heaven on the right hand of the Father, and at the same time on the earth. Besides the Lord's Supper is administered at a great many different places

and to a great many different persons at the same time. Has Christ so many different bodies, yet all the same? (5). It is preposterous that a mere man —and often a very bad one—can become a creator and make God! (6). The doctrine makes cannibals of Christians. They are said to eat the real body and blood of Jesus Christ. They eat God! Can anything be more horrible and blasphemous! (7). This monstrous doctrine is justified on the ground that it is a sacrifice made for sin in behalf of the participants, the officiating priest conducting the sacrifice. This is ruinous to the souls of those who trust in such a sin-offering, and draws them away from the true sacrifice for sin. We read of crucifying Christ afresh, but the act is not at all commended. (Heb. vi · 6). We are told (Heb. vii : 27), "He needeth not, daily, as those high priests, to offer up sacrifice first for his own sins and then for the sins of the people, for this He did once when He offered himself up." Again it is declared (Heb. ix : 25), "Nor yet he that should offer himself often * * for then must He have often suffered since the foundation of the world; but now once in the end of the world hath He appeared to put away sin by the sacrifice of himself." And yet we are told that He must suffer often for the sins of the people, as if His own sacrifice were insufficient, thus drawing men from the true sacrifice for sin, and imperiling their souls in the face of the positive declaration that "there remaineth no more sacrifice for sin." (Heb. x: 26)—that "Christ made an offering of himself once for all and by that offering perfected forever them that are sanctified." (Heb. x: 10–14.)

A modification of this doctrine is to be found in the consubstantiation of the Greeks. They deny that the bread and wine are really turned into the body and blood of the Lord, but that His body and blood are really present, imparting everlasting life to the participants. This is liable to the same objections urged against transubstantiation, except those against creating and eating God.

The passages relied on to prove these objectionable and unscriptural doctrines: "This is my body" and "this is my blood," no more prove that the bread and wine become the real body and blood of Christ, or that He is really present in them than the declaration: "Thou art a stone (Petros)" made the stone really Peter, or caused Peter to be present in the stone. This form of speech is common in the Scriptures, and is to be explained as elsewhere. The stone represents the character of Peter; so the bread and wine represent the body and blood of the Lord. This furnishes an easy and satisfactory explanation without the contradictions involved in the other.

4. There are two fundamental ideas in the plan of salvation; the resurrection, which embraces the redemption of the soul from sin, and the body from the grave, symbolized in baptism; and the sacrificial offering of Christ which is typified in the bloody rites of the former dispensations and symbolized in the ordinance of the Lord's Supper. These two doctrines are the keystone of the arch, without which the whole structure of Christianity would topple into ruins. They embrace in their comprehensive scope an epitome of the gospel, and hence the necessity for making them conspicuous, by perpetuating them in visible symbols, that the memory of these great truths might be understood and preserved.

1. The bloody rites of the former age pointed to the vicarious sufferings of Christ. (1). The sacrifice of Abel was accepted while that of Cain was not. "By faith Abel offered unto God a more acceptable sacrifice than Cain." Abel brought the

bloody victim. His sacrifice owned himself a sinner, deserving to die; and implies faith as Paul says, in the promised Messiah. He looked through the bleeding victim which he laid upon the altar to the Lamb of God which taketh away the sin of the world. (2). The offering of Isaac also points to the same event. How beautifully it foretells the coming event. Man is led to the altar of God's justice. The sword is uplifted to slay him; but God provides himself a sacrifice, and the child of faith goes free. (3). The paschal lamb, while commemorative of a remarkable providence of God, also typified the efficacy of Christ's blood. It was in connection with this that the Lord's Supper was instituted and the close connection between them may serve to explain the latter. As those whose door-posts were sprinkled with the blood of the paschal lamb, escaped the vengeance of the destroying angel, so by the Christian passover, we are constantly reminded that it is the blood of Christ sprinkled upon our hearts that saves us from the wrath of God. (4). The sin-offerings under the law illustrate the same truth. The victim was without blemish. Over him was there made a confession of the sins of the people, which were typically laid upon his head; and then he was slain in acknowledgment of the fact that they deserved to be slain. So, the "Lamb of God that taketh away the sins of the world" is a perfect victim, who "bore our sins in His own body in the tree."

2. So the ordinance of the Lord's Supper symbolizes and was intended to preserve the memory of the same great truth. Like baptism it is commemorative. The divine author declares this at the time of its institution: "This do in remembrance of me." And Paul declares the same thing: "As oft as ye eat this bread and drink this cup ye do shew forth the Lord's death till He come." It was

meant to commemorate the dying love of Christ.

The bread symbolizes His body which was crucified. This is my body which is broken for you. As bread sustains our animal life, so our spiritual life is sustained by feeding upon Christ, who is the bread of life. His doctrines are the nourishment and His spirit the life of our spiritual natures. The unleavened bread that is broken and consumed fitly represents our unsanctified natures in the room of which Christ, assuming our human nature, suffers.

The wine represents His blood which was shed for us. "This is my blood which was shed for you." The wine is a fitting emblem of this. As it revives a man sinking from weariness, and exhausted by disease, so the application of the blood of Christ imparts new life to the believer.

SECTION 2. *Its Limitation.*—It can hardly be supposed that this ordinance of the Lord's house has been left without any safeguard to protect it from the unworthy. But who is to be the judge of those who are to approach the Lord's table; and what qualifications are to be required?

Many, misinterpreting the language of Paul in 1 Cor. xi: 28: "But let a man examine himself and so let him eat of that bread and drink of that cup," suppose that each is to be the judge of his own qualifications, and that the church has only to spread the table and allow all who choose to participate. But Paul meant to teach no such thing. It should be borne in mind that this language is addressed to the members of the church, and cannot, therefore, be construed to extend any further. Paul means to counsel the members to self-examination before partaking, in order to divest themselves of every unworthy motive, lest eating and drinking unworthily they bring condemnation upon themselves.

The church is made the depository of the laws and ordinances of the gospel and is charged with their safe keeping. Paul praised the Corinthians for having kept the ordinances as they were delivered. It would be monstrous if every blasphemer had the privilege, and no one could gainsay it, of thrusting himself among the people of God and desecrating that ordinance which commemorates the broken body and shed blood of our Lord, whom he despises.

If all, therefore, who choose may not partake, it becomes us to inquire what are the Scriptural qualifications, and under what circumstances the ordinance is to be observed.

1. In regard to the terms of admission to the Lord's Supper there is much less difference than is generaly supposed. With a very few exceptions the standards of all denominations are agreed that conversion, baptism, church membership and an orderly walk are indispensable qualifications. It is in the application of these terms that they differ. They differ as to the nature of conversion, as to what constitutes baptism and church membership and an orderly walk. It is this difference in the application of terms that renders the communion of some closer than that of others. Absolutely free communion is tolerated nowhere. Those who believe there can be no visible church without baptism (and all believe this); and that only immersion performed by an administrator duly authorized by an orderly church, is baptism, must necessarily be more restricted in their invitations than those who believe differently.

1. But let us endeavor to settle what was the practice of the apostles. What are the Scriptural qualifications?

(1). *Regeneration.*—This is the starting point of every act of obedience. Except a man be born again he cannot see the kingdom of God. There is no spiritual discernment without it; for spiritual things are spiritually discerned. Those who partook unworthily discerned not the Lord's body, said Paul. No unconverted person comprehends the great truth commemorated in this ordinance. We have already shown that conversion is an indispensable prerequisite to baptism, and that the church is built upon faith in the Lord Jesus Christ, which is the fruit of the Spirit, and we find only those who professed to be believers, who assembled to participate in this ordinance. It was first instituted among the most eminent disciples. It was disciples who were to be taught to observe "all things whatsoever he had commanded." It was the disciples who continued steadfast in the apostles' doctrine and fellowship and in breaking bread. It was the church at Corinth that administered it. It was the disciples who assembled with Paul at Troas to celebrate the Lord's Supper; and no instance can be found where it was administered to an unbeliever. To give it to such is to cast pearls before swine. They can have no appreciation of its lessons; and "eating and drinking unworthily, they eat and drink condemnation to themselves, not discerning the Lord's body."

(2). Baptism is a necessary prerequisite. The apostolic practice was to admit none who had not been baptized. We may not transpose the order of God's house. The commandment is first to make disciples, then to baptize them, and then they were to be taught to observe the commandments—this among them. On the day of Pentecost they that gladly received the word were baptized, and then continued steadfast in the apostles' doctrine and fellowship, and in breaking bread. It was instituted after baptism, was instituted and committed to men who had been baptized.

Nor may each be the judge when he has complied with the law of baptism. The law of Christ and not the conscience of the applicant must determine whether he has complied. Robert Hall, the great champion of loose communion, admits that the apostles would not have permitted one to commune who refused to be baptized, however pious he might have been otherwise, because he refused to obey Christ. And is disobedience less a sin to-day than it was eighteen hundred years ago? But it is urged that those who err in respect to the law of baptism now, have not the same means of ascertaining the truth that they had under the personal instruction of the apostles. Why not, pray? Have we not the same commandment that they had? Have we not the same means to know the meaning of terms? Have we not the instructions of the same apostles? Or, forsooth, has God delivered us such an imperfect revelation of His will that we cannot at this distance of time, with reasonable certainty learn our duty? Surely His word is not deficient. He has preserved enough to guide us into all truth, and we are left without excuse; and there is no charity in conceding to error that there is reason to doubt on this or any other subject connected with our duty. The apostles have not done their work so bunglingly in delivering His laws that error is to be indulged and permitted to enjoy privileges which it could not have enjoyed in the apostles' days. They preserved and embodied in the books of the New Testament all of their personal instructions that they deemed sufficient to guide Christians in all ages in their duty. But when the apostolic practice is conceded, the whole ground is conceded. He who reveres the apostolic order will be in no hurry to depart from it.

I take it therefore as sufficiently established that the neglect or abuse of the ordinance of baptism is a sufficient ground of exclusion from the communion. To allow him this privilege is to encourage the neglect of the ordinance of baptism, but the church cannot encourage the neglect or abuse of its initiatory rite; for, as we have seen, it is required to keep the ordinances as they were delivered.

No one has a right to complain of a privation when his own act furnishes the ground of exclusion; and when he has it in his own power to remove the obstacle. His own willful rejection of the law of Christ affords no ground to set aside the law for his accommodation.

(3.) Church membership is also necessary. I do not think this will be controverted. All those who partook in apostolic times were undoubtedly church members. As the table is set within the church of course none can rightfully approach it but those within. Why should we take it to the door and offer it to those who stand without and refuse to enter.

But the membership must be in an orderly church. Now disorder respects not only the morality of the church, but its faith and practice. The command is to withdraw from every brother that walketh disorderly and not according to the apostolic tradition. But the apostles delivered only the immersion of believers as proper baptism, and a form of church government in which the assembled church exercised the highest authority under Christ. To substitute aspersion for Scriptural baptism and to admit unconscious infants as subjects contrary to the command of Christ, is to walk disorderly and not according to the tradition of the apostles. The commemoration of the Lord's death is the most important act of churchship, and to admit disorderly persons to a participation is far from obeying the injunction.

2. Having thus settled the kind of persons who should participate, it becomes us to inquire under

what circumstances they should celebrate the Supper.

It was without doubt the practice of the Apostolic Church to assemble on the first day of the week to break bread, but as the apostle Paul, in speaking of this ordinance, uses the language, "as oft as ye eat this bread," &c., it is thought that the frequency of its celebration is left to the discretion of the church. But it cannot be objected that the apostolic practice repeated the ordinance too often, and as it has many advantages it is to be regretted that it has so generally been abandoned.

The celebration of the Supper was the public, official act of the church, and not of individuals in their individual capacity. It was the assembled church that celebrated it. It was the united testimony of the whole to the great truth symbolized. It was never celebrated under other circumstances. It was a church, and not an individual ordinance. Hence the practice of some to give the communion to persons under peculiar circumstances, as when they are sick or dying, is in violation of the law of the Supper, and the demand for it under such circumstances is from a superstitious belief in its sacramental efficacy, and should always be refused.

SECTION 3. *Feet Washing not a Church Ordinance.*

1. *Was Feet Washing appointed as a church ordinance?* — A church ordinance is something appointed to be done by the church in its collective capacity, or by its authority. It is an essential part of its organization, without which it cannot exist. It is founded upon divine authority, must be literally performed and is perpetually binding. Does feet washing answer this definition? Is it appointed to be done by the church in its collective capacity, or by its authority? I think not, and will proceed to give my reasons.

1. It is strenuously maintained by the **advocates** of feet washing, so far as I know without exception, that the event recorded in the thirteenth chapter of John took place in connection with the Lord's Supper. Without at all admitting the correctness of this assumption, I will discuss the question upon that supposition. Its advocates suppose they derive strength from this fact, and if they cannot maintain their cause on grounds of their own choosing, much less can they upon any other. Those who practice it, always practice it in this connection; and if authorized by Christ, we would naturally expect to find it mentioned when the Lord's Supper is mentioned by the Apostles, who must have understood the Lord's meaning. And when they gave an account of the celebration of the Supper, or furnished particular directions for its observance, that the other would be mentioned also in immediate succession. But if we find that the latter is entirely overlooked, we must conclude that the writers did not regard it of the same importance. But if it be an ordinance to be celebrated in connection with the Lord's Supper, it must be equally important; for all ordinances are of the same force. They all rest solely upon divine authority for their obligation, and one cannot be said to be more important and binding than another.

In Acts ii: 41, 42, we read: "Then they that gladly received the word were baptized, and the same day there were added unto them about three thousand. And they continued steadfastly in the Apostles' doctrine and fellowship, and in breaking of bread and in prayer." Why omit this important rite if it formed a part of the service on the occasion of breaking bread? Certainly the Apostles understood the Saviour's words differently from some of the moderns.

In the tenth chapter of 1 Corinthians the Apostle

gives a particular account of the Supper, and yet no mention is made of the washing of the saints' feet. If it formed a part of the ceremony, as now practiced, the failure of the Apostle to mention it is unaccountable, particularly as he prefaces his remarks by saying: "For I have received of the Lord that which I also delivered unto you," a plain declaration that he was about to describe the services as he received them.

The omission in these two instances seems to me conclusive that the Apostles did not regard it as an ordinance of the church, to be practiced in connection with the Supper.

2. Again, that which was intended to be performed by the whole church could not rightly be performed by an individual. An individual might break bread ever so frequently, but it would not be the eucharist, because that is a church act.

The only place, so far as I know, where the washing of the saints' feet is mentioned after this act of Christ, is in 1 Tim. v: 10, where it is represented as a personal act, and is classed with other good works, such as hospitality, relief of the afflicted, &c.

3. It is remarkable that but one of the evangelists mentions this transaction, if regarded as an ordinance of the church, to be observed in connection with the Supper; and it is equally remarkable that the Apostles, writing to distant Gentile churches, should never have enforced its observance. It is also strange, considered from this point of view, that it is not mentioned by any of the Apostolic Fathers, who were the companions and immediate successors of the Apostles. Moreover, Justin Martyr, who flourished A. D. 140 in his Apologies, minutely describes the worship of the Christians of his day, and particularly the celebration of the Lord's Supper. Had feet washing been a part of

the exercises in his day, he could not have failed to mention it.

4. If it indeed be a church ordinance, the church is incomplete without it. A mutilated church is no church at all! Now, whatever may have been the institution of Christ and the practice of the Apostles, feet washing was not perpetuated in the church. Through long ages we search in vain for evidence of the existence of a practice so remarkable that it could not escape notice. That there was a time when it was not practiced by any body of Christians claiming to be the Church of Christ, proves that it could not have formed a part of the original constitution of the church, else the gates of hell have prevailed against it to that extent. At present there is but one inconsiderable body of Christians who practice this ceremony. These are the Anti-mission Baptists of the United States, and even among them the practice is not universal. About fifty years ago it was practiced by many of the Baptists of this country. But we can trace it to its fountain-head, and ascertain how it was introduced among us. Previous to 1788 it was not practiced by the regular Baptists, but was introduced at that time by the incorporation of the Separate Baptists. This denomination was an offshoot of Presbyterianism, or rather of Congregationalism, as the indirect fruit of the labors of Whitefield. They supposed that it was their peculiar mission to restore the gospel order, which they believed to be lost. They held to nine ordinances, to-wit: *baptism, Lord's Supper, love feasts, laying on of hands, feet washing, anointing the sick, right hand of fellowship, the kiss of charity,* and *devoting children.* They also retained the offices of *Ruling Elders, Elderesses* and *Deaconesses.* See *Leland's Virginia Chronicle, p. 42; Benedict's History of the Baptists, pp. 686, 939.*

The union of these denominations brought in

some of their practices, which continue to the present day.

II. If not a church ordinance, has it been appointed to be observed by Christians as a religious ceremony?

Those who attempt to defend it at all claim for it the dignity of a church ordinance, and none consider it a mere ceremony. Indeed, a religious ceremony to be observed by Christians in their church capacity is nothing less than an ordinance. This, I have shown, it could not be. But is it a religious ceremony intended to be observed by individual Christians?

1. A religious ceremony relates to the worship of God; but this act was not performed by Christ as an act of worship, and, as it is fair to presume that he intended, if observed at all literally, that it should be observed in the same sense in which he practiced it; and it was not enjoined upon them collectively, but individually.

2. If we may reason from analogy in other cases, ceremonial observances belong to the church as such. Individual observances are founded upon moral law; or some exceptional order that ceases with the particular individual. A positive ordinance. which is not binding upon the body corporate of Christ, the church, cannot descend in succession from one to another.

3. Individual duties and obligations are always modified by circumstances. If it be an individual duty to wash one of the saints' feet, that duty is founded upon the need of the brother who is the recipient of the service. When the necessity ceases the obligation is at an end. Men having long since ceased to travel either totally or partially barefooted, the feet of the guest need not be washed whenever they enter the house. Hence the obligation in that particular form has long since ceased.

III. How are we to understand the command, "Ye ought also to wash one another's feet?" This is one of those beautiful examples of illustrative teaching which abound in the Bible, intended to make the lesson more impressive. What, then, was meant to be taught by this example?

1. Hospitality. As the washing of the feet of visitors was an important and very necessary act among the ancients and the first performed upon entering the house, it became the signal of welcome, and by a figure of speech by which a part is put for the whole, it signified hospitality. And the Saviour meant in part to impress the duty of hospitality. It was this duty that Paul often commends and enjoins.

2. But the main lesson meant to be taught is the subordination of Christians to each other, regardless of official rank. He foresaw that some would assume to lord over God's heritage, and He designed to teach His true disciples that they should seek rather to serve one another than to play the Master. He was their Lord and Master. But he condescended to perform the lowest menial service for his brethren; so ought every person occupying the same relation to the flock as teacher and guide, to be ready to lay aside the garments of his official dignity, and in humility perform any service the necessities of his brethren may require. That it respects those in authority in the church is evident from the sixteenth verse: "The servant is not greater than his lord. Neither he that is sent greater than he that sent him." If, therefore, it is to be observed as a ceremony, a literal obedience can only be rendered by the pastor washing the feet of the flock, thereby acknowledging his subordination to the church. And Christ adds; "For I have given you an example, that ye should do as I have done to you," *i. e.*, serve the brethren.

To content ourselves with the letter of this injunction is tame and powerless. It is in the spirit of this noble lesson that we rise to a proper conception of the grace of humility.

PART III.

INSTITUTION AND PERPETUITY OF THE CHURCH.

CHAPTER I.

THE IDENTITY OF THE CHURCH UNDER BOTH DISPENSATIONS, CONSIDERED.

Pedobaptists, in defence of Infant Baptism and other innovations upon the body of Christ, driven from the New Testament, have entrenched themselves in the old Dispensation; and declare that the church is substantially the same under both dispensations. But this is only an adroit maneuver to shift the burden of proof; for the reason, if the church is the same, as children were admitted under the old, it requires an express command to exclude them under the new. But the strength of their position consists in the obscurity with which it is surrounded. It masks itself behind obscure generalities and by a mass of doubtful assertions, contrives to present an appearance of strength which the position by no means possesses.

But they are no more willing to accept the consequence of this assumption than we are. If the church was really set up in the Jewish dispensation, then the whole Jewish polity has descended to us, except what has been changed by express enactment. This would force the Episcopalian to accept the Presbyterian government of the synagogue, and the Presbyterian to accept the priesthood as received by Episcopalians and Catholics; and all Christendom, with the early New England Puritans, accept no other laws than those of Moses. But each is willing to accept only so much as suits his own case. The Presbyterians accept the synagogue government, and the Catholic and Episcopalian the priesthood, and all accept its infant membership. All reject the greater part of the rites and ceremonies of the Jews, although there is no express law repealing them, that does not apply with equal force to the whole polity. Thus they present a false issue.

Another false issue is made in the comparison instituted. They do not directly compare the external visible organization of the Christian church, with the visible organization of the Jews; but some vague conception of the former with an invisible, intangible something that existed under the Jewish dispensation. They conceive of the church as the true people of God, as they appear to His eye, abstracted from the visible organizations with which they are associated; and as many truly pious men existed under both dispensations whose moral and spiritual characteristics were the same, they conclude, not that good men were the same under both dispensations, but that the visible organizations with which they were associated are identical. That Freemason is a believer and a pious man; so is that Oddfellow; therefore the institutions of Oddfellowship and Freemasonry are identical!! Such is the reasoning on this subject when divested of its generalities. But this is an evasion of the true issue. The contest is not in regard to believers under both administrations but in regard to visible organizations. It is necessary to keep in the mind constantly the thing under comparison. If they are correct in their conception of what the church is, the visible organizations which they represent are not churches, for all their members are not believers; and it is not possible to introduce unconscious infants into the church, because they cannot believe; and therefore the correspondence between what they call the church under the two dispensations affords no advantage to them. But the comparison should be made between the external visible organizations and not that ideal body which is sometimes called the invisible church, which is not a church really but only figuratively; and the term church can only be applied to it as an assembly of the faithful conceived in the mind. We are to compare real—not figurative organizations.

If we inquire for a visible organization we will find two existing among the Jews at different periods of their history, the patriarchal, and the hierarchical.

Is the visible organization set up by Christ the same as either or both of these? It is to this question that I now address myself. The identity claimed, to avail anything in this argument must respect *the kind of persons composing each, the terms of admission, the external forms of government, i.e. the method of administering the laws, the rites and ceremonies connected with their public worship;* and lastly *their connection by successions.*

In this case it should also be remembered that it is an effort to infer the institutions of the gospel from those of the former dispensations; and not the comparison of institutions admitted to exist by the authority of the Scriptures.

1. The New Testament nowhere declares the church the same under both dispensations. It is true that the term *ekklesia* usually employed in the New Testament to designate the Christian Church is often used in the Old Testament, but never in regard to the establishment. Every assembly of the people was called an *ekklesia* (congregation) not in respect to their organization, but with respect

to their assemblage without regard to the character of those that assembled. It is applied to all the people in the wilderness because they were one body like an assembly.

The figurative language of Paul in Rom. 11th chapter is often quoted to prove that the institutions of Christ were grafted upon the old Jewish stock, and derived their strength from its fatness. But the grafting of the wild olive (Gentile believers) among the branches (unbelieving Jews) which were cut off furnishes no exception to my statement. Paul is not discussing the relation of the Gentiles to the church; but to the grace of God. The Jews were a representative nation, with whom the covenant of Grace had been made. The bestowal of His grace upon believing Jews was according to the covenant, but there was no covenant to extend this favor to even believing Gentiles. The heathen therefore had no reason to exult over those Jews who from unbelief were excluded from the terms of the covenant.

2. If ever so striking a resemblance could be shown, resemblance does not constitute identity. Indeed two things may be exactly alike and yet not the same. Illustrations of this will readily occur to the reader. The constitution and the laws of two States may be exactly alike and yet the two States be different. A more intimate connection must be shown. It must be shown that the Christian church is only an amendment of what is called the Jewish church: an introduction of some new forms while the old, not expressly abrogated, continue in force. The Jews themselves seemed to have entertained some such idea. But Jesus corrected their error, by the parable of sewing a peice of new cloth into an old garment, thus making the rent worse, and putting new wine into old bottles. New wine is to be put into new bottles.

The new rites which I ordain are not to be sewed as patches of new cloth upon the old garment of the Jewish polity. The new wine of the gospel is not to be put into the old bottles of the law. The whole was to be new.

3. The two institutions, though resembling in some particulars are organically different.

The patriarchal was properly a civil government. There were no established forms of worship; there was only a single rite, that of circumcision, and no officers except the natural head of the family. Abraham, Isaac, and Jacob, each succeeded the other in the government of his own family. Then as the heads of families increased, as in the family of Jacob, each family was governed by its own head; and was separate and independent in its government. And no connection existed between them except confraternity. And in this respect they bore some resemblance to the independent societies the apostles organized. But they differ from the Christian Churches in this. Each family of Christians does not form a church. The patriarchal was not a segregation of families, and gives no countenance to the idea that the church is arranged upon the family principle. Christian Churches are made up of members from many families. The patriarchal embraced but one family. Circumcision was the only visible rite that belonged to it and did not make them members of the patriarchal families; but was administered because they were.

The patriarchal government continued until Moses established the hierarchy, with all its rites and ceremonies. To this institution the Christian Church bears still less resemblance.

(1.) The Jewish establishment was national; the Christian Church is not, indeed cannot be, because it is not confined to any particular nation as the Jewish was. The Jewish polity embraced the whole people; the Christian Church is made up of persons separated from the world—a chosen race—in the state but not the state, as was the case with the Jews.

(2.) The Jewish order was built upon the flesh, and respected a temporal possession; it was perpetuated by natural generation. The Christian Church is of a Spiritual character, designed to secure only Spiritual blessings. It does not depend upon natural descent. The circumcised Jew became at once entitled to all the blessings promised to Abraham; but the baptized child of a Christian is no more a Christian than he was before. The Jews were the natural descendants of Abraham; but Christians are his Spiritual seed. The child of a Jew was necessarily a Jew and like himself the natural seed of Abraham; but the child of a Christian is not of the Spiritual seed of Abraham; and baptism cannot make him such: for only those who are in Christ Jesus are of the Spiritual seed of Abraham, and heirs according to the promise.

(3.) Flesh and not faith was a qualification for membership in the Jewish order. Every natural descendant of Abraham whether a believer or not, was entitled to admission. Every Jewish child was admissible by reason of his descent, irrespective of the faith of his father; but faith is the door into the Christian Church. No adult is received into any church without professing faith; and even Pedobaptist churches require a profession of faith on behalf of the child before they baptize him.

(4.) Every parent might circumcise himself and all his family, but an official administrator is required in baptism.

(5.) No such thing as excommunication for immorality was known to the Jews. The punishments for the violation of the law were corporeal, embracing in some instances the death-penalty. But the church has no such power. It has no authority to inflict corporeal punishment. It can only excommunicate the offender. There its power ends.

(6.) Its ordinances were different. Baptism bears no resemblance to circumcision, and the Passover, although a meal, differed from the Lord's Supper in its commemorative design, in the substance eaten, and the periodic character of its celebration. The Passover was eaten by any number of Jews who chanced to come together. The Lord's Supper is celebrated by the church as an official act.

(7.) Its officers were different. The officers of the Jews were Priests, and Levites, and Elders. The officers of the Christian Church are bishops, elders and deacons. The Jewish priesthood was confined to a particular family, and the office was hereditary. The son of a priest became a priest although a wicked man. In the church all are priests—"a nation of priests." None of the offices are hereditary. The son of a minister does not by reason of his natural relation become a minister. The office is conferred on account of moral and spiritual endowments. The elders of the Jews were judicial officers; the elders of the Christian Church are preachers.

(8.) The sacrifices were different. Under the Jewish dispensation the sacrifices were carnal; under the Christian, spiritual.

4. Whatever resemblance may be traced between the two institutions, before their identity is established, it must be shown that the Christian was a continuance of the old and not an independent organization.

(1.) A conclusive fact going to show that the church was not a successor to the Jewish hierarchy is that they existed at the same time. They maintained a separate existence side by side. John did not begin his mission by declaring the Jewish economy at an end. Christ declared that he had not come to destroy the law but to fulfill it, and he foretold when the Jewish dispensation should come to an end, but it was not until the gospel should be preached in all parts of the world. If the Jewish economy ended with the destruction of Jerusalem by Titus, as is usually believed, long before this, churches had been planted in every principal city in the Roman empire.

(2.) Converted Jews who joined the disciples were said to be "added to the church." They could not be added if already members. Long before the gospel was preached among the Gentiles a church was organized at Jerusalem, composed only of Jews; and it was to this body that converted Jews were added.

(3.) Daniel prophesied that in the days of these kings, the Lord would set up a kingdom. It is generally agreed that the kings referred to were the Roman Emperors. If already set up in Abraham or Moses, Daniel could not refer to it as a future event. John the Baptist began his ministry by declaring: "The kingdom of heaven is at hand." [*engike*—is coming and close at hand]. He could not have so spoken if it had come hundreds of years before.

(4.) The Lord, by Jeremiah (xxxi: 31) declared that he would make a new covenant with the house of Israel. Paul applied this prophecy to the church—the Spiritual Israel—and declares that "God hath made the first OLD." (Heb. viii: 13). And in the subsequent chapter, running the parallel between the two dispensations, declares (v. 11): "But Christ being come an high priest of good things to come, by a greater and more perfect tabernacle, not made with hands, that is to say, NOT OF THIS BUILDING."

(5.) It is also declared: "That the law and the prophets were until John; since that time the kingdom of heaven is preached, and every man presseth into it." If the Jews were already in this kingdom; how could they be said to press into it? The expression clearly imports that with the preaching of John began a new order of things and not the perpetuation of the old under a new form.

(6.) Many of the epistles were written to correct and oppose the errors of Judaizing teachers, and it is remarkable that this identity was never invoked by either party to the controversy, and it would have been referred to so naturally in the contest that arose about the circumcision of the Gentile converts. It would have settled the matter so satisfactorily, if the church at Jerusalem could have assured those troubled on the subject, that the church was but a continuation of the Jewish polity, with baptism substituted for circumcision, and other changes to adapt it to the new order of things. But as they did not do what would have been so natural to do we must conclude that they did not so understand the matter.

CHAPTER II.

SETTING UP THE CHURCH.

I have shown in the last chapter that the church is not the perpetuation of the Jewish hierarchy under a modified form, but that it is a new organization. The next inquiry will be when it was set up. I will endeavor to trace it from its tender beginnings to its complete development.

SECTION 1. *Mission of John the Baptist.*—His was a preparatory work. Before a church could be organized—before a kingdom could be set up, materials must be prepared, subjects must be made ready. And this was the holy mission assigned to the Harbinger. The Evangelists apply to him the prophecy of Isaiah (xl: 3:) "The voice of one crying in the wilderness; prepare ye the way of the Lord make straight in the desert a pathway for our God." The angel that announced the birth of John to his father Zacharias, said: (Luke i: 6-19) "And many of the children of Israel shall he turn to the Lord their God. And he shall go before Him in the power of Elias, to turn the hearts of the fathers to the children and the disobedient to the wisdom of the just; to make ready a people prepared for the Lord." And Zacharias afterwards prophesied of his son (Luke i: *76 et seq:*) "And thou child shalt be called the prophet of the Highest; for thou shalt go before the face of the Lord to prepare His ways; to give knowledge of salvation to His people by the remission of their sins through the tender mercy of God, whereby the day-spring from on high hath visited us, and to give light to them that sit in darkness and the shadow of death; to guide our feet into the way of peace." This shows the kind of preparation he was charged to make. It was to make ready a people prepared for the Lord. We will presently consider in what that readiness consisted. Notice the thoroughness of that preparation. It was to make a straight pathway. Mountains were to be leveled and valleys filled. Nothing was to be left undone for the proper ushering in of His kingdom. A people must be made ready, prepared for the Lord; not merely apprised of His coming, and prepared to expect Him; but also ready to receive Him by joining His standard. He should not only precede the Highest, to announce His speedy coming, but also to prepare to receive Him. He was to give knowledge of salvation to His people by the remission of their sins by the tender mercy of God. This was to be the condition of the people prepared to receive Him. This preparation embraced several particulars which we proceed to consider.

1. Instruction.—He was to give knowledge of salvation. Hence he came preaching in the wilderness. That preaching must have embraced the whole gospel plan of salvation; for it was to transform their characters by turning the hearts of the fathers to the children and the disobedient to the wisdom of the just, and to give knowledge of salvation. This necessarily included the means of salvation through faith in Him who was to come.

2. But the instruction was rendered effective. He was to come in the wisdom and power of Elias. The preparation embraced a *change of heart.* "Except a man be born again he cannot see the kingdom of God." A change of heart is necessarily implied in the word *metanoia* (repentance), employed in connection with his preaching. The repentance which John preached was a thorough reformation, which can only take place by a radical change of the

desires, and this is the work of the Holy Spirit. Some urge in opposition to this view the example of those disciples whom Paul found at Ephesus and who said they had been baptized unto the baptism of John, but declared that they had never so much as heard whether there be any Holy Ghost. But these persons could not have been baptized by John himself and instructed by him; but by some ignorant or careless disciple of John; for their very declaration proves that they could not have been converted under the preaching of John the Baptist who constantly spoke of the Holy Spirit. He preached, "I indeed baptize you with water unto repentance; but he that cometh after me is mightier than I, whose shoes I am not worthy to bear; He shall baptize with the Holy Ghost and with fire." He also told the people after the baptism of Jesus: "I saw the Spirit descending from heaven like a dove and it abode upon Him. And I knew Him not; but He that sent me to baptize with water the same said unto me: "Upon whom thou shalt see the Spirit descending and remaining on Him, the same is He which baptizeth with the Holy Ghost." Could any true disciple of John be ignorant of the Holy Spirit?

3. *Repentance.*—"Then came John the Baptist, preaching in the wilderness of Judea, and saying: Repent, for the kingdom of heaven is at hand." This is exactly the language in which Jesus opened His own personal ministry. The same repentance which Jesus preached, John the Baptist preached. And when multitudes came to his baptism he required them to bring forth fruits becoming repentance.

4. *Faith.*—In his discourses he constantly refers to the Messiah as the Lamb of God that taketh away the sins of the world. His disciples were ready to join the standard of Jesus as soon as John

made known the person. Repentance of the kind of which he preached includes faith, for there can be no true repentance without it. Remission of sins also implies faith, for there could be no forgiveness of sins without it; for unbelief is itself the chief sin. Paul declares that John preached faith in Christ: "John verily baptized with the baptism of repentance, saying unto the people that they should believe on him, which should come after him, that is on Christ Jesus." (Acts xix: 4.) He declares himself that he came baptizing with water that Christ might be manifest to Israel. (John i: 31). And John the Evangelist declares that John the Baptist came to "bear witness of the light that all through him might believe." (John i: 7.)

5. *Baptism.*—Many were "baptized of him in the river Jordan, confessing their sins." This proves that the subjects were adults, for only such could be conscious of sin. It also shows that they had exercised repentance and faith, for only such would make a sincere confession of their sins. We have already shown that the action performed by him was immersion and that the same word was used to describe the action performed by Christ and His apostles. The persons therefore baptized by John possessed the same qualifications both as to subject and to action as were required for admission into the church.

But did Christ organize His church in the first instance out of the disciples of John. I think this can be made to appear with sufficient clearness to satisfy any reasonable mind. Unless the material prepared by John was used by Christ, the work of John was useless; and there is no propriety in saying that he prepared a people, made ready for the Lord, if the Lord did not accept them when He began to organize His kingdom. But we are not left without some positive proof on the subject.

Jesus himself, a member of the church which He constituted and its first pastor, was baptized by John, declaring that this was necessary to fulfill all righteousness. If necessary for Him it was to say the least, equally necessary for His disciples also. We learn from the first chapter of John that Andrew and John (or at least another disciple, supposed to be John, whose well-known modesty would lead him to conceal his name) were disciples of the Baptist who followed Jesus when He was pointed out to him by John. When the disciples were met at Jerusalem to select a successor to the apostate Judas Iscariot, Peter said: "Wherefore of these men who have companied with us all the time that the Lord went in and out among us, beginning FROM THE BAPTISM OF JOHN unto that same day that he was taken up from us, must one be ordained to be a witness with us of His resurrection." (Acts i: 21).

Here Peter connects himself and others directly with the baptism of John, and makes it a qualification for the apostolic office that one should have companied with them all the time from the baptism of John. The apostles were the eye witnesses of the acts of Christ from the beginning. We read that Christ, through His disciples, made and baptized more disciples than John. He was accustomed to baptize the disciples He made, therefore the apostles must have been baptized, and it is not material whether by himself or John the Baptist.

SECTION 2. *Collection of the Material.*—Immediately after His baptism Jesus was led up of the Spirit into the wilderness to be tempted of the devil, and His public ministry did not begin until after this event. But very soon afterward He began the work of gathering His church. While John was pursuing his mission Jesus walked in the midst of the people. This afforded an opportunity to the

Harbinger to point out the person of the Saviour to his disciples. "Behold the Lamb of God." And two of his disciples, Andrew and John followed Him. This was the small beginning of the church. Andrew immediately sought his own brother. The day following He found Philip, and said unto him: "Follow me," and Philip findeth Nathaniel who also joined the little company of disciples. We are not informed precisely when others were added but we soon find Him appearing in public, accompanied by His disciples and engaged in the work of His ministry. His popularity was very great. Multitudes hung upon His ministry and the report soon reached the ears of John that Jesus made and baptized more disciples than he.

As the work enlarged He selected out of the company of disciples He had collected twelve apostles, who should receive special instruction, and He ordained them to go forth and preach. Subsequently He sent out seventy others by whom the gospel was widely disseminated among the Jews, to whom alone it was first preached.

Just before His crucifixion He instituted the Lord's Supper to commemorate His death. The church was then complete in its ordinances. It was gathered and accustomed to assemble about His person. It was composed of clergy and laity, to use terms that have been much abused, but which are the only ones at my command to express the distinction between official and unofficial members. They were voluntarily associated, and Jesus himself was the pastor.

It has been stoutly disputed at what time the formal organization of the church took place. But no such formal organization was necessary, and in my opinion ever took place with that formality with which we now constitute and recognize churches. Its organization was a work of growth. But when the first disciples gathered around the great teacher they possessed all the elements of a church *i. e.* voluntary association and the choice of a spiritual guide. We find the Saviour in the 18th of Matthew giving instruction in regard to discipline, and He expressly recognizes the existence of the church, and in such a way as shows that the idea was well understood by the disciples. Before the day of Pentecost we find the church assembled as an organized body and transacting business.

On the day of Pentecost a large accession was made to its membership and the account of it clearly implies that they were added not to an organization then first formed, but to an organization already formed.

Such was the increase that it became necessary, under the direction of the Holy Spirit, to add seven deacons. As the disciples multiplied the sphere of labor enlarged and zealous preachers of the gospel went into all parts of the world, making and baptizing disciples, and organizing new churches after the model of the first church at Jerusalem. To instruct these in the doctrines and duties of Christianity, a number of epistles were written and the historical portions of the New Testament by men inspired of God for the purpose. These compose the written code of the church and serve to direct Christians in all questions of faith and practice.

CHAPTER III.

PERPETUITY OF THE CHURCH.

I have already (Part I, chapter III) considered the legislative power of the church, promising to revert to the subject in considering the perpetuity of that order which was set up by Christ and his apostles. I now propose to show that the Holy Spirit was not guided by mere accident, caprice, or expediency in selecting that form of church government which was established at the beginning; but that it was selected because of its adaptability to the wants of God's people which have continued the same in all ages; and therefore there can arise no necessity under the present order of things for any change.

1. I showed that not only no legislative power was bestowed upon the church, but that it was forbidden to exercise any such power. And this shall form our first argument. If no provision has been made for a change it affords a strong presumption that no change was intended. At any rate it furnishes conclusive proof that the church was not endowed with power to alter its external form; and that Christ has reserved to himself that power if such changes were ever contemplated in the divine economy. The Jews did not dare to change their institutions without the authority of God; or if they desired or attempted even indirectly such a thing, they thereby incurred the displeasure of the Almighty and often received the severest punishment. If the Jews could not of their own accord change their institutions, much less can Christians alter that order which Christ introduced without some authority to do so. But we have seen that

they possessed no such power, and as Christ has not interfered to make or authorize any change it follows that no change has been allowed.

2. The Holy Spirit was not guided by mere accident, or caprice, or temporary expediency in the selection of that form which was adopted at the beginning. We cannot dissociate God from the idea of design. He would not be God without purpose. It derogates from His sovereign power to suppose that He is the subject of accident. Can He whose power can dispose all events and whose providence regulates even the falling of the sparrow, be the sport of chance in the choice of means to accomplish his ends? Neither is he governed by caprice. While he is an absolute sovereign this by no means imports that he is a capricious tyrant, governed by his whims. He is directed in the use of means by the eternal fitness of things. What he does is always the best and most appropriate to be done. But we are told he was governed by temporary expediency in the choice of the eternal form of the church, and that what suited one state of things might not suit under different circumstances. This is to assume what is very necessary to prove, viz.: That the particular circumstances which directed his choice have materially changed. Certainly he has given no intimation that such changes have taken place, and in his silence we must infer that no such changes have taken place as require his interference.

But mere temporary expediency cannot account for the external forms of the church. In no instance are they such as circumstances would suggest. What events could have suggested the initiatory rite that does not apply with equal force to any period of the church's history. I can conceive of no circumstances under which immersion is more convenient than aspersion. It is a more conspicuous act than aspersion. If a notable act was required then it is equally so now. If publicity was dangerous it was a circumstance against, rather than in favor of, the temporary expediency of immersion. So of the Lord's Supper. Bread and wine could not have been required by expediency, and circumstances could not have suggested the use of both substances. The participation of the multitude of the disciples in the government of the church was inconvenient in some respects and exposed the church to the hatred of the Imperial government under which they lived because it was naturally jealous of everything that encouraged a return to the republic. Indeed I am at a loss to find a single institution of the Apostolic Church, demanded by mere expediency, and I find many which mere human prudence would never have suggested.

3. The positive institutions of the gospel were selected because of their adaptability to the wants of God's people, not in that age only, but in all time to come. The cotemporaries of the apostles did no more need the lessons of instruction conveyed by the commemorative ordinances than we do to-day. We need as many props to our halting faith as they; and whatever the design and significance of these ordinances, they are as necessary to us as to them. The human race is affected by the same depravity now as then. The same wicked unbelief, the same carnal enmity to God is to be removed. The same renovation must be brought about. The same gospel is to be preached. The same discipline is to be sustained; and whatever relations the external forms of the church bore to these then, they bear now. The spiritual necessities of men are the same, and are to be supplied in the same way. The same opposition to the progress of the gospel exists. Though victorious in a thousand conflicts, the church turns everywhere to encounter

the same foe. "The weapons of her warfare are not carnal, but spiritual and mighty." They neither grow old, nor decay; but they grow brighter and stronger by use.

The laity shared in the government, not because the times then more than now demanded it, but because the good of the whole in all ages is promoted thereby. It is because the government in which all participate is that which is best adapted to the accomplishment of the end designed. The obligations of religion are personal, and that form of government which calls into exercise the greatest number of personal endowments is the most effective. The gospel theory of a church contemplates a body of persons sanctified and enlightened, and each becomes a power felt in proportion to the responsibilites devolved upon him; and hence that is the most effective church which moves as a whole. Nor can it be objected that such bodies are more liable to corruption and dissension. If composed of the kind of persons designed by Christ, holy men taught of God, they will not be guided by evil passions; nor will they depart readily from the truth. I grant that a popular assembly directed by unregenerate men would be a very inefficient agency for propagating the gospel, and the more so in proportion to the want of piety. But I am discussing the efficiency of that church which is composed as Christ designed it should be.

The popular form of government is the more fitting, because the interests of all being common, it is reasonable that they should share in common the administration of their mutual interest; and all will prize more highly what they all feel to be peculiarly their own. The recruits of the church are from the masses of mankind and that government appeals most to their sympathies which accords to them the greatest share of privileges.

It is thought by some that the Apostolic Churches, as an aggressive power, were defective from their independent characters. But the history of the church, during the first century, while yet the churches were independent of each other, shows the contrary. At no period have the disciples multiplied more rapidly. The same is true of churches organized upon this plan in subsequent times. The church only propagates itself by contact with society, hence each local church segregates the pious near it. When the materials are exhausted it throws out colonies to be new centers of influence. Unity of faith and a common brotherhood and fellowship of the Spirit are stronger bonds of union than any mere organic connection, and such a union exists in every true Church of Christ.

CHAPTER IV.

THE SOURCE OF KNOWLEDGE.

The Bible is the only depository of divine knowledge, and the only accessible source of information pertaining to the world to come. Here God has revealed all that is necessary or desirable to be known. It furnishes a sufficient guide in all matters of faith and practice. A proper knowledge of its truths is all that is needful. It contains all that God intends to reveal of Himself, His will and the state of the dead; and the only supernatural aid afforded is His Holy Spirit, which prepares the mind to receive the divine knowledge conveyed in His Word.

But men are not content with this source of knowledge. They seek to put themselves in communication with the spirit world. This has given rise to a class of persons who pretend to be *media* of communication with departed spirits, and to convey new truths in regard to the state of the dead. It is not my design to discuss the question whether such communications are possible; nor to attempt to explain the phenomena that attend the seances of Spiritualists; but to consider the pretended revelations of Spiritism as a source of divine knowledge. The desire of knowledge, properly directed, meets the approbation of God, and tends to promote the happiness and well-being of man. To this desire we are indebted for all the useful improvements in the arts and sciences, and all the practical appliances that surround us with comforts in this life. Of this desire God avails Himself to put Himself into communication with men. He has placed within our reach all that is useful or necessary for us to know in our present state. But he has set bounds to our inquiries. To attempt to go beyond is presumptuous rebellion, and incurs the displeasure of God. Such was the sin of our first parents. So long as they were content to confine their investigations to things lawful, they were innocent and happy. But not satisfied with this, they sought for hidden knowledge. They were prohibited from eating the fruit of the tree of the knowledge of good and evil, which grew in the midst of the Garden; and ruin was the result of their rash disobedience. And whoever attempts to follow their mischievous example may expect a like result.

Whatever is placed within the reach of man's senses, or is palpable to his own consciousness, is a legitimate field of inquiry; because he treads on *terra firma*, and others may follow his footsteps, and correct his observations. But whenever he goes beyond and attempts to invade the realm of the invisible, he treads on air and deals with flitting shadows; and his conclusions are as unstable as "the baseless fabric of a vision." He goes forth on a perilous voyage with only conjecture for his pilot, and no wonder that he is wrecked.

To prevent such dangerous excursions, God himself stands in the vestibule of the invisible world, and becomes himself the sole medium of its dread secrets. For man's own good he is prohibited from seeking any other guide to its secrets, and he who makes the rash attempt finds his punishment in being given up to strong delusions, to believe a lie and be damned.

The injunction of the Scripture is, "If any of you lack wisdom, let him ask of God who giveth to all men liberally and upbraideth not." (James v: 1). The exposition of this text will present what I desire to say on the subject.

If we knew nothing of the history of the past, we

might suppose this Scripture written expressly for our own times. But that prying disposition which seeks to wring from the dread unknown its guarded secrets, has existed in all ages, and men and women have been found who offered themselves as janitors to unlock the spirit world and communicate with its inhabitants.

The proper elucidation of the subject leads me to inquire:

1. *What is wisdom!* It is not every species of knowledge that constitutes wisdom. A man may know a great deal, and yet be very unwise. True wisdom consists in the knowledge of what is best to be known, and the ability to apply that knowledge to useful purposes. The wisdom spoken of in this text is a knowledge of divine things. It is the possession of what God desires us to know. It embraces a knowledge of the duties we are called upon to perform; the service we are required to pay to God; what he sees proper to reveal of the future; such doctrines as he has made known for our comfort and growth in grace; and such views of the invisible world as he has chosen to disclose. To be content with that knowledge, striving to gain the greatest advantage from it, is true wisdom, that wisdom which is from above, which is "first pure, then peaceable, gentle, and easy to be entreated, full of mercy and good fruits, without partiality, and without hypocrisy."

2. The lack of wisdom is the need of what is proper and best to be known. We do not need injurious information. Hurtful knowledge is not a need of our condition here. In our blindness and folly we may desire to know what will be hurtful to know; but God has not promised that. We may from idle curiosity desire unprofitable knowledge; but we cannot be said to need it.

He promises to give whatever knowledge we

need. We are, therefore, under no necessity to seek information from any other source in regard to the future, or in regard to that unexplored world that lies beyond the present sphere. From the benevolent character of God, we must conclude that He has revealed, or will make known, whatever is beneficial to us; and that what he has not revealed cannot benefit us to know.

If it should be said that we need the testimony of those who have gone before us into the world of spirits to strengthen our faith, the blessed Saviour has answered it in the parable of the rich man and Lazarus, where he introduces Abraham as saying: "If they hear not Moses and the prophets, neither will they be persuaded though one rise from the dead." (Luke xvi : 31).

3. The passage we are considering recognizes God as the true source of wisdom, the fountain of true knowledge. Will any one dare to say that God has not made known in His blessed Word all that is necessary for us to know to regulate our duties or promote our happiness; or that there is any better source of knowledge than God? His intelligence would furnish Him with a knowledge of the wants of man in life, and his benevolence would prompt him to make it known. Hence we find him communicating directly with man. He talked face to face with Adam before the fall. It is said of Enoch that he walked with God. To the patriarchs he sent messengers to communicate His will. He talked with Moses in the mount, and made known his will. By His Holy Spirit He inspired the Prophets and Apostles to write, and He Himself, in the person of the Son, condescended to mingle with men and teach them his word; and we have the result of their labors in the Book of Books. Is that word incomplete that men are under the necessity of opening a new fountain to supply its

deficiences? Do His promises need confirmation by pretended seers, and the spirits of the departed, speaking through so-called media? Does His word need to be verified by spirits called from the vasty deep? The closing chapter of Revelation clearly imports that God had finished the work of communicating his will to man, and what was proper to be known of that world which is next to ours, but separated from it by an impassable gulf. Granting that we may reasonably expect Him to continue His revelations, He will guard His elect from imposition by attesting the mission of His Prophets in some unmistakable manner. In the past, God ratified the mission of His true Prophets by endowing them with power to work miracles. Let those who claim to speak to-day as the oracles of God, stand forth and attest their mission as did the Apostles of old by restoring the dead to life. They did not ask the world to believe them prophets upon their own mere declaration. God himself bore witness to it. Even Jesus himself did not deem it below His dignity to receive divine attestation.

4. We cannot rely on any revelation, not made by God Himself, or attested by him. But here are pretended revelations, made independent of God, and, as I will directly show, in direct violation of His commandments, and even contradicting what He has hitherto revealed. Can this information thus surreptitiously obtained be relied on?

Bating a vast amount of impostures that have confessedly attended these manifestations; bating the scientific theory on the one hand that attributes these phenomena so far as they are real to some psychic force not yet fully understood, and in many instances unconsciously exerted by the medium; and on the other hand, the theological theory that attributes them to Satanic agencies; giving full credit to the integrity and sincerity of the medium;

and admitting for the nonce, that the strange things witnessed are really produced by departed spirits, attempting to communicate their thoughts to us, how are we to know with any degree of certainty, that we have correctly interpreted their signs? The difficulty of understanding arbitrary signs, without the intervention of language, is well illustrated in the efforts to decipher the celebrated Rosetta Stone. Chompollion, a French savant, who spent his life, in exploring the antiquities of Egypt, as he thought, hit upon the key by which he was enabled to read the hieroglyphic monuments of the country. On applying it he read inscription after inscription, it seemed impossible that there should be any mistake. But a few years ago two young men, students at Harvard University, engaged in the study of Archæology, hit upon an entirely different key, with which they readily interpreted the monumental remains of Egypt, but with entirely different results. Both made good sense, but conveyed entirely different meanings, so that the learned world are as much puzzled as before to know what the ancient Egyptians meant. Who shall say that the Chompollion of the spirits may not find, some day, some beardless Hale, just weaned of his *Alma Mater*, stepping forth with a new key to the raps and tilts of Spiritism that will put an entirely different face upon the knowledge gained.

The very uncertainty that attaches to the proper interpretations of these manifestations would deter any prudent man from relying upon them, especially in making their supposed revelations the ground of religious belief.

5. But it is said: "If any of you lack wisdom, let him ask of GOD,"—not of some muttering wizard who pretends to hold the keys of divine knowledge—not of some phrenzied Pythoness, inflated over the fumes of her tripod, whose inco-

herent ravings shall be taken for the oracles of God; not of some witch of Endor, invoking her familiar spirit; not of some modern medium, calling spirits from the vasty deep; but "ask of GOD, who giveth to all men liberally and upbraideth not."

I add some of the denunciations of God against the terrible sin, against which this chapter is directed.

Lev. xix : 31 : Regard not them that have familiar spirits, neither seek after wizards.

Lev. xx : 6 : And the soul that turneth after such as have familiar spirits, and after wizards, to go a whoring after them, I will even set my face against that soul, and will cut him off from among his people.

Lev. xx : 27 : A man also, or a woman, that hath a familiar spirit, or is a wizard, shall be put to death.

Here in the commonwealth of Israel, they were punished as murderers, because they murdered the misguided souls who sought their forbidden knowledge.

Deut. xviii : 11 : The consulter with familiar spirits is declared to be an abomination to the Lord. It was one of the abominable sins that destroyed Saul, that he consulted the Witch of Endor, who was a spiritual medium.

2 Kings xxi : 6 : It is mentioned as one of the gross sins of Manassah, that he dealt with familiar spirits.

Isaiah viii : 19 : And when they shall say unto you, Seek unto them that have familiar spirits, and unto wizards, that peep and that mutter; should not a people seek unto their God? for the living to the dead?

The learned Adam Clarke, supplying the ellipsis. renders the latter clause, " Should not a nation seek unto its God? Why should you seek unto the dead concerning the living?" And to-day we might ask the people, why should the living go to the dead for knowledge? Why should they not seek unto God?

6. Lastly, let us notice some of the encouragements to seek wisdom of God. *"He giveth to all liberally."* He withholds nothing that we need. He bestows all the light that is necessary to guide our erring footsteps. Nothing is lacking. He giveth to all men who ask him in faith, nothing wavering. Why should any suppose that because he has hung a veil over the future, that he meant otherwise than in kindness to his creatures? Why should we seek to reach across the line that separates between the visible and invisible worlds, and attempt to pluck fruit which He has forbidden, to gain knowledge which He has withheld. We may be sure that whatever, pertaining to the world to come, will be of service to us, He will communicate to us. Here in His Word He has given us glimpses of the New Jerusalem, enough to spur our tardy resolutions to press thither. Here also He has so far pulled aside the veil as to give us some faint conception of the fate of the sinner. Whatever else He may have withheld, we may rest assured it will not benefit us to know.

He is not dipleased with the earnest inquirer after wisdom. He upbraideth not. When Solomon asked wisdom of God, He was greatly pleased because he had not asked long life for himself, nor riches, nor the life of his enemies; but asked for understanding, to discern judgment. Freely we may come to the school of Christ, not fearing a rude repulse, but assured that He will impart all the knowledge now necessary, and after awhile will impart more when he invites us to come up higher.

Let us then not doubt the sufficiency of the Scriptures for instruction, reproof and doctrine, and distrust every proposal to seek knowledge elsewhere.

CHAPTER V.

CHURCH SUCCESSION.

The church of Christ was not a transient institution, to pass away with its founders and to be lost in the convulsions of society. But it has survived to the present day; not mutilated and shorn of its fair proportions, but preserving the identity of its form and doctrines. That order which was established at the beginning has continued in all its essential features from generation to generation until now. Not a link in the chain has been broken. We may not be able in every instance to furnish the historical proofs showing the connection of the churches with each other any more than I can name the succession of ancestors that connects me with Adam. The proof of my relationship does not depend upon the genealogical tables which I may be able to present. The fact is sufficiently established when I have shown that I am a man like Adam, and that beings of the same order have existed in all ages since creation. He who contests the fact of my descent must show positively a different origin. So that if we are able to find churches to-day agreeing in doctrine and external form with the pattern of the Apostolic Church, which we trace in the Scriptures, and find similar churches existing at no very remote period from each other, during all the ages of Christianity, the proof of a succession is sufficiently made out to put the burden of proof upon those who contest the succession. Add to this the declaration of Christ, that the gates of hell should not prevail against His church, and the proof is complete, unless forsooth, the Son of God was a false prophet. But if His church has continued to exist without interruption where shall we look to find it, but in those organizations that are most like the visible church which He established at the beginning.

It must be borne in mind that the church is a visible organization and not an imaginary body composed of all Christians. It embraces certain external forms which were instituted by Christ and His apostles, and is composed of persons qualified according to the law of Christ; and when I speak of church succession I mean that bodies of Christians organized according to the Apostolic Church, have succeeded each other from the apostles until now.

During the first and second centuries the departure from the apostolic order was slow and scarcely perceptible. But even then there were many single bodies that preserved the ancient purity of doctrine and practice; and when the great mass became corrupt there were always some who resisted the corruptionists and preserved the original order; and the History of the Apostate Church is chiefly made up of efforts to suppress the societies of those who sought to preserve and restore the apostolic order.

Those who have given but a superficial examination to church history suppose that after the purer days of the apostles and primitive Christianity, the whole church became gradually corrupt, until it merged into the great Roman Apostasy; and that whatever parties existed outside of the Roman communion, they had sloughed off from it and were, if possible, more corrupt in doctrine and practice; or, if they occasionally recognized a purer class, they suppose that they broke away from Rome and revived the New Testament order for a time, to be again absorbed in the general apostasy, until Luther, in the early part of the sixteenth century, established a more general and permanent reformation.

Those who take this view generally admit the claim of Rome to be the mother church, placing themselves in an awkward dilemma. If they deny Rome to be a true church of Christ, they destroy the validity of their own ordinances, because if transmission is necessary to their validity, as most believe, it can hardly be admitted that valid ordinances can be transmitted by a false church. But if they confess Rome to be a true church, then they acknowledge themselves schismatics in having forcibly separated from the true church. There is but one escape from this dilemma, and that is to show that the validity of ordinances does not depend on the authority of a church of Christ. But it will hardly be questioned that succession in some sense is necessary to the validity of ordinances; in other words, that they must have been received by regular tradition from Christ and his apostles, through an uninterrupted chain of persons succeeding each other. No company of persons, however pious, can *originate* ordinances independent of, and outside of this line of succession, and the ordinances presented by such a *sporadic* organization would not be received as genuine coin at any counter in Christendom. For it strikes the common sense of mankind that no man can confer what he has never received. Hence all denominations are anxious to make it appear that they are in the line of succession, and thus remove all suspicion of validity in their ordinances. The command was to keep the ordinances as they were delivered, and only such as have thus kept them can deliver them to others. The Scriptures reveal the fact that there is a true and a false church in the world. Such being the case, can it be a question which of them Christ has made the depository of everything which pertains to the administration of the external affairs of his kingdom? And where any organization has ceased to adhere to the apostolic pattern it has lost the power of transmission; for how can they transmit what they do not practice?

But mere succession alone is not sufficient; it must be a succession in the truth. Only those are successors to the apostles who have continued in the apostles' doctrine and fellowship. It is no doubt true that the church of Rome can trace historical connection with the Apostolic Church. But that does not prove her to be a true church, for she has ceased to be like the true church. By degrees she departed from the original model until she ceased to be in any way the perpetuation of the gospel church; for as she departed from the original model she also departed from the true line of succession.

Now, if no irregular organization can transmit the ordinances it follows for a greater reason that Anti-Christ cannot be the channel through which they have been handed down to us. Protestants are agreed that Rome is the great apostate church —the Anti-Christ, exalting himself above all that is called God. If this be true how can any candid, conscientious member of any of those ecclesiastical organizations which derive their ordinances from Rome, be satisfied with their validity? How can any minister feel himself possessed of valid ordination who has received it from the unholy hands of Anti-Christ? Can Anti-Christ properly set aside a minister of Christ's true church? As well might the priests of Baal attempt to consecrate an altar to the true and living God, and sanctify and invest with priestly authority the priesthood of Jehovah! God has permitted no such absurdities, nor allowed any such necessities in His government, but has graciously provided against such an apparent excuse for neglecting His true church in the world.

Christ is under no necessity to depend upon any

such organizations for the preservation of His institutions; for there has been no time since its organization when His church did not exist in the world. The body of Christians for whom I claim the honor of being the true successors of the apostles, is not one of those sects that have arisen in this prolific age of isms, but it is venerable for its antiquity; distinguished for the simplicity of its doctrines and worship; and having its garments dyed in the blood of its martyred saints. Its history is written in flame, and blood, and exile. It is the only living Christian organization that can successfully contest the palm of antiquity with the Roman Hierarchy and which can trace the line of its spiritual genealogy outside of the line of Romish succession, in which all the others sooner or later terminate. It derives neither its ordinances nor its succession from Rome, and the validity of neither is affected by her apostasy.

The difficulty of furnishing connected historical proofs of our succession must be apparent when we consider that until a hundred years past our people have been under the ban of both civil and ecclesiastical authorities; that there was no greater offense against either than to be a Baptist, that they were subject to the most fiery persecutions, their congregations broken up and dispersed; and that they were exiles in every country; that for their own security they sheltered themselves as much as possible from the public eye; that their accusers had every motive to misrepresent them; and that they were denied the opportunity to defend themselves; that all their books and papers were seized and burned whenever found. As yet there has been no organized effort to exhume from the archives of the old world the monuments of their history. Those archives have always been and are still in the hands of our enemies, and scarcely yet fully accessible to us, so that their history is yet really to be written. As yet we have often to trace it through dark periods, and sift the truth from the perverted statements of our enemies. And yet with all these difficulties God has preserved sufficient monuments; and new ones are being brought to light every year, to enable us to trace our succession with such reasonable certainty as to satisfy the mind of any impartial inquirer after the truth. I do not mean to say that we can name all the persons that form the links in this chain, as the Roman Catholic may trace the connection between Pope Pio Nono and Pope Sylvester; but I do say that there has been no period since the days of the apostles when there did not exist persons having no connection whatever with the Church of Rome, who held substantially the same sentiments we hold; and such has always been the proximity of time and place as to show beyond a rational doubt, the connection between them.

CHAPTER VI.

HERESY AND SCHISM.

I have in another part of this work discussed the Rights of Conscience and Private Judgment. I have fully conceded the right of every man to judge for himself in matters of religion, subject only to his responsibility to God, who will hold him accountable for the correctness of his faith. The only limit to this right is the right of every other man to do the same thing. I use the term right in a modified sense, not in respect to the abstract character of the action, but to express what a man may do without any interference on the part of his fellowmen. This right does not import that religion is a mere matter of taste, and that each may choose a religion which shall be acceptable to God. In respect to God no man has a right to do wrong. It is therefore, meant only to affirm that one may not punish another for the exercise of his religious faith, by the privation of his civil rights, or by inflicting upon him any corporeal punishment. If in the exercise of his judgment he errs, he is not guiltless, but God, and not man, is his judge.

The object of this chapter is to inquire how one may exercise this right with respect to others; for each must exercise his right in such a manner as not to interrupt others in pursuing the same right; and to ascertain what is the duty of the church in respect to those who may err. If men in the exercise of the right thus accorded to them judge wrong and separate themselves from the church and organize opposition to the truth, is the church bound to regard and treat them with the same consideration as those who love and maintain the truth; and preserve the unity and fellowship of the brotherhood? Is it one of the rights of private judgment to teach and practice error in the very bosom of the church, without censure or restraint? Has the church no rights which he is bound to respect?

The term heresy and schism are often used to express dissent from a State religion. But originally they had no such signification. It is into their Scriptural meaning that I propose to inquire.

Heresy (Gr. *hairesis*) originally signified a choice, and related to the selection between conflicting religions, and the act of identifying one's-self with a party, who hold views similar to his own. At first it was applied to a class without respect to the correctness, or incorrectness of their opinions. Thus it is used in reference to both the heterodox Sadducees (Acts xv: 17,) and the orthodox Pharisees (Acts xv: 5) alike. Tertullus uses it as a term of reproach to the whole body of Christians as distinguished from the Jews. (Acts xxiv: 5–14).

Very soon after the introduction of Christianity false teachers began to multiply and false doctrine to be taught, and the term heresy acquired an application to every system of doctrine contrary to apostolic teaching, and it is in this sense we consider it.

Schism (Gr. *Schisma*) primarily signifies rupture or division. As heresy is a departure from the divine doctrines of the apostles, so schism is a separation from the fellowship of the church. Heresy respects doctrine, schism the order of the church.

As the church is charged with the administration of the laws of Christ and the preservation of that order which he established, it is plain that schism, which defies the authority of the church, and rends the body is no trifling offense; and hence we find the apostles constantly warning the disciples against divisions. *Rom. xxi: 17.* " Now, I beseech you brethren, mark them which cause divisions and heresies contrary to the doctrines which ye have learned, and avoid them." Here the church is enjoined to do two things, to *watch* and to *avoid.*

1. To Watch—Error is very insidious in its approaches. It grows from small beginnings. Intercepted at the outset it is easily arrested; but if disregarded it becomes a huge gangrene, corrupting and destroying the body. Watch with the view to prevent the weak and unstable from falling into error. Watch, that the advocates of error be not placed in positions where they may propagate error. Those who are to be admitted to official positions as teachers or rulers, are to be subject to the closest scrutiny to ascertain if they are "sound in the faith." This precaution is also to be observed with reference to those without who have assumed the office of instruction.

No man may claim exemption from this scrutiny. He may not draw around him the mantle of offended dignity, and repel the inquiry, declaring that it is nobody's business what he believes or teaches. It is no infringement of his rights for those under the cover of whose fellowship he seeks to gain respectability for his error, to mark his departure from the doctrine of Christ in terms of distinct disapprobation.

2. To avoid them. Evil communications corrupt good manners. Familiarity with error lessens our abhorrence for it. Men of pleasing address, and some excellent qualities gain us to their errors before we are aware. When the heart is won to the person, the head is half convinced. Hence the injunction to "avoid them that cause divisions contrary to the doctrines of Christ." John admonishes us: "If there come any unto you and bring not this doctrine [the doctrine of Christ] receive him not into your houses, neither bid him God speed, for he that biddeth him God speed is partaker of his evil deeds." "Withdraw yourself from every brother that walketh disorderly and not according to the traditions ye have received from us."

That heresy, or departure from the doctrine of Christ is no trifling offense, is evident from the kind of offenses with which it is classed. *Gal. v: 19.* "Now the works of the flesh are manifest which are adultery, fornication, uncleanness, lasciviousness, idolatry, witchcraft, hatred, variance, emulation, strife, seditions, heresies, envyings, murders, drunkenness, revelings, and such like, of the which I tell you before, as I have told you in time past that they which do such things, shall not inherit the kingdom of God."

The manner of dealing with the heretic is expressly laid down. (Titus iii: 10). "The man that is an heretic after the first and second admonition reject."

1. He must be admonished. A faithful effort must be made to reclaim him from his error. This must be done kindly, but faithfully. He who is teaching what is not recognized as truth, may not claim exemption from this admonition. The efforts to reclaim him from his error must not be abandoned with the first effort. He must be admonished the second time. He should not be abandoned as long as there is reasonable hopes of reclaiming him.

2. But if after the second admonition he remains incorrigible he must be rejected. No man may shelter himself in the bosom of the church, and claim immunity for his departure from the truth, on the plea of his right of private judgment. If he choose to dissent from the church he may do so; but he has no longer any claims upon her fellowship. "Reject"—This imports that he should be cast out

of the church. So long as he remains in the fellowship of the church, unmarked by her censure, he is tacitly endorsed.

If there is an obligation to reject those within, who depart from the faith it is equally as important, and equally as obligatory to reject those who approach from without.

It is only by enforcing the law against heretics, and schismatics that the church can preserve the purity of her discipline, and maintain the faith once delivered to the saints, with the preservation of which she is charged.

CHAPTER VII.

THE BASIS OF CHRISTIAN UNION.

As much is being said and many efforts put forth to accomplish a closer union of Christians, I have reserved for the concluding chapter some remarks upon that subject.

It cannot be denied that the unhappy divisions among Christians do much to retard the gospel, and it should be the earnest desire of all to see every barrier to Christian union removed.

The Saviour of mankind had partaken the last memorial Supper with His disciples, and had given them a remarkable proof of His humility. He had startled them with the disclosure of the perfidy of Judas Iscariot. He had opened to them His impending death, and poured tender, parting words into their sorrow-stricken hearts, and bade them be of good cheer, "for," said He, "I have overcome the world."

And then in that last sad interview with His chosen friends, He lifted up His eyes and prayed. He poured His full heart into His Father's ear and the burden of His prayer was that those whom God had given Him might be kept from the evil of the world; and then He prayed that they might be one as He and the Father are one. (John xvii: 20-21).

Was this outpouring of the Saviour's great heart unmeaning or unavailing? If any, surely, ever possessed the key that unlocks the treasure house of God's rich grace, that one was the Son of God. Nay, He once said to the Father: "Thou hearest me always." If this be so—and what Christian can doubt it?—we may expect the realization of that prayer.

When we look over the Christian world and witness the strife, and divisions, and contentious among the professed followers of God, we are ready to conclude that the answer is far distant. But if we look more closely we will find that all these commotions is but the effort of the people of God to cast off the shackles of Anti-Christ; and like the heaving sea they are purifying themselves by their own agitation. There are two principles at work, divine truth and the Holy Spirit, purifying and assimilating the heaving mass. Nor can we reasonably doubt the ultimate result. But truth is the means, and the Holy Spirit the efficient agent for the accomplishment of this end.

If Christ prayed for the unity of His people it is right for Christians to desire it, to pray for it, and labor for its attainment; and in no age of Christianity has there been so much attention paid to this subject. From all quarters we hear men talk of union and Christian alliance; but I believe there is no subject so much talked of and so little understood. As it is a question destined to excite a deeper interest than almost any other of the present age, it is necessary that the subject should be properly understood, and I propose to discuss it, not particularly from a Baptist point of view; but as a question in which all Christians have an interest.

If Christian unity is a thing to be desired, then it is important to know the basis upon which it may be attained, the obstacles in the way of its attainment; and to know clearly in what that unity consists.

I. *The Basis.*—It must strike every practical mind that the only basis upon which we can hope successfully to build the fabric of Christian union, is one which must be fair and just to all parties; and requires none to disregard the conscientious scruples of another or sacrifice his own. For this reason I remark,

1. It cannot be attained by the union of discordant elements on the basis of agreeing to disagree. The consolidation of two Christian denominations on the platform of mutual forbearance, allowing each to preach and practice according to his own standard, if the thing were practicable, would not be the kind of unity the Saviour prayed for. It would only be a foolish attempt to blend incongruous elements, that would result as all such efforts have always resulted, in producing wider discord and greater alienation; for "how can two walk together except they be agreed?" Separately they may each, by his own course, seek the attainment of his ends without collision; but brought together the repulsive features in each appears to the other. They are like two magnets which do not affect each other so long as they are kept apart; but as soon as they are brought within the sphere of each other's influence, they begin to repel each other. Hence it usually happens that the efforts of Christians, radically different from each other, to co-operate, result in collisions, that arouse mutual jealousies, and separate them in their feelings wider than ever. For this reason many good men have concluded that the surest way to keep the peace among the different sects of Christianity is for each to pursue his own course without attempting any impracticable alliances, that only result in greater alienation. I think it must be apparent to every one that where two differ essentially on the fundamentals of religion, the attempt to co-operate, each presenting his own views of truth, must at once array them in hostile attitude towards each other. Such a union is not the unity prayed for by the Saviour, for He prayed that they may be one as He and the Father are one. The oneness of the Father and the Son is not a oneness of differences, not an attempt to blend incompatibles, to harmonize irreconcilable elements. Hence I conclude that the unity prayed for is not a union upon the principle that each may insist upon his own peculiarities.

2. But perhaps some may say. Let them unite upon the basis that they teach the doctrines upon which they agree and suppress those upon which they disagree. This is objectionable as a basis of union.

(1). Because such is the diversity of religious opinions that if the terms of the union were faithfully carried out it would result in the total suppression of all religious teaching; or religious teachers would be compelled to deal in such unmeaning platitudes as would be destitute of any vital power; for there is hardly a doctrine of any one denomination that is not called in question by some other. Hence it could never be used as an universal bond.

(2). Our theological views are interwoven in the very texture of our minds, and give shape to the expression of our thoughts. In our conversation, in our sermons, in our very prayers they crop out in spite of ourselves. The apparent bad faith thus manifested would be the source of continual distrust that would result in a state of bad feeling that is wholly incompatible with that unity of which I am speaking.

(3). It reduces the Christian faith to the level of a political platform, which may be changed, abated or ignored altogether at pleasure, according to the shifting scenes of political exigency. Such a view of divine truth is calculated to lesson its dignity as emanating from God; and to weaken its force in the moral renovation of the world. It subverts the authority of God's word and leaves His law to be interpreted by the caprice of man, who, by nature is inclined to evade God's requirements; and introduces a spirit of innovation that would not spare the most sacred things.

(4). It supposes a pliancy of conscience as great

as that of mere political trimmers, who shape their opinions according to circumstances; just as if conscientious men could take up and lay down at will their convictions of duty and slip them off and on with the ease of an old garment. But no conscientious Christian can consent to ignore what he honestly believes to be the truth or to abate the least of what he believes to be God's requirements. And any alliance that requires this does violence to the conscience and must of necessity be demoralizing in its tendency. Hence this mode of producing unity is as impracticable as the other. And this truth the Christian world has recognized by separating into sects, each of which consists of those who are agreed in religious sentiments. I know there are exceptions to this rule in those who from some peculiar circumstances take an asylum from the world in some religious body with whose creed their own is at variance. But such connections are always more or less unhappy according to the conscientiousness of the individual, and the depth of his convictions. Hence I would never encourage one to change his church relations unless he found sentiments more congenial with his own. I would convince all men if I could; but I would not induce anyone to become a member of the Baptist Church who was not also thoroughly and from earnest conviction a Baptist. For I would be sure his happiness would not be advanced and he would be a dead weight to us; for what was gained in the number would be lost in the unity.

3. But there is a basis of union that requires no sacrifice and violates no scruples of conscience. It is God's eternal truth; His everlasting word. If men know the truth and are content with the simple truth, they have a firm basis of real union. Each may safely adopt the teachings of God's word; and no Christian man can hesitate to do this to the extent of his knowledge.

The only practical difficulty in the case is that men from the imperfection of their reason mistake God's teaching; but that does not alter God's truth which is immutable. The want of light may prevent us from discovering the objects around us; but those objects are nevertheless there; and if through imperfect vision we should mistake an ox for a horse it would not alter the fact. So in discerning God's truth we may be blind, or only see partially and make great mistakes; but the truth of God remains the same, wholly unaffected by those things which affect us.

We can only ask the divine guidance and strive earnestly to attain the light of truth, divesting ourselves of every hindrance; to dig deep into the sacred mine of God's word; to make that our guide; to receive and obey its teachings implicitly; and recognize nothing else as authoritative. When Christians do this they will have taken the first step in the direction of that unity for which the Saviour prayed. A kind comparison of opposing views and a candid examination of the grounds of our faith by the standard of the gospel will do much to remove the barriers that separate us.

II. *The obstacles to Christian Union.* God has put in motion the causes by the silent, but effectual operation of which that unity will in His own good time, be accomplished. His truth enforced by the Holy Spirit has long battled with error, winning many a noiseless triumph, and preparing the arena of this world for that blessed period when men "shall see eye to eye, and none shall say to another, knowest thou the Lord? for all shall know Him from the least unto the greatest." One by one the obstacles that interpose to prevent the ultimate success of true religion, and the consequent unity of the church, fall before the triumphant march of divine truth.

1. The efforts of men to produce that unity have

proved a serious obstacle to its attainment. The powers of this world have endeavored to stereotype creeds, and bind the consciences of men. But the dark, damp dungeons of inquisitorial tyranny, and the martyr flames that have lighted the pathway of truth amid the surrounding darkness, attest the utter failure of these efforts to enforce a unity of faith and practice by the arm of civil power, aside from the earnest convictions of truth itself. But the independence of thought, and the self-assertion of individual consciousness have always and will always manifest themselves. The present age has done much to strike off the shackles that have sought to bind the conscience.

But the danger at present is in a different direction. Men are pushing forward to this unity with imprudent haste. Forgetting that uniformity may exist without that unity for which the Saviour prayed, they vainly imagine that they have attained this unity by agreement, without respect to the basis upon which that unity is sought to be founded. So that it becomes the lovers of true unity to be firm and watchful to resist this tendency, and to uphold the truth, as the only sure basis of real unity.

2. Before this unity can be attained, Christians must give up all that is merely human and traditional; those false adornments of the bride of Christ, which mar her beauty and hinder her progress. As long as men insist upon preserving their own inventions, so long will they differ, for each thinks his own invention the best. When men look to the Word of God alone for guidance, and require a plain and positive precept or example to continue any observance, or support any doctrine, then will an important step be taken towards the attainment of that unity which is so much desired.

3. Another obstacle is to be found in the natural indolence of men. They accept a certain creed because it is the creed of their fathers, or of some

person in whom they have confidence. This saves the trouble of thinking for one's self, which, with many people, is no small matter. Thus passively receiving their creed, they are naturally fretted at every effort calculated to disturb their repose. They love peace and quiet, because it costs no labor; and they equally dislike the clash of contending opinions, because it obliges them to think. Their position is merely accidental, and if they happen to take it short of the truth, they never advance to it.

4. Pride of opinion also interposes to prevent men from acknowledging the truth, even when convinced of it. It is humiliating to confess that we have erred, particularly in a matter of judgment. Men will more readily confess a sin than a mere error of reason. The heart may err, but the head is infallible! Until this pride is broken down, no man will seriously set to work to discern the truth, and correct his faith.

5. Prejudice and party spirit also stand in the way. Men often adopt opinions without examination, and these are generally the most obstinate. I had much sooner attack an opinion deliberately formed, than one of those which is the result of mere prejudice, particularly when it is joined with party spirit; that spirit which determines to sustain at all hazards the dogmas of a sect, regardless of their truth, simply because they are held by the party to which they belong. If such persons happen to mistake the truth, they can never be induced to come upon this the only platform upon which all can stand.

III. Let us, lastly, consider in what that unity consists. I have already shown that the only basis upon which it can be established is the truth; and it consists in unity of faith, unity of practice and unity of feeling.

1. *Unity of faith.* How can two walk together

except they be agreed? The truth of God has no variations, and those who attain to that unity for which the Saviour prayed, must not only believe the same things, but they must all believe the truth, all the truth, and no more than the truth. It was not unity in error that Christ desired; a union simply for the sake of union, regardless of the basis. They must endeavor to keep the unity of the spirit in the bonds of peace, and strive to attain a unity of the faith. They must be one in the faith, as the Father and Son are one in faith.

2. *Unity of practice.* They must not only believe alike, and believe right, but they must also conform in their outward conduct to that faith. There must be uniformity in conduct. The same forms of worship must regulate their devotions, and the same external ordinances manifest their obedience to God's simplest positive laws.

3. *Unity of feeling.* But more than all they must possess a unity of feeling. Oneness of faith and practice will remove those causes of dissension that engender strife and discord, and will promote that cordiality of feeling that marks the intercourse of those who agree in the truth; that love without dissimulation that elevates Christian fellowship into the harmonious unity of the Godhead himself.

May the time speedily come when men will seek the truth with pure hearts fervently; when love shall flow like a river from heart to heart; when, divested of the imperfections of reason, and the bias of passion, the clear mind shall grasp the truth of God; and Christians shall see eye to eye, because they see the one truth.

THE END.

A
Biographical Sketch
of
William Edwards Paxton
(1823-1883)

by
John Franklin Jones

A Biographical Sketch of William Edwards Paxton (1823-1883)

William Edwards Paxton was born June 23, 1823 (*ESB*) (GPM cited 1825) in Little Rock, Pulaski County, Arkansas to David Coulter (born ca. 1784 in Rockbridge Co, Virginia to Samuel and Sarah Coulter) and Lucy Edwards Paxton (born ca. 1802 in Woodford County, Kentucky). David, a Baptist preacher, and Lucy were married November 17, 1818 in Woodford County, Kentucky (GPM).

The family moved to Hempstead County in Southern Arkansas during the 1830s. William's early schooling occurred in an academy run by a Presbyterian minister. He began to write verse at age thirteen. Some of that prose and poetry was published in the Washington, Arkansas Telegraph (WEPB).

They moved back to Kentucky in 1842. Paxton attended a private school for fifteen months, preparing to enter college (WEPB). Paxton received the A.B. degree from Georgetown College in 1847 and the A.M. degree in 1849 (*ESB*) (GCSC said 1850). Following graduation he taught school and served as school headmasters in Woodford, Mercer, and Scott counties Kentucky while he studied law. He was admitted to the Kentucky state bar and married Sarah J. Mothershed in 1851. She died that same year (WEPB).

John Franklin Jones

He moved to Sparta, Louisiana, became headmaster at Mt. Lebanon Baptist Academy and studied for the Louisiana state bar. He passed the bar and established a civil law practice. He married Rebecca Wardlaw on February 24, 1857. To the marriage were born Willie, a son, and Lucy, a daughter (WEPB).

The 1850s pre-Civil War years found Paxton vocally advocating southern causes, raising the first company of volunteers from his parish following Ft. Sumter, and editing the *Southern Banner* (WEPB).

He began his Confederate military service in October, 1861, stationed at New Orleans to defend against possible Union attacks. He served at Corinth, Mississippi and the battle of Shiloh. He resigned his commission on July 10, served in a Calvary unit west of the Mississippi, and then as a assistant enrolling office in Bienville Parish in 1864. The same year Rebecca died. He was paroled from the army June 20, 1865 (WEPB).

Paston surrendered to preach at the Sparta Baptist Church in 1864 and thereafter, preached somewhere most every week. The Minden Baptist Church called him as pastor in March 1865 (PM said 1866), at which he served until 1872 (WEPB).

In 1866, he married a war widow, Margaret Eugenia Hargrove Fuller. Over seventeen years of marriage, they parented nine children. Of the children, only three daughters reached adulthood: Lizzie Clare, Eloise, and Viva (WEPB).

At the 1870 US Census, William and his wife, Eugina Marguerite Hargrove (born November 13, 1843 in Georgia) lived in Claibourne County Louisiana (the Minden Post Office). The household contained Lucy (13, born in Louisiana); William E. (10, born in Louisiana); Josie B (2, born in Louisiana); Claude E. (7 months, born in Louisiana); and Lucy S. (68, born in Kentucky) (GPM).

A Biographical Sketch of William Edwards Paxton

Paxton served as pastor at Summer Grove, Shreveport (1872-1877) (WEPB). Among the Georgetown College Alumni, Paxton is listed as having served as the president of Shreveport Univeristy, Shreveport, Louisiana in 1873 (GCSC).

He served as pastor of the Baptist Church in Warren Arkansas, (1878-1882)(WEPB) and as president at Centennial Institute, Warren, Arkansas, 1878-? (GCSC).

At the 1880 US Census, the family lived in Bradley County Arkansas (Pennington). The household consisted of William E. Paxton (54, born in Arkansas of a Virginia father and a Kentucky mother); M. E. (39, born in Georgia of a Georgia father and a Georgia mother); W. E. Jr. (age 19); Lizzie (age 9); Eloise (age 7); Vera (age 4 (all the children born in Louisiana of an Arkansas father and a Georgia mother); and Lucy (78, born in Kentucky of a North Carolina father and a North Carolina mother) (GPM).

He had conferred upon him the D.D. by Keatchie College in 1882 (*ESB*). He served as associate editor or correspondent for papers in several states--Louisiana (the *Louisiana Baptist*), the *Arkansas Evangel* (WEPB), Mississippi, Tennessee, Kentucky, and Texas (*ESB*).

The First Baptist Church, Ft. Smith Arkansas called him to be its pastor on February 11, 1883 (GPM).

He wrote many pamphlets and books. Among the books are *The Apostolic Church: Being An Inquiry into the Constitution...*(1876) and *A History of the Baptists of Louisiana: From the Earliest Times to the Present* (1888) (*ESB*), published posthumously (WEPB).

Paxton died of congestive malarial fever at Fort Smith, Arkansas Saturday June 9, 1883 (GPM), two weeks short of his fifty-eighth birthday, June 9, 1883 (WEPB). He was buried at Oak Cemetery in Fort Smith, Arkansas. Following his death, the family moved back to Louisiana (GPM).

BIBLIOGRAPHY

Encyclopedia of Southern Baptists. S.v. "Paxton, William Edwards," by T. W. Gayer.

http://ftp.rootsweb.com/pub/usgenweb/la/bienville/bios/paxton we.txt. Accessed July 1, 2006. (Cited as KD).

http://genforum.genealogy.com/paxton/messages/1089.html. Accessed July 1, 2006. (Cited as GPM).

http://genforum.genealogy.com/paxton/messages/296.html. Accessed July 1, 2006. (Cited as PM).

http://library.georgetowncollege.edu/Special_Collections/Colle ge_Presidents.htm. Accessed July 1, 2006. (Cited as GCSC).

Paxton, W. E. *A History of the Baptists of Louisiana: From the Earliest Times to the Present.* St. Louis: C.R. Barnes, 1888.

— *The Apostolic Church: Being An Inquiry into the Constitution...*Memphis, TN: Southern Baptist Tract Society, 1876.

Paxton, William McClung. *The Paxtons: We Are One.* Platte City, MO: N.p., 1903.

BY JOHN FRANKLIN JONES
CORDOVA, TENNESSEE
JULY 2006

THE BAPTIST STANDARD BEARER, INC.

a non-profit, tax-exempt corporation
committed to the Publication & Preservation
of the Baptist Heritage.

CURRENT TITLES AVAILABLE IN
THE BAPTIST *DISTINCTIVES* SERIES

KIFFIN, WILLIAM — A Sober Discourse of Right to Church-Communion. Wherein is proved by Scripture, the Example of the Primitive Times, and the Practice of All that have Professed the Christian Religion: That no Unbaptized person may be Regularly admitted to the Lord's Supper. (London: George Larkin, 1681).

KINGHORN, JOSEPH — Baptism, A Term of Communion. (Norwich: Bacon, Kinnebrook, and Co., 1816)

KINGHORN, JOSEPH — A Defense of "Baptism, A Term of Communion". In Answer To Robert Hall's Reply. (Norwich: Wilkin and Youngman, 1820).

GILL, JOHN — Gospel Baptism. A Collection of Sermons, Tracts, etc., on Scriptural Authority, the Nature of the New Testament Church and the Ordinance of Baptism by John Gill. (Paris, AR: The Baptist Standard Bearer, Inc., 2006).

CARSON, ALEXANDER	Ecclesiastical Polity of the New Testament. (Dublin: William Carson, 1856).
BOOTH, ABRAHAM	A Defense of the Baptists. A Declaration and Vindication of Three Historically Distinctive Baptist Principles. Compiled and Set Forth in the Republication of Three Books. Revised edition. (Paris, AR: The Baptist Standard Bearer, Inc., 2006).
BOOTH, ABRAHAM	Paedobaptism Examined on the Principles, Concessions, and Reasonings of the Most Learned Paedobaptists. With Replies to the Arguments and Objections of Dr. Williams and Mr. Peter Edwards. 3 volumes. (London: Ebenezer Palmer, 1829).
CARROLL, B. H.	*Ecclesia* - The Church. With an Appendix. (Louisville: Baptist Book Concern, 1903).
CHRISTIAN, JOHN T.	Immersion, The Act of Christian Baptism. (Louisville: Baptist Book Concern, 1891).
FROST, J. M.	Pedobaptism: Is It From Heaven Or Of Men? (Philadelphia: American Baptist Publication Society, 1875).
FULLER, RICHARD	Baptism, and the Terms of Communion; An Argument. (Charleston, SC: Southern Baptist Publication Society, 1854).
GRAVES, J. R.	Tri-Lemma: or, Death By Three Horns. The Presbyterian General Assembly Not Able To Decide This Question: "Is Baptism In The Romish Church Valid?" 1st Edition.

	(Nashville: Southwestern Publishing House, 1861).
MELL, P.H.	Baptism In Its Mode and Subjects. (Charleston, SC: Southern Baptist Publications Society, 1853).
JETER, JEREMIAH B.	Baptist Principles Reset. Consisting of Articles on Distinctive Baptist Principles by Various Authors. With an Appendix. (Richmond: The Religious Herald Co., 1902).
PENDLETON, J.M.	Distinctive Principles of Baptists. (Philadelphia: American Baptist Publication Society, 1882).
THOMAS, JESSE B.	The Church and the Kingdom. A New Testament Study. (Louisville: Baptist Book Concern, 1914).
WALLER, JOHN L.	Open Communion Shown to be Unscriptural & Deleterious. With an introductory essay by Dr. D. R. Campbell and an Appendix. (Louisville: Baptist Book Concern, 1859).

For a complete list of current authors/titles, visit our internet site at:
www.standardbearer.org
or write us at:

he Baptist Standard Bearer, Inc.

NUMBER ONE IRON OAKS DRIVE • PARIS, ARKANSAS 72855
TEL # 479-963-3831   FAX # 479-963-8083
EMAIL: Baptist@centurytel.net   http://www.standardbearer.org

Thou hast given a standard to them that fear thee; that it may be displayed because of the truth. — Psalm 60:4

www.ingramcontent.com/pod-product-compliance
Lightning Source LLC
Chambersburg PA
CBHW021135230426
43667CB00005B/119